Workbook/Laboratory Manual

to accompany

¡Apúntate!

español introductorio

Volume 1

Alice A. Arana
Formerly of Fullerton College

Oswaldo Arana
Formerly of California State University, Fullerton

María Sabló-Yates
Delta College

Higher Education

Boston   Burr Ridge, IL   Dubuque, IA   New York   San Francisco   St. Louis
Bangkok   Bogotá   Caracas   Kuala Lumpur   Lisbon   London   Madrid   Mexico City
Milan   Montreal   New Delhi   Santiago   Seoul   Singapore   Sydney   Taipei   Toronto

 **Higher Education**

Workbook/Laboratory Manual (Volume 1) to accompany
¡Apúntate! español introductorio

Published by McGraw-Hill, an imprint of The McGraw-Hill Companies, Inc., 1221 Avenue of the Americas, New York, NY 10020. Copyright © 2010 by The McGraw-Hill Companies, Inc. All rights reserved. No part of this publication may be reproduced or distributed in any form or by any means, or stored in a database or retrieval system, without the prior written consent of The McGraw-Hill Companies, Inc., including, but not limited to, in any network or other electronic storage or transmission, or broadcast for distance learning.

This book is printed on acid-free paper.

2 3 4 5 6 7 8 9 0 QDB/QDB 0

ISBN-13: 978-0-07-728981-2
ISBN-10: 0-07–728981–1

Vice president and Editor-in-chief: *Michael Ryan*
Editorial director: *William R. Glass*
Executive editor: *Christa Harris*
Director of development: *Scott Tinetti*
Development editor: *Pennie Nichols*
Marketing manager: *Jorge Arbujas*
Senior production editor: *Mel Valentín*
Editorial assistant: *Margaret Young*
Production supervisor: *Louis Swaim*
Composition: *10/12 Palatino by Eisner/Martin Typographics*
Printing: *40# Alt Book 690 Quad/Graphics*
Illustrators: *Wayne Clark, David Bohn, Axelle Fortier, Lori Heckelman, Judith Macdonald, Stephanie O'Shaughnessy, Barbara Rienerison, Katherine Tillotson, Stan Tusan, and Joe Veno.*

The Internet addresses listed in the text were accurate at the time of publication. The inclusion of a Web site does not indicate an endorsement by the authors or McGraw-Hill, and McGraw-Hill does not guarantee the accuracy of the information presented at these sites.

Contents

To the Student

Welcome to Volume 1 of the combined Workbook/Laboratory Manual to accompany *¡Apúntate! An Introduction to Spanish.* Each chapter of this Workbook/Laboratory Manual is based on the corresponding chapter of the text, so that you may practice and review on your own what you are learning in class. For ease of identification, the exercises appear under the same headings as in *¡Apúntate!* Once a section from the textbook has been introduced, you can do the same section in the Workbook/Laboratory Manual with assurance that no new vocabulary or structures from later sections of that chapter will be encountered.

Special Feature

This Workbook/Laboratory Manual also contains a unique and convenient feature: within each chapter, each individual **paso** can be torn out and handed in without disturbing the remainder of the chapter. This means that you can have your instructor check your work on previous **pasos** while you continue to practice the current class material. It also means that the study materials are clearly organized and easy for you to use.

Integrated Written and Oral Exercises

Because your different senses and skills (writing, reading, listening, and speaking) reinforce one another, written and oral exercises for each point in the text appear together in the Workbook/Laboratory Manual. Oral exercises are coordinated with the Audio Program, available in compact disc format, which you can use at home or at your school's language laboratory. The audio program can also be found on the Online Learning Center at **www.mhhe.com/apuntate.** The oral exercises are marked with a headphones symbol:

To get the most out of the Audio Program, you should listen to the audio after your instructor covers the corresponding material in class, and you should listen as often as possible. You will need the Workbook/ Laboratory Manual much of the time when you listen to the audio, since many of the exercises are based on visuals, realia (real things—such as advertisements, classified ads, and so on—that you would encounter in a Spanish-speaking country), and written cues.

Organization

The structure of the **Capítulo preliminar** of the Workbook/Laboratory Manual parallels that of the **Capítulo preliminar** in the main text. **Capítulos 1–9** are organized as follows.

- **Paso 1: Vocabulario** allows you to practice the thematic vocabulary of each chapter through a variety of fun and interesting exercises. Here and in **Pasos 2** and **3,** written and oral exercises appear together for each point. The **Pronunciación y ortografía** pronunciation and spelling exercises provide focused practice of Spanish pronunciation, with explanations all in English. **Paso 1** closes with a comprehension activity for the **Lectura cultural** sections from the textbook.

- **Paso 2: Gramática** presents a variety of exercises on each grammar point in the corresponding section of the main text.

- **Paso 3: Gramática,** as in **Paso 2,** gives you the opportunity to practice chapter structures through written and oral exercises. In addition, **Un poco de todo** combines grammar points and vocabulary included in the current chapter as well as in previous chapters.

Following the three **pasos** are synthesizing and testing sections.

- **¡Repasemos!** is a focused review of grammar and vocabulary from preceding chapters. It includes reading selections, tense transformation, and paragraph completion. Each **¡Repasemos!** section includes an oral interview, in which you write your responses to personalized questions. Answers for **¡Repasemos!** sections are *not* provided in the Appendix.

- **Mi diario** is a chapter culminating activity in which you are encouraged to write freely about your own experiences, applying the material you have been studying in that chapter.

- **Ponte a prueba** is a two-part testing section. The first part is a short quiz called **A ver si sabes...** , which focuses on some of the more mechanical aspects of the language-learning process, such as memorization of verb forms and syntax. By taking this quiz, you can evaluate your knowledge of the most basic aspects of the language before moving on to the second part, **Prueba corta,** where you will complete a brief quiz that contains more contextualized written and oral practice.

Answers to most oral exercises are given on the Audio Program. In a few cases, as required, they appear in the Appendix at the back of this Workbook/Laboratory Manual. Answers to most written activities also appear in the Appendix. No answers are provided for exercises requiring personalized answers, indicated with this symbol: ❖.

About the Authors

Alice A. Arana is Associate Professor of Spanish, Emeritus, at Fullerton College. She received her M.A.T. from Yale University and her Certificate of Spanish Studies at the University of Madrid. Professor Arana has also taught Spanish at the elementary and high school levels and has taught methodology at several NDEA summer institutes. She is coauthor of the first edition of *A-LM Spanish*, of *Reading for Meaning—Spanish*, and of several elementary school guides for the teaching of Spanish. Professor Arana has been named Staff Member of Distinction at Fullerton College and was subsequently chosen as a nominee from Fullerton College for Teacher of the Year. She has also served as Academic Senate President. Professor Arana is coauthor of the *Workbooks to Accompany Puntos de partida* and *Puntos en breve*, as well as the *Workbook/Laboratory Manual to Accompany ¿Qué tal?*

Oswaldo Arana is Professor of Spanish, Emeritus, at California State University, Fullerton, where he has taught Spanish American culture and literature. He received his Ph.D. in Spanish from the University of Colorado. Professor Arana has taught at the University of Colorado, the University of Florida (Gainesville), and at several NDEA summer institutes. He served as a language consultant for the first edition of *A-LM Spanish*, and is coauthor of *Reading for Meaning—Spanish* and of several articles on Spanish American narrative prose. Professor Arana is coauthor of the *Workbooks to Accompany Puntos de partida* and *Puntos en breve*, as well as the *Workbook/Laboratory Manual to Accompany ¿Qué tal?*

María Sabló-Yates is a native of Panama. She holds a B.A. and and M.A. from the University of Washington (Seattle). She has taught at the University of Washington and Central Michigan University (Mt. Pleasant, Michigan), and is currently an Assistant Professor of Spanish at Delta College (University Center, Michigan). She is author of *Laboratory Manual to Accompany Puntos de partida*, the *Workbook/Laboratory Manual to Accompany ¿Qué tal?*, and the *Laboratory Manual to Accompany Puntos en breve*.

Primer paso
Saludos y expresiones de cortesía

A. Saludos. Greet the following people in an appropriate manner.

1. a classmate, at any time of day _____

2. la señora Alarcón, at 9:30 P.M. _____

3. el señor Ramírez, at 2:00 P.M. _____

4. la señorita Cueva, at 11:00 A.M. _____

¡RECUERDA! (*REMEMBER!*)

¿Tú o (*or*) usted?

1. What form do you use when speaking to a professor?   **tú** ☐   **usted** ☐

2. What form do you use when speaking to another student?   **tú** ☐   **usted** ☐

3. To ask a classmate his or her name, say: ¿_____?

4. To ask your instructor his or her name, say: ¿_____?

B. ¡Hola, Carmen! On your way to class, you meet Carmen, a student from Spain, and exchange greetings with her. Complete the brief dialogue.

TÚ: Hola, Carmen, ¿_____?[1]

CARMEN: Bien, gracias. ¿_____?[2]

TÚ: Regular.

CARMEN: Adiós, _____[3] mañana.

TÚ: Adiós, Carmen. _____.[4]

C. Diálogo. Complete the following dialogue between you and your new Spanish instructor. Be sure to use your own name and that of your instructor in the appropriate blanks.

TÚ: _____[1] noches, profesor(a) _____ (*instructor's name*).

¿Cómo _____[2]?

PROFESOR(A): Bien, _____.[3] ¿Cómo _____[4] usted?

TÚ: _____[5] (*your name*).

PROFESOR(A): Mucho _____.[6]

TÚ: _____.[7]

Paso 1. In the following dialogues, you will practice greeting others appropriately in Spanish. The dialogues will be read with pauses for repetition. After each dialogue, you will hear two summarizing statements. Circle the letter of the statement that best describes each dialogue. First, listen.

1.

MANOLO:	¡Hola, Maricarmen!
MARICARMEN:	¿Qué tal, Manolo? ¿Cómo estás?
MANOLO:	Muy bien. ¿Y tú?
MARICARMEN:	Regular. Nos vemos, ¿eh?
MANOLO:	Hasta mañana.

Comprensión: **a. b.**

2.

ELISA VELASCO:	Buenas tardes, señor Gómez.
MARTÍN GÓMEZ:	Muy buenas, señora Velasco. ¿Cómo está?
ELISA VELASCO:	Bien, gracias. ¿Y usted?
MARTÍN GÓMEZ:	Muy bien, gracias. Hasta luego.
ELISA VELASCO:	Adiós.

Comprensión: **a. b.**

3.

LUPE:	Buenos días, profesor.
PROFESOR:	Buenos días. ¿Cómo te llamas?
LUPE:	Me llamo Lupe Carrasco.
PROFESOR:	Mucho gusto, Lupe.
LUPE:	Igualmente.

Comprensión: **a. b.**

4.

MIGUEL RENÉ:	¡Hola! Me llamo Miguel René. ¿Y tú? ¿Cómo te llamas?
KARINA:	Me llamo Karina. Mucho gusto.
MIGUEL RENÉ:	Mucho gusto, Karina. Y, ¿de dónde eres?
KARINA:	Yo soy de Venezuela. ¿Y tú?
MIGUEL RENÉ:	Yo soy de México.

Comprensión: **a. b.**

Paso 2. Now you will participate in a conversation, partially printed in your Manual, in which you play the role of Karina. Complete the conversation using the written cues. When you hear the corresponding number, say Karina's line. Then you will hear Miguel René's response. Continue until you complete the conversation. (If you wish, pause and write the answers.) Here are the cues for your conversation.

buenas tardes	cómo te llamas	de dónde eres
me llamo	mucho gusto	yo soy

Now, begin the conversation.

KARINA: _____.¹

MIGUEL RENÉ: Muy buenas.

KARINA: _____² Karina. ¿_____³?

MIGUEL RENÉ: Me llamo Miguel.

KARINA: _____,⁴ Miguel. ¿_____⁵?

MIGUEL RENÉ: Soy de Puerto Rico. ¿Y tú?

KARINA: _____⁶ de Puerto Rico también.

E. **¿Formal o informal?** You will hear a series of expressions. Indicate whether each expression would be used in a formal or in an informal situation.

1. **a.** formal   **b.** informal
2. **a.** formal   **b.** informal
3. **a.** formal   **b.** informal
4. **a.** formal   **b.** informal
5. **a.** formal   **b.** informal

F. **Situaciones**

Paso 1. You will hear a series of questions or statements. Each will be said twice. Circle the letter of the best response or reaction to each.

1. **a.** Me llamo Ricardo Barrios.   **b.** Bien, gracias.
2. **a.** Encantada, Eduardo.   **b.** Muchas gracias, Eduardo.
3. **a.** Regular. ¿Y tú?   **b.** Mucho gusto, señorita Paz.
4. **a.** Con permiso, señor.   **b.** No hay de qué.
5. **a.** De nada, señora Colón.   **b.** Buenas noches, señora Colón.
6. **a.** Soy de Guatemala.   **b.** ¿Y tú?

Paso 2. Now, listen to the questions and statements again and read the correct answers in the pauses provided. You will hear each item only once. Be sure to repeat the correct answer after you hear it.

1. ...   2. ...   3. ...   4. ...   5. ...   6. ...

A. El alfabeto español. Answer the following questions about the Spanish alphabet.

1. What are the two letters in the Spanish alphabet that are not found in the English alphabet?

    _____ _____

2. What letter in the Spanish alphabet is never pronounced? _____

B. ¿Cómo se escribe... ? (*How do you write . . . ?*) Write only the name of the underlined letter.

MODELO: ¿Se escribe <u>J</u>osé con (*with*) ge o con jota? → Con jota.

1. ¿Se escribe <u>g</u>eneral con ge o con jota? Con _____.

2. ¿Se escribe Oli<u>v</u>ia con be o con ve (uve)? Con _____.

3. ¿Se escribe e<u>x</u>perto con equis o con ese? Con _____.

4. ¿Se escribe Pére<u>z</u> con ese o con zeta? Con _____.

5. ¿Se escribe <u>C</u>ecilia con ese o con ce? Con _____.

6. ¿Se escribe opt<u>i</u>mista con i o con i griega? Con _____.

7. ¿Se escribe <u>h</u>asta con o sin (*without*) hache? _____.

❖**C. ¿Cómo se llama usted?** Spell your complete name in Spanish.*

MODELO: Me llamo Juan Martínez. → Jota-u-a-ene, eme-a-ere-te-i acentuada-ene-e–zeta

Me llamo _____.

Nota comunicativa: Los cognados

❖**A. Pronunciación.** Read aloud the following pairs of words. The stressed syllable is italicized. Note how the stress shifts in most of the Spanish words. These adjectives can be used to describe a man or a woman.

	ENGLISH	SPANISH		ENGLISH	SPANISH
1.	*nor*mal	nor-*mal*	8.	*te*rrible	te-*rri*-ble
2.	e*mo*tional	e-mo-cio-*nal*	9.	res*pon*sible	res-pon-*sa*-ble
3.	*el*egant	e-le-*gan*-te	10.	*va*liant	va-*lien*-te
4.	*cru*el	cru-*el*	11.	*ho*rrible	ho-*rri*-ble
5.	pesi*mis*tic	pe-si-*mis*-ta	12.	im*por*tant	im-por-*tan*-te
6.	opti*mis*tic	op-ti-*mis*-ta	13.	in*tel*ligent	in-te-li-*gen*-te
7.	materia*lis*tic	ma-te-ria-*lis*-ta	14.	re*bel*lious	re-*bel*-de

---

*Exercises marked with this symbol (❖) do *not* have answers in the Appendix nor on the Audioscript.

B. Los cognados

❖**Paso 1.** Scan the following selection, then underline all the cognates and other words that look familiar to you.

Un producto natural, protector de la salud

El aceite de oliva, especialmente el aceite de oliva virgen, es un producto que cada día gana mayor aceptación en la preparación de las comidas. Contiene mucha vitamina E, un antioxidante por excelencia. Además, el aceite de oliva virgen no contiene colesterol. En efecto, su uso reduce la concentración de colesterol en la sangre. Por lo tanto, es preferible a las grasas de origen animal, que son malas para el sistema cardiovascular.

Paso 2. Based on your understanding of the article, check the box for either **cierto** (**C**) (*true*) or **falso** (**F**) (*false*). ¡**OJO!** The sentences can help you understand the meaning of the paragraph.

		C	F
1.	Olive oil is gaining more acceptance in the preparation of meals.	☐	☐
2.	One of the benefits of this oil is that it contains a lot of vitamin C.	☐	☐
3.	Olive oil contains as much cholesterol as animal fats.	☐	☐
4.	Animal fats are unhealthy because they are bad for the heart.	☐	☐
5.	The use of olive oil reduces the amount of cholesterol in our blood.	☐	☐
6.	Olive oil is beneficial for the cardiovascular system.	☐	☐

¿Cómo eres? (Part 1)

❖**A. Adjetivos.** Read aloud the following adjectives, then choose those that best describe you and use them to complete the sentence.

arrogante	irresponsable
egoísta	optimista
emocional	paciente
idealista	pesimista
impaciente	realista
independiente	rebelde
inteligente	responsable

Yo soy _____, _____, _____ y _____.

❖**B. ¿Qué opinas?** (*What do you think?*) Describe the following people by using appropriate adjectives from the preceding list and from the list in **Los cognados** in your textbook.

1. Jennifer López es _____, _____ y _____.

2. Enrique Iglesias es _____, _____ y _____.

3. Madonna es _____, _____ y _____.

4. Justin Timberlake es _____, _____ y _____.

5. Salma Hayek es _____, _____ y _____.

❖C. Mi mejor amigo/a (*My best friend*). Tell your best friend what you think he/she is like. What verb form will you use with **tú: soy, eres, es**?

Tú (soy / eres / es) _____, _____, _____ y _____.

D. ¿Cómo es usted? You will hear the following brief conversation. It will be read with pauses for repetition. First, listen to the conversation. (Then repeat as directed.)

—¿Cómo es usted?
—Bueno... Yo soy moderna, independiente, sofisticada...

❖E. Encuesta (*Survey*). You will hear a series of questions. For each question, check the appropriate answer. No answers will be given. The answers you choose should be correct for you!

1. ☐ Sí, soy independiente.
   ☐ No, no soy independiente.

2. ☐ Sí, soy sentimental.
   ☐ No, no soy sentimental.

3. ☐ Sí, soy eficiente.
   ☐ No, no soy eficiente.

4. ☐ Sí, soy flexible.
   ☐ No, no soy flexible.

F. Descripción. In this exercise, you will practice gisting, that is, getting the main idea, an important skill in language learning. Although some of the vocabulary you hear will not be familiar to you, concentrate on the words that you *do* know. After the exercise, pause and choose the statement that best describes the passage.

1. ☐ This person is describing her country and the sports that are played there.

2. ☐ This person is describing herself, her studies, and her outside interests.

Now resume listening.

G. Preguntas (*Questions*). Ask the following persons about their personalities, using **¿Eres... ?** or **¿Es usted... ?** as appropriate, and the cues you will hear. Follow the model. (Remember to repeat the correct question. If you prefer, pause and write the questions.) You will hear answers to your questions.

MODELO: (*you see*) Marcos   (*you hear*) tímido →
(*you say*) Marcos ¿eres tímido?   (*you hear*) Sí, soy tímido.

1. Ramón, ¿_____?

2. Señora Alba, ¿_____?

3. Señor Castán, ¿_____?

4. Anita, ¿_____?

H. Dictado: ¿Cómo son? (*What are they like?*) You will hear five sentences. Each will be said twice. Listen carefully and write the missing words. (Check your answers in the Appendix.)

1. El hotel es _____.

2. El estudiante es muy _____.

3. El _____ no es difícil (*difficult*).

4. El museo es muy _____.

5. Íñigo no es _____.

Pronunciación y ortografía • El alfabeto español

A. El alfabeto español. You will hear the names of the letters of the Spanish alphabet, along with a list of place names. Listen and repeat, imitating the speaker. Notice that most Spanish consonants are pronounced differently than in English. In future chapters, you will have the opportunity to practice the pronunciation of most of these letters individually.

a	a	la Argentina	**ñ**	eñe	España
b	be	Bolivia	**o**	o	Oviedo
c	ce	Cáceres	**p**	pe	Panamá
d	de	Durango	**q**	cu	Quito
e	e	el Ecuador	**r**	ere	el Perú
f	efe	Florida	**rr**	erre	Monterrey
g	ge	Guatemala	**s**	ese	San Juan
h	hache	Honduras	**t**	te	Toledo
i	i	Ibiza	**u**	u	el Uruguay
j	jota	Jalisco	**v**	ve	Venezuela
k	ca	(*Kansas*)	**w**	doble ve	(*Washington*)
l	ele	Lima	**x**	equis	Extremadura
m	eme	México	**y**	i griega	el Paraguay
n	ene	Nicaragua	**z**	zeta	Zaragoza

B. Repeticiones. Repeat the following words, phrases, and sentences. Imitate the speaker and pay close attention to the difference in pronunciation between Spanish and English.

1.	c/ch	Colón	Cecilia	Muchas gracias.	Buenas noches.
2.	g/gu	Ortega	gusto	Miguel	guitarra
3.	h	La Habana	Héctor	hotel	historia
4.	j/g	Jamaica	Jiménez	Geraldo	Gilda
5.	l/ll	Lupe	Manolo	Sevilla	me llamo
6.	y	Yolanda	yate	Paraguay	y
7.	r/rr	Mario	arte	Roberto	carro
8.	ñ	Begoña	Toño	señorita	Hasta mañana.

C. Más repeticiones. Repeat the following Spanish syllables, imitating the speaker. Try to pronounce each vowel with a short, tense sound.

1.	ma	fa	la	ta	pa		4.	mo	fo	lo	to	po
2.	me	fe	le	te	pe		5.	mu	fu	lu	tu	pu
3.	mi	fi	li	ti	pi		6.	sa	se	si	so	su

D. Las vocales. Compare the pronunciation of the following words in both English and Spanish. Listen for the schwa, the *uh* sound in English, and notice its absence in Spanish.

English: *banana*   Spanish: **banana**

capital   **capital**

Now, repeat the following words, imitating the speaker. Be careful to avoid the English schwa. Remember to pronounce each vowel with a short and tense sound.

1.	hasta	tal	nada	mañana	natural
2.	me	qué	Pérez	usted	rebelde
3.	sí	señorita	permiso	imposible	tímido
4.	yo	con	cómo	noches	profesor
5.	tú	uno	mucho	Perú	Lupe

E. ¿Español o inglés? You will hear a series of words. Each will be said twice. Circle the letter of the word you hear, either a Spanish word (**español**) or an English word (**inglés**). Note that Spanish vowels are short and tense; they are never drawn out with a *u* or *i* glide as in English.

	ESPAÑOL		INGLÉS
1.	**a.** mi	**b.**	*me*
2.	**a.** fe	**b.**	*Fay*
3.	**a.** es	**b.**	*ace*
4.	**a.** con	**b.**	*cone*
5.	**a.** ti	**b.**	*tea*
6.	**a.** lo	**b.**	*low*

F. Dictado

Paso 1. You will hear a series of words that are probably unfamiliar to you. Each will be said twice. Listen carefully, concentrating on the vowel sounds, and write in the missing vowels. (Check your answers in the Appendix.)

1. r____d____ll____

2. M____r____b____l

3. ____n____l____t____r____l

4. s____lv____v____d____s

5. ____lv____d____d____z____

Paso 2. Imagine that you work as a hotel receptionist in Miami. Listen to how some Hispanic guests spell out their last names for you. Write down the names as you hear them. (Check your answers in the Appendix.)

1. _____

2. _____

3. _____

4. _____

Nota cultural: Spanish Around the World

A. Match the geographical area of the United States with the largest Spanish-speaking group(s) that has (have) settled in each area.

1. _____ Northeast   **a.** Central Americans
    b. Cubans
2. _____ Southwest   **c.** Mexicans
3. _____ Southeast   **d.** Puerto Ricans

❖**B.** Do you know people who have come from Spanish-speaking countries? Which countries?

_____

⏵ Segundo paso

Los números del 0 al 30; *Hay*

A. Cantidades (*Quantities*). Write out the numbers indicated in parentheses. Remember that the number **uno** changes to **un** before a masculine noun and to **una** before a feminine noun.

1. (1) _____ clase (*f.*)

2. (4) _____ dólares

3. (7) _____ días

4. (13) _____ personas

5. (11) _____ señoras

6. (1) _____ estudiante (*m.*)

7. (20) _____ señoras

8. (23) _____ personas

9. (26) _____ clases

10. (21) _____ señores (*m.*)

11. (21) _____ profesoras (*f.*)

12. (30) _____ estudiantes

B. Problemas de matemáticas. Complete each equation, then write out the missing numbers in each statement.

1. 14 + _____ = 22   Catorce y _____ son veintidós.

2. 15 – 4 = _____   Quince menos cuatro son _____.

3. 2 + 3 = _____   Dos y tres son _____.

4. 8 + _____ = 14   Ocho y _____ son catorce.

5. 13 + _____ = 20   Trece y _____ son veinte.

6. 15 + 7 = _____   Quince y siete son _____.

7. _____ – 3 = 27   _____ menos tres son veintisiete.

❖**C. Preguntas** (*Questions*). Answer the following questions that a friend has asked about your university.

1. ¿Cuántas clases de Español I hay? _____

    _____

2. ¿Cuántos estudiantes hay en tu (*your*) clase de español? _____

    _____

3. ¿Y cuántos profesores hay en el Departamento de Español? _____

4. ¿Hay clase de español mañana? _____

5. ¿Hay un teatro en la universidad? _____

D. Canción infantil. You will hear a reading of the following children's song. It will be read with pauses for repetition. First, listen to the reading of the song.

Canción infantil

Dos y dos son cuatro,
cuatro y dos son seis,
seis y dos son ocho,
y ocho dieciséis.

E. ¿Cuántos hay? (*How many are there?*) Read the following phrases when you hear the corresponding numbers. (Remember to repeat the correct answer.)

1. 21 personas (*f.*)
2. 18 profesores
3. 1 señora (*f.*)
4. 21 días (*m.*)
5. 30 cafés

F. ¿Qué hay en el salón de clase? (*What is there in the classroom?*) You will hear a series of questions. Each will be said twice. Answer based on the following drawing. (Remember to repeat the correct answer.)

1. ...   2. ...   3. ...   4. ...

Los gustos y las preferencias (Part 1)

A. ¿Qué le gusta? (*What do you like?*) Imagine that you are asking your instructor and several classmates whether they like the following items and activities. Form your questions by combining phrases from the two columns. Then write the answers you think they *might* give.

le gusta	la música jazz	beber café
te gusta	el chocolate	estudiar
(no) me gusta	el programa «American Idol»	jugar a la lotería / al tenis /al fútbol
	esquiar	

1. —Profesor(a), ¿_____?

   —Sí (No), _____.

2. —Profesor(a), ¿_____?

   —Sí (No), _____.

3. —_____, ¿_____?
      (*classmate's name*)

   —Sí (No), _____.

4. —_____, ¿_____?

   —Sí (No), _____.

❖**B. ¿Qué te gusta?** (*What do you like?*)

Paso 1. You will hear a series of questions. For each question, check the appropriate answer. No answers will be given. The answers you choose should be correct for you.

1. ☐ ¡Sí, me gusta!   ☐ ¡No, no me gusta!

2. ☐ ¡Sí, creo que (*I think*) es fantástico!   ☐ ¡No, no me gusta!

3. ☐ Sí, me gusta.   ☐ No, no me gusta.

4. ☐ Sí, me gusta.   ☐ No, no me gusta.

Paso 2. Interview Professor Morales about his likes and dislikes using the oral cues. Remember to use **¿Le gusta... ?** and to repeat the correct question. You will hear his answer.

MODELO: (*you hear*) la universidad →
          (*you say*) ¿Le gusta la universidad?   (*you hear*) Sí, me gusta mucho.

1. ...   2. ...   3. ...   4. ...

C. Los gustos y las preferencias. You will hear a series of questions. Each will be said twice. You should be able to guess the meaning of the verbs based on context. Answer based on your own experience. You will hear a possible answer. (Remember to repeat the answer.)

MODELO: (*you see*) jugar
          (*you hear*) ¿Te gusta jugar al tenis? →
          (*you say*) Sí, me gusta jugar al tenis. OR No, no me gusta jugar al tenis.

1. jugar   2. estudiar   3. tocar   4. comer

A. Son las... Match the following statements with the clock faces shown.

1. _____ Son las cinco y diez de la tarde.

2. _____ Son las diez menos veinte de la noche.

3. _____ Es la una y cuarto de la mañana.

4. _____ Son las once y media de la mañana.

5. _____ Son las cuatro menos cuarto de la tarde.

6. _____ Son las nueve y veinte de la noche.

a.   b.   c.   d.   e.   f.

Nota comunicativa: Para expresar la hora

¿Qué hora es? Write out the times indicated. Use **de la mañana, de la tarde,** or **de la noche,** as required.

1. It's 12:20 A.M. _____

2. It's 1:05 P.M. _____

3. It's exactly 2:00 A.M. _____

4. The reception (**La recepción**) is at 7:30 P.M. _____

5. The class is at 10:50 A.M. _____

6. It's 9:45 P.M. _____

7. It's 1:30 A.M. _____

8. It's 8:15 A.M. _____

9. It's at 3:25 P.M. _____

10. It's 4:10 A.M. _____

¡OJO!

In Spain, as in most of Europe, times in transportation schedules are given on a 24-hour clock. A comma is often used instead of a colon. Convert the following hours from the 24-hour system to the A.M./P.M. system.

a. 16,05 = _____   b. 20,15 = _____   c. 22,50 = _____

B. ¿Qué hora es?

Paso 1. You will hear a series of times. Each will be said twice. Circle the letter of the clock face that indicates the time you hear.

MODELO: (*you hear*) Son las diez de la mañana. → (*you circle the letter* ***a***)

(a.)   **b.**

1. a.   **b.**

2. a.   **b.**

3. a.   **b.**

4. a.   **b.**

Paso 2. Now when you hear a number, tell the time that you see on the corresponding clock. Repeat the correct answer.

MODELO: (*you see*) **1.**

(*you hear*) uno →
(*you say*) Son las tres y media de la tarde.

2.    **3.**    **4.**    **5.**

C.   ¿A qué hora es... ? You will hear a series of questions about Marisol's schedule. Answer based on her schedule. (Remember to repeat the correct answer.) First, pause and look at the schedule.

MODELO: (*you hear*) ¿A qué hora es la clase de español? →
(*you say*) Es a las ocho y media de la mañana.

1. ...   **2.** ...   **3.** ...   **4.** ...

Horario escolar*
Nombre: Marisol Abad
Dirección: Calle Alfaro, 16
Teléfono: 72-45-86

8:30	Español
9:40	Ciencias
11:00	Matemáticas
12:25	Inglés
2:15	Arte

*School schedule

Lectura cultural: La geografía del mundo hispánico

Un poco de (*A little bit of*) **geografía.** Match these geographical names with the category to which they belong.

1. _____ los Andes

2. _____ Titicaca

3. _____ Cuba

4. _____ el Caribe

5. _____ el Amazonas

6. _____ Yucatán

a.   una cordillera
b.   una isla
c.   un lago
d.   una península
e.   un río
f.   un mar

❖ **¡Repasemos!** (*Let's review!*)*

A. En el periódico (*newspaper*). You will hear a series of headlines from a Spanish newspaper. Each will be said twice. Write the number of the headline next to the section of the newspaper in which it most likely appears. Try not to be distracted by unfamiliar vocabulary; concentrate instead on the key words in the headline. First, listen to the list of sections.

_____ Política   _____ Espectáculos (*Entertainment*)   _____ Economía

_____ Libros (*Books*)   _____ Deportes (*Sports*)

B. Entrevista. You will hear a series of questions. Each will be said twice. Answer based on your own experience. Pause and write the answers.

1. _____

2. _____

3. _____

4. _____

5. _____

6. _____

7. _____

❖ **Mi diario**

Yo soy... It is a good idea to have a separate notebook for your **diario** entries. Before you begin writing, reread the pages about **Mi diario** in *To the Student* (page vi). Include at least the following information in your first entry:

- First, write today's date in numerals. Note that in Spanish the day comes first, then the month, and finally the year. Thus, 8/9/08 is September 8, 200**8.**
- Now greet your diary as you would a friend and introduce yourself.
- Write down what time it is. (Write out the hour.)
- Describe your personality, using as many adjectives as you can from page 5 of the Workbook/ Laboratory Manual.
- List two things you like (or like to do) and two things you do *not* like (or do not like to do).

⏵ Ponte a prueba

A ver si sabes...

A. ¿Cómo eres? Fill in the blanks with the appropriate form of **ser.**

1. yo _____   2. tú _____   3. usted, él, ella _____

_____

*No answers are given for **¡Repasemos!** activities.

B. **Saludos y expresiones de cortesía.** Complete the following phrases.

1. To a friend: ¡_____! ¿Qué tal?

2. Fill in the blanks with the correct form of **bueno.**

   _____ días.   _____ tardes.   _____ noches.

3. To ask a classmate her name, you say: ¿Cómo _____?

4. The responses to **muchas gracias** are: _____ _____

C. **Los gustos y las preferencias.** Fill in the blanks with the appropriate word(s).

   —¿Te _____¹ el chocolate?

   —No, no _____.²

D. **¿Qué hora es?**

1. To ask what time it is, you say:

   ¿_____?

2. To answer, use:

   _____ la una (y cuarto, y media).

   _____ las dos (tres, etcétera).

Prueba corta

A. **Preguntas.** Contesta en español.

1. Ask your instructor what his or her name is. _____

2. Ask the student next to you what his or her name is. _____

3. Now ask where he/she is from. _____

4. What do you say when someone gives you a gift? _____

5. How does that person respond? _____

6. Tell your best friend what he or she is like. Use at least three adjectives.

   _____

7. Ask your instructor if he or she likes **el jazz.** _____

8. Ask a classmate if he or she likes **el chocolate.** _____

9. Write out the numbers in the following series: tres, _____, nueve, _____,

   _____, dieciocho, _____, veinticuatro, veintisiete, _____.

10. Express 11:15 P.M. in Spanish: _____

B. **Hablando** (*Speaking*) **de las clases.** You will overhear a conversation between Geraldo and Delia. Listen carefully. Try not to be distracted by unfamiliar vocabulary; concentrate instead on what you do know. Then, you will hear a series of statements. Circle **C** (**cierto**) if the statement is true and **F** (**falso**) if it is false.

   1. C   F   2. C   F   3. C   F   4. C   F   5. C   F

CAPÍTULO 1

Paso 1 Vocabulario

En el salón de clase

A. Identificaciones. Identify the person, place, or objects shown in each drawing.

1. _____   2. _____

3. _____   6. _____

4. _____   7. _____

5. _____   8. _____

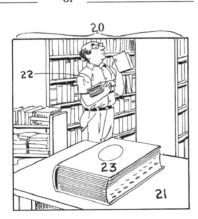

9. _____   14. _____   20. _____

10. _____   15. _____   21. _____

11. _____   16. _____   22. _____

12. _____   17. _____   23. _____

13. _____   18. _____

19. _____

B. **¡Busca el intruso!** (*Look for the intruder!*) Write the item that does not belong in each series of words and explain why.

> **Categorías posibles**
>
> un lugar
>
> un objeto
>
> una persona
>
> MODELO: el bolígrafo / el estudiante / el profesor / el hombre →
> El bolígrafo, porque (*because*) es un objeto. No es una persona.

1. la consejera / la profesora / la calculadora / la compañera de clase

_____

2. la residencia / la librería / la biblioteca / la mochila

_____

3. el papel / el lápiz / el hombre / el bolígrafo

_____

4. el diccionario / el libro / el cuaderno / el salón de clase

_____

5. la bibliotecaria / la cafetería / la biblioteca / la oficina

_____

C. **Dictado: ¿Qué necesita?** (*What does she need?*) Luisa is making a list of things that she will need for her classes this semester. Listen carefully to her list and check the items that she needs. If she mentions a number, write it in the space provided. Don't be distracted by unfamiliar vocabulary; concentrate instead on the words that you *do* know. ¡OJO! Not all items will be mentioned. First, listen to the list of possible items. (Check your answers in the Appendix.)

COSAS	SÍ	NO	¿CUÁNTOS O CUÁNTAS?
mochila(s)			
lápiz (lápices)			
bolígrafo(s)			
libro(s) de texto			
cuaderno(s)			
diccionario(s)			
calculadora(s)			
papel			
pizarra(s)			

D. Identificaciones. Identify the following items when you hear the corresponding number. Begin each sentence with **Es el...** or **Es la...** (Remember to repeat the correct answer.)

1.	...	**6.**	...
2.	...	**7.**	...
3.	...	**8.**	...
4.	...	**9.**	...
5.	...	**10.**	...

Las materias

A. Materias. What classes would you take if you were majoring in the following areas? Choose your classes from the list.

Astronomía   Contabilidad (*Accounting*)   Antropología   Sicología del adolescente
Biología 2   La novela moderna   Francés 304   Física
Gramática alemana   Química orgánica   Sociología urbana   Computación
Cálculo 1   Trigonometría

1. Lenguas y literatura

a. _____

b. _____

c. _____

3. Ciencias sociales

a. _____

b. _____

c. _____

2. Matemáticas y administración de empresas

a. _____

b. _____

c. _____

d. _____

4. Ciencias naturales

a. _____

b. _____

c. _____

d. _____

❖**B. ¿Qué estudias?** (*What are you studying?*) Write about the courses you need or like or do not like to study by combining phrases from the two columns.

Necesito estudiar... (No) Me gusta estudiar...	**+**	japonés, chino, inglés, ruso, español, italiano cálculo, computación, contabilidad historia, ciencias políticas biología, química sicología

MODELO: Necesito estudiar inglés.

1. _____

2. _____

3. _____

Nota comunicativa: Las palabras interrogativas (Part 1)

A. Palabras interrogativas. Complete the sentences with the most appropriate interrogative word or phrase from the following list. In some cases more than one answer is possible. To use this exercise for review, cover the answers with a piece of paper.

¿A qué hora?	¿Cuándo?	¿Dónde?
¿Cómo?	¿Cuánto?	¿Qué?
¿Cuál?	¿Cuántos?	¿Quién?

1. ¿_____ es por el libro (*for the book*)? ¿Tres o cuatro dólares?

2. ¿_____ es la clase de historia? ¿A la una o a las dos?

3. —Buenos días, Sr. Vargas. ¿_____ está Ud. hoy?

4. ¿_____ es la capital de la Argentina? ¿Buenos Aires o Lima?

5. ¿_____ estudias (*do you study*), en casa (*at home*) o en la biblioteca?

6. —¿_____ es Ud.?

   —Soy María Castro.

7. ¿_____ es el examen, hoy o mañana?

8. ¿_____ es esto? ¿una trompeta o un saxofón?

B. El Cine Bolívar. Your friend asks you some questions about a movie (**una película**) at the Cine Bolívar. Use an appropriate interrogative phrase to complete each of his questions.

AMIGO: ¿_____¹ se llama la película?

USTED: *Casablanca.*

AMIGO: ¿_____² es el actor principal?

USTED: Humphrey Bogart.

AMIGO: ¿_____³ es la película?

USTED: Es romántica.

AMIGO: ¿_____⁴ es por la entrada (*for the admission*)?

USTED: Siete pesos.

AMIGO: ¿_____⁵ está el Cine Bolívar?

USTED: Está en la Avenida Bolívar.

AMIGO: ¿_____⁶ es la película?

USTED: A las siete de la tarde.

AMIGO: ¿_____⁷ hora es ahora?

USTED: Son las cinco y cuarto.

C. Preguntas y respuestas (*Questions and answers*). Imagine that your friend Marisa has just made some statements that you didn't quite understand. You will hear each statement twice. Circle the letter of the interrogative word or phrase you would use to obtain information about what she said.

1. **a.** ¿a qué hora?   **b.** ¿cómo es?
2. **a.** ¿quién?   **b.** ¿dónde?
3. **a.** ¿cuál?   **b.** ¿dónde está?
4. **a.** ¿cuántas?   **b.** ¿cuándo?
5. **a.** ¿qué es?   **b.** ¿cómo es?
6. **a.** ¿cómo está?   **b.** ¿qué es?

Pronunciación y ortografía • Diphthongs and Linking

A. Las vocales. Complete the sentences.

1. Spanish has _____ (*number*) vowels.

2. The strong vowels are _____.

3. The weak vowels are _____.

4. A diphthong consists of one _____ vowel and one _____ vowel,

   or two successive _____ vowels pronounced in the same syllable.

B. Los diptongos. Underline the diphthongs in the following words.

1. es-tu-dian-te   4. cua-der-no   7. es-cri-to-rio
2. dic-cio-na-rio   5. bi-lin-güe   8. sie-te
3. puer-ta   6. gra-cias   9. seis

C. Repaso: Las vocales. Repeat the following words, imitating the speaker. Pay close attention to the pronunciation of the indicated vowels.

WEAK VOWELS

(i, y)   Pili   silla   soy   y
(u)   gusto   lugar   uno   mujer

STRONG VOWELS

(a)   calculadora   Ana   banana   lápiz
(e)   trece   papel   clase   general
(o)   profesor   hombre   Lola   bolígrafo

D. Los diptongos. Diphthongs are formed by two successive weak vowels (**i** or **y, u**) or by a combination of a weak vowel and a strong vowel (**a, e, o**). The two vowels are pronounced as a single syllable. Repeat the following words, imitating the speaker. Pay close attention to the pronunciation of the indicated diphthongs.

1. (ia) media   gracias
2. (ie) bien   siete
3. (io) Julio   edificio
4. (iu) ciudad (*city*)   viuda (*widow*)
5. (ua) cuaderno   Managua
6. (ue) buenos   nueve
7. (ui) muy   fui (*I was / I went*)
8. (uo) cuota   arduo
9. (ai) aire   hay
10. (ei) veinte   treinta
11. (oi) soy   estoy
12. (au) auto   pausa
13. (eu) deuda (*debt*)   Ceuta

Más sobre (*about*) **los diptongos**

Paso 1. Diphthongs can occur within a word or between words, causing the words to be "linked" and pronounced as one long word. Repeat the following phrases and sentences, imitating the speaker. Pay close attention to how the words are linked.

    1. (oi/ia)   Armando‿y‿Alicia

                              las letras o‿y‿hache

    2. (ei/ie)   el tigre‿y‿el chimpancé

                              Vicente‿y‿Elena

    3. (oi/ie/ai/io)   Soy‿extrovertida‿y‿optimista.

    4. (ai/iu)   Elena‿y‿Humberto necesitan una mochila‿y‿unos libros.

Paso 2. Linking also occurs naturally between many word boundaries in Spanish. Repeat the following sentences, imitating the speaker. Try to say each without pause, as if it were one long word.

    1. ¿Es usted eficiente?
    2. ¿Dónde hay un escritorio?
    3. Tomás y Alicia están en la oficina.
    4. Están en la Argentina y en el Uruguay.
    5. No hay estudiantes en el edificio a estas horas (*at these hours*).

🎧 **F.** **Dictado.** You will hear a series of words containing diphthongs. Each will be said twice. Listen carefully and write the missing vowels. (Check your answers in the Appendix.)

    1. c_____nc_____s   **3.** s_____s   **5.** _____to

    2. Patric_____   **4.** b_____nos   **6.** s_____

Lectura cultural: Los Estados Unidos

¿Cierto o falso? Contesta según las **Lecturas culturales 1** y **2*** del libro de texto.

	C	F
1. La población (*population*) hispana de los Estados Unidos es más grande que (*bigger than*) la población hispana de México.	☐	☐
2. La Misión San José de Laguna está en California.	☐	☐
3. Unos cuatro millones de puertorriqueños (*Puerto Ricans*) viven (*live*) en la Pequeña Habana de Miami.	☐	☐
4. Hay muchos músicos (*musicians*), escritores (*writers*), atletas y actores hispanos en los Estados Unidos.	☐	☐
5. En marzo (*March*) celebran el Festival de la Calle Ocho en Los Ángeles.	☐	☐
6. Un periódico (*newspaper*) importante que se publica (*that is published*) en español es *La Opinión*.	☐	☐

---

*These sections quiz the **Lectura cultural 1** reading between **Paso 1: Vocabulario** and **Paso 2: Gramática** as well as **Lectura cultural 2** between **Paso 2: Gramática** and **Paso 3: Gramática**.

Paso 2 Gramática

1. Identifying People, Places, Things, and Ideas (Part 1) • Singular Nouns: Gender and Articles

A. ¿El o la? Escribe el artículo definido apropiado, **el** o **la.**

1. _____ tarde   3. _____ nación   5. _____ día   7. _____ clase

2. _____ libertad   4. _____ profesor   6. _____ mujer   8. _____ hombre

B. ¿Un o una? Escribe el artículo indefinido apropiado, **un** o **una.**

1. _____ diccionario   3. _____ lápiz   5. _____ salón   7. _____ mesa

2. _____ universidad   4. _____ dependienta   6. _____ mochila   8. _____ programa

C. Una cuestión de gustos. Indicate how you feel about the following places or things. Remember to use the article **el** or **la.**

MODELO: programa «Sixty Minutes» → (No) Me gusta el programa «Sixty Minutes».

1. clase de español   _____

2. universidad   _____

3. música de Bach   _____

4. Mundo de Disney   _____

5. limonada   _____

6. comida (*food*) mexicana   _____

7. física   _____

8. programa «American Idol»   _____

D. Gramática en acción: La lista de José María.
You will hear the list of supplies and texts that
José María needs for two of his classes. Check the
items you hear for each class. Not all items you
hear are on the list, and the items are not in order!
(Check your answers in the Appendix.)

	ESPAÑOL 30	CÁLCULO 2
un cuaderno	☐	☐
un diccionario español-inglés	☐	☐
una calculadora	☐	☐
los libros de texto	☐	☐
la novela *Don Quijote*	☐	☐
la tarjeta de acceso para el cuaderno en línea	☐	☐

E. En la clase del profesor Durán: El primer día

Paso 1. Dictado. The dialogue below will be read twice. Listen carefully the first time; the second time, write in the missing words. (Check your answers in the Appendix).

PROFESOR DURÁN: Aquí está _____¹ _____² del curso. Son necesarios

_____³ _____⁴ de texto y _____⁵ diccionario.

También hay _____⁶ _____⁷ de _____⁸

y libros de poesía.

ESTUDIANTE 1: ¡Es una lista infinita!

ESTUDIANTE 2: Sí, y los libros cuestan demasiado.

ESTUDIANTE 1: No, _____⁹ _____¹⁰ no es el precio de los libros. ¡Es

_____¹¹ _____¹² para leer los libros!

Paso 2. ¿Cierto o falso? Now pause and read the following statements about the dialogue. Circle **C** (**cierto**) if the statement is true or **F** (**falso**) if it is false.

1. C F En la clase del profesor Durán es necesario leer muchos libros.

2. C F Para los estudiantes, el problema es el tiempo para leer los libros.

3. C F Los estudiantes necesitan una calculadora para la clase.

Now resume listening.

F. ¿Qué te gusta? Tell a friend what you like, using the oral cues and the correct definite article. (Remember to repeat the correct answer.)

MODELO: (*you hear*) profesora → (*you say*) Me gusta la profesora.

1. ... 2. ... 3. ... 4. ... 5. ...

G. ¿Qué hay en estos (*these*) lugares? Identify the items in each drawing after you hear the corresponding number. Begin each sentence with **Hay un...** or **Hay una...** (Remember to repeat the correct answer.)

MODELO: (*you see*) diccionario → (*you say*) Hay un diccionario en la mesa.

1.

2.

estudiante

3.

consejero

4.

2. Identifying People, Places, Things, and Ideas (Part 2) • Nouns and Articles: Plural Forms

A. Singular → plural. Escribe la forma plural.

1. la amiga _____

2. el bolígrafo _____

3. la clase _____

4. un profesor _____

5. el lápiz _____

6. una extranjera _____

7. la universidad _____

8. un programa _____

B. Plural → singular. Escribe la forma singular.

1. los edificios _____

2. las fiestas _____

3. unas clientas _____

4. unos lápices _____

5. los papeles _____

6. las condiciones _____

7. unos problemas _____

8. unas mujeres _____

C. Gramática en acción: Un anuncio

Paso 1. You will hear the following ad. Listen carefully and read along with the speakers. Do not be distracted by unfamiliar vocabulary. Focus instead on the words that you *do* know.

Paso 2. Pause and complete the following sentences based on the preceding ad. (Check your answers in the Appendix.)

1. The plural of **curso** is

   _____.

2. The plural of **idioma** is

   _____.

3. The plural of **universidad** is

   _____.

Cursos de Idiomas en el Extranjero

Financiación **SIN INTERESES** en 3, 6 ó 12 meses

- Cursos para jóvenes de 7 a 17 años
- Cursos para adultos a partir de 18 años
- Cursos en Universidades: Idioma general y/o técnico
- Minimasters en Universidades USA, Inglaterra e Irlanda
- Programa residencial en Sevilla y/o Madrid con inglés
- Preparación para TOEFL, GMAT, SAT, GRE, USMLE
- Cursos de idiomas en Madrid

Instituto ProLengua ofrece pagar su curso aplazado en 3, 6 ó 12 meses

🌐 INSTITUTO PROLENGUA

Infórmate **902-253 797**

4. To express **residential program** in Spanish, you would say _____.

Now resume listening.

D. Descripción: El cuarto de Ignacio. You will hear Ignacio describe his room. As you listen, circle the number of the drawing that best matches his description. First, pause and look at the drawings.

1.   **2.**   **3.**

E. Cambios (*Changes*). You will hear a series of nouns and articles. Give the plural forms of the first four nouns and articles and the singular forms of the next four. (Remember to repeat the correct answer.)

SINGULAR → PLURAL   PLURAL → SINGULAR

1. ...   **2.** ...   **3.** ...   **4.** ...   **5.** ...   **6.** ...   **7.** ...   **8.** ...

F. Los errores de Inés. You will hear some statements that your friend Inés makes about the following drawing. She is wrong and you must correct her. (Remember to repeat the correct answer.)

MODELO: (*you hear*) Hay dos libros. → (*you say*) No. Hay tres libros.

1. ...   **2.** ...   **3.** ...   **4.** ...   **5.** ...   **6.** ...

G. Dictado. You will hear a series of sentences. Each will be said twice. Listen carefully and write the missing words. You will be listening for words that are either singular or plural. (Check your answers in the Appendix.)

1. Hay _____ _____ en _____ _____.

2. _____ _____ están en _____ _____.

3. No hay _____ en _____ _____.

4. ¿Hay _____ _____ en _____ _____?

Paso 3 Gramática

3. Expressing Actions • Subject Pronouns (Part 1); Present Tense of -ar Verbs; Negation

A. Los pronombres personales. What subject pronouns would you use to speak *about* the following persons?

1. your female friends _____
2. your brother _____
3. yourself _____

4. your friends Eva and Jesús _____
5. your male relatives _____
6. you and your sister _____

B. Más sobre (*about*) **los pronombres.** What subject pronouns would you use to speak *to* the following persons?

1. your cousin Roberto _____

2. your friends (*m.*) _____   _____
                    (*in Spain*)   (*in Latin America*)

3. your instructors _____

4. the store clerk _____

5. your friend _____   _____
            (*in Spain*)   (*in Latin America*)

C. ¡No, no! Correct the following statements by making them all negative. Use subject pronouns in your answers. Then write two sentences telling about things *you* do *not* do. Use only verbs that you have studied so far.

1. Shaquille O'Neal trabaja en una oficina.

    _____

2. Shakira canta en japonés.

    _____

3. Tomamos cerveza (*beer*) en la clase.

    _____

4. La profesora regresa a la universidad por la noche.

    _____

5. Los estudiantes bailan en la biblioteca.

    _____

6. Enseño español.

    _____

❖7. _____

❖8. _____

D. En la universidad. Describe what the following people are doing, using the verbs given. Not all verbs will be used.

bailar
cantar
hablar
pagar
tocar
tomar
trabajar

1. *En el bar:* Yo _____ por teléfono. Madonna _____ en la

   televisión y Jaime y Ana _____. Tomás y Carlos _____ cerveza y

   Carlos _____ las bebidas (*drinks*). El mesero (*waiter*) _____ mucho.

buscar
escuchar
necesitar
pagar

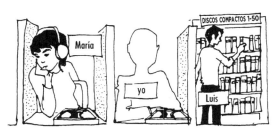

2. *En el laboratorio de lenguas:* María y yo _____ la lección de español. Luis

   _____ el CD #2. Él _____ preparar la lección de francés.

desear
enseñar
estudiar
practicar
regresar

3. *En la clase:* La profesora Cantellini _____ italiano, y los estudiantes

   _____ y _____ mucho. A las nueve y media, ella

   _____ a su (*her*) oficina.

❖4. Now write three sentences that describe what you and your friends do on a typical weekend.
   Use only verbs that you have studied so far. (Use **nosotros** forms.)

   En un fin de semana típico, _____

   _____.

E. Preguntas. Answer the questions with real information. Use subject pronouns to replace nouns. Note that normally the subject follows the verb in questions.

MODELO: ¿Cantan o estudian Uds.? → Nosotros estudiamos.

1. ¿Baila o canta Enrique Iglesias?

_____

2. Wynton Marsalis, ¿toca la guitarra o la trompeta?

_____

3. En clase, ¿desean Uds. cantar o escuchar?

_____

4. Por la noche, ¿estudia Ud. en la biblioteca o en casa?

_____

5. ¿Toma Ud. Coca-Cola o café?

_____

6. ¿Y sus (*your*) amigos?

_____

7. ¿Practican Uds. español o francés?

_____

F. Gramática en acción: Una escena en la biblioteca. You will hear a description of the following drawing. After listening, pause and read each statement about the description. Circle **C** (**cierto**) if the statement is true or **F** (**falso**) if it is false. If the information is not contained in or cannot be inferred from the description, circle **ND** (**No lo dice** [*It doesn't say*]). In this exercise, you will be listening for specific information.

1. C F ND Cuatro estudiantes trabajan hoy en esta (*this*) sección de la biblioteca.

2. C F ND La narradora (*The narrator*) trabaja en la biblioteca.

3. C F ND Manuel y la narradora estudian para un examen de matemáticas.

4. C F ND El amigo del profesor (*The professor's friend*) trabaja en la biblioteca.

G. ¿Quién habla? You will hear a series of sentences. Each will be said twice. Listen carefully and circle the letter of the *subject* of each sentence. In this exercise, you will practice listening for specific information.

1. **a.** yo   **b.** ella
2. **a.** él   **b.** tú
3. **a.** Ana y yo   **b.** los estudiantes
4. **a.** Alberto   **b.** Alberto y tú
5. **a.** Uds.   **b.** nosotras

H. ¿Quién... ? Answer the following questions using the oral cues. (Remember to repeat the correct answer.)

1. ¿Quién canta bien?

    MODELO: (*you hear*) Juan → (*you say*) Juan canta bien.

    a. ... **b.** ... **c.** ... **d.** ...

2. ¿Quién practica deportes (*sports*)?

    MODELO: (*you hear*) yo → (*you say*) Yo practico deportes.

    a. ... **b.** ... **c.** ... **d.** ...

I. Mis compañeros y yo. Form complete sentences about yourself and others, using the oral and written cues. (Remember to repeat the correct answer.)

    MODELO: (*you see and hear*) yo   (*you hear*) pagar la matrícula →
    (*you say*) Pago la matrícula.

1. Ana y yo
2. Chela y Roberto
3. el estudiante de Chile
4. Jaime, tú...
5. profesor, Ud. ...

Nota comunicativa: The Verb *estar*

A. ¿Dónde están todos ahora? Tell where you and your classmates are. Form complete sentences by using the words provided in the order given.

    MODELO: Ud. / cafetería → Ud. está en la cafetería.

1. Raúl y Carmen / salón de clase _____

2. yo / biblioteca _____

3. tú / clase de biología _____

4. Uds. / laboratorio de lenguas _____

B. ¿Dónde están y qué hacen (*what are they doing*)**?** Completa las oraciones con el verbo apropiado de la lista.

bailar	escuchar	tocar
cantar	estar	tomar

1. Mis (*My*) amigos y yo _____ en una fiesta.

2. José, Elena, Roberto y Carmen _____.

3. Isabel y Julio _____ «La bamba».

4. Yo _____ la guitarra.

5. Pablo _____ café y _____ la música.

Un poco de todo

A. Situaciones. You and your friend have just met Daniel, a new student at the university. It is about half an hour before class. He asks you the following questions. Answer them in complete sentences.

1. ¿Estudian Uds. español? _____

2. ¿Quién enseña la clase? _____

3. ¿De dónde es él/ella? _____

4. ¿Cuántos estudiantes hay en la clase? _____

5. ¿Te gusta la clase? _____

6. ¿El profesor / La profesora habla inglés en la clase? _____

7. ¿Uds. necesitan practicar en el laboratorio todos los días? _____

   _____

8. ¿A qué hora es la clase? _____

B. De compras (*Shopping*). Martín necesita comprar unos libros. Contesta las preguntas según el dibujo (*according to the drawing*).

1. ¿Dónde compra libros Martín? _____

2. ¿Hay libros en italiano en la librería? _____

3. ¿Qué otros objetos hay? _____

   _____

4. ¿Cuántos libros compra Martín? _____

5. ¿Hablan alemán la dependienta y Martín? _____

6. ¿Paga Martín doce dólares? _____

¡Repasemos!

A. **¿Cómo se dice en español?** Sigue (*Follow*) el modelo. Usa un verbo conjugado + un infinitivo.

MODELO: I need to study. → Necesito estudiar.

1.   I want to work. _____

2.   We need to work. _____

3.   We need to buy a dictionary. _____

4.   We need to pay for the dictionary. _____

5.   He needs to look for some books. _____

B. **En la cafetería.** En español, por favor. Escribe el diálogo en otro papel.

ANA: Hi, Daniel! How are you?
DANIEL: Fine, thanks. (At) What time are you going (returning) home today?
ANA: At two o'clock. I work at four.
DANIEL: How many (**¿Cuántas**) hours do you work today?
ANA: Six. And tonight (**esta noche**) I need to study. Tomorrow there is an exam in (**un examen de**) history.
DANIEL: Poor thing! (**¡Pobre!**) You work a lot.
ANA: Well, I need to pay for my (**mis**) books and tuition. See you tomorrow.
DANIEL: Good-bye. See you later.

C. **Entrevista.** You will hear a series of questions about your classes and your life at the university. Each will be said twice. Answer based on your own experience. Pause and write the answers.

Note: The word **tu** means *your,* and **mi** means *my.*

1.   _____

2.   _____

3.   _____

4.   _____

5.   _____

6.   _____

Mi diario

Una introducción. Write the date first. (*Remember:* In Spanish the day comes first, then the month: 15/9/2010.) Write about yourself. Be sure to write in complete sentences. Include the following information:

- your name and where you are from
- how you would describe yourself as a student (**Como estudiante, soy...**); review the cognates in **Capítulo preliminar** if you need to
- the courses you are taking this term (**este semestre/trimestre**) and at what time they are given
- the school materials and equipment that you have (**tengo...**) and those you need
- what you like to do (**me gusta...**) at different times of the day (**por la mañana, por la tarde, por la noche**).

Limit yourself to vocabulary you have learned so far. Do *not* use a dictionary!

Ponte a prueba

A ver si sabes...

A. Gender and Articles. Escribe el artículo apropiado.

DEFINITE ARTICLES (*the*) INDEFINITE ARTICLES (*a, an, some*)

	SINGULAR	PLURAL			SINGULAR	PLURAL
1. *m.*	_____	_____	**3.** *m.*	_____	_____
2. *f.*	_____	_____	**4.** *f.*	_____	_____

B. Present Tense of *-ar* Verbs. Escribe la forma correcta del verbo **buscar.**

1. yo _____   **4.** nosotros/as _____

2. tú _____   **5.** vosotros/as _____

3. Ud., él, ella _____   **6.** Uds., ellos, ellas _____

C. Negation. Place the word **no** in the appropriate place to form negative sentences.

1. Yo _____ deseo tomar _____ café.

2. _____ hablamos _____ alemán en la clase.

D. El verbo *estar*. Escribe la forma plural.

SINGULAR   PLURAL

yo estoy → _____   _____ 1

tú estás → vosotros   _____ 2

          Uds.   _____ 3

él está → _____   _____ 4

Prueba corta

A. Los artículos definidos. Da el artículo definido.

1. _____ papel **4.** _____ libro de texto **7.** _____ lápices

2. _____ mochila **5.** _____ nación **8.** _____ programas

3. _____ universidad **6.** _____ días

B. Los artículos indefinidos. Da el artículo indefinido.

1. _____ librería **4.** _____ problema **7.** _____ mujer

2. _____ señores **5.** _____ clase **8.** _____ horas

3. _____ hombres **6.** _____ tardes

C. **Los verbos.** Completa las oraciones con la forma apropiada de un verbo de la lista.

enseñar   estudiar   hablar   necesitar   practicar   regresar   tocar

1. Los estudiantes _____ en la biblioteca.

2. Yo _____ español en el laboratorio de lenguas.

3. En la clase de español (nosotros) no _____ inglés.

4. ¡Alberto es fantástico! _____ el piano como (*like*) un profesional.

5. La profesora García _____ ciencias naturales.

6. (Yo) _____ comprar un diccionario bueno.

7. ¿A qué hora _____ el consejero a su (*his*) oficina?

D. **Cosas de todos los días**

Paso 1. Practice talking about your university, using the written cues. When you hear the corresponding number, form sentences using the words provided in the order given, making any necessary changes or additions. (Remember to repeat the correct answer.)

MODELO: (*you see*) **1.** profesores / llegar / temprano / a / universidad   (*you hear*) uno →
(*you say*) Los profesores llegan temprano a la universidad.

2. consejeros / trabajar / en / oficina
3. mi amiga y yo / estudiar / en / biblioteca
4. en clase / nosotros / escuchar / a / profesores
5. fin de semana / mis amigos y yo / bailar / en / discoteca
6. por la mañana / (yo) / practicar / vocabulario
7. por la noche / (yo) / mirar / televisión

Paso 2. ¿Qué recuerdas? Now you will hear a series of questions. Each will be said twice. Answer based on the preceding sentences. If you prefer, pause and write the answers. (Remember to repeat the correct answer.)

1. _____

2. _____

3. _____

4. _____

CAPÍTULO **2**

Paso 1 Vocabulario

La familia y los parientes

A. Identificaciones. Identifica a los parientes y mascotas de Julián.

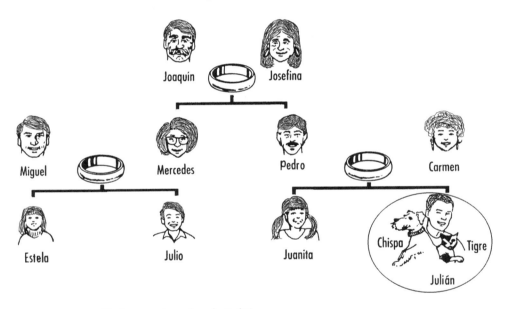

MODELO: Pedro es el padre de Julián.

1. Joaquín _____ de Julián.

2. Julio _____ de Julián.

3. Miguel y Mercedes _____ de Julián.

4. Estela y Julio _____ de Julián.

5. Juanita _____ de Julián.

6. Pedro y Carmen _____ de Julián.

7. Chispa _____ de Julián.

8. Tigre _____ de Julián.

B. **¿Qué son?** Complete the sentences logically. Use each item only once. Some items will not be used.

abuela   hermana   mascota   padres   sobrino
abuelos   hermano   nieta   parientes   tía

1. El hijo de mi hermano es mi _____.

2. La madre de mi primo es mi _____.

3. Los padres de mi madre son mis _____.

4. La madre de mi madre es mi _____.

5. Yo soy la _____ de mis abuelos.

6. Hay muchos _____ en mi familia. Tengo seis tíos y veintiún primos.

7. El perro o gato de una familia es su (*their*) _____.

Nota cultural: Los apellidos hispánicos

¿Cómo se llama?

1. Miguel Martín Soto married Carmen Arias Bravo. Thus, their daughter Emilia's legal name is
   a. Emilia Soto Bravo
   b. Emilia Martín Bravo
   c. Emilia Martín Arias
   d. Emilia Soto Arias

2. Ángela Rebolleda Castillo married César Aragón Saavedra. Their son Francisco's name, therefore, is
   a. Francisco Castillo Saavedra
   b. Francisco Aragón Rebolleda
   c. Francisco Saavedra Castillo
   d. Francisco Rebolleda Saavedra

C. **La familia Muñoz.** You will hear a brief description of Sarita Muñoz's family. Listen carefully and complete the following family tree according to the description. First, pause and look at the family tree. (Check your answers in the Appendix.)

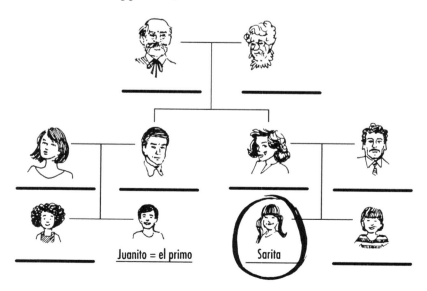

Juanito = el primo   Sarita

D. Definiciones. You will hear a series of definitions of family relationships. Each will be said twice. Listen carefully and write the number of the definition next to the word defined. First, listen to the list of words.

_____ mi (*my*) abuelo   _____ mi hermano   _____ mi tío

_____ mi tía   _____ mi prima   _____ mi abuela

Los números del 31 al 100

A. Situaciones. You've been asked to make a list of some equipment and supplies in the university library. Write out the numbers. ¡RECUERDA! (*Remember!*) **Uno** becomes **un** before a masculine noun and **una** before a feminine noun.

1. 100 _____ discos compactos

2. 31 _____ computadoras

3. 57 _____ enciclopedias

4. 91 _____ diccionarios

5. 76 _____ escritorios

Nota comunicativa: Expressing Age

❖**¿Cuántos años tienen?** (*How old are they?*) Completa las oraciones con información acerca de (*about*) tu (*your*) familia o amigos: **padre, madre, abuelo/a, amigo/a, ¿ ?**

1. Mi _____ tiene _____ años.

2. Mi _____ tiene _____ años.

3. Mi _____ tiene _____ años.

4. Y yo tengo _____ años.

B. Dictado: El inventario. Imagine that you and a friend, Isabel, are taking inventory at the university bookstore where you work. Write out the numerals as she dictates the list to you. She will say each number twice. ¡OJO! Items are given in random order. First, listen to the list of words. (Check your answers in the Appendix.)

_____ mochilas

_____ lápices

_____ cuadernos

_____ novelas

_____ calculadoras

_____ libros de español

Los adjetivos

❖**A. ¿Qué opinas?** Do you agree or disagree with the following statements? Check the appropriate box.

	ESTOY DE ACUERDO.	NO ESTOY DE ACUERDO.
1. David Letterman es cómico.	☐	☐
2. Danny DeVito es alto y delgado.	☐	☐
3. Christina Aguilera es morena y gorda.	☐	☐
4. Brad Pitt es guapo.	☐	☐
5. El Parque Yosemite es impresionante.	☐	☐

B. Descripciones. Describe the drawings using adjectives from the following list. Some items will not be used.

1.　　　　2.　　　　3.　　　　4.

gordo　grande　guapo　joven　listo　moreno　nuevo　pequeño　perezoso　trabajador　viejo

1. El libro es _____ y _____.

2. El libro es _____ y _____.

3. El hombre es _____, _____ y _____.

4. El hombre es _____, _____ y _____.

C. Anuncios personales. Lee (*Read*) los anuncios y corrige (*correct*) los comentarios falsos.

Profesor, 48 años, rubio, guapo. Me gusta el ciclismo, la música clásica. Tel: 2-95-33-51, Luis

Ejecutivo, Banco Internacional, 32 años, graduado en MIT, soltero, delgado. Aficiones: basquetbol, viajar, bailar, ciencia ficción. Tel: 9-13-66-42, Carlos

Secretaria ejecutiva bilingüe, alta, morena, 28 años. Me gusta la playa, el *camping*, la comida francesa. Tel: 7-14-21-77, Diana

1. Diana es joven y rubia. _____

2. Luis tiene cincuenta y ocho años. _____

3. Carlos es casado y gordo. _____

4. A Luis le gusta escuchar la música rock. _____

5. El teléfono de Diana es el siete, cuarenta, veintiuno, setenta y siete. _____

_____

D. ¿Cómo son Ricardo y Felipe? Ricardo is the opposite of Tomás, and Felipe is the opposite of Alberto. What are Ricardo and Felipe like?

1. Tomás es alto, guapo, tonto y perezoso, pero Ricardo es _____,

   _____, _____ y _____.

2. Alberto es casado, joven, antipático y rubio, pero Felipe es _____,

   _____, _____ y _____.

E. ¿Cómo son estas personas famosas? Escribe todos los adjetivos apropiados.

1. Will Ferrell es _____.

2. Antonio Banderas es _____.

3. Madonna es (¡OJO! Remember to use the **-a** ending.) _____

   _____

4. Penélope Cruz es (¡OJO!) _____.

F. ¿Cuál es? You will hear a series of descriptions. Each will be said twice. Circle the letter of the item or person described.

1. **a.**    **b.**    2. **a.**    **b.**

3. **a.**    **b.**    4. **a.**    **b.**

5. **a.**    **b.**

Pronunciación y ortografía • Stress and Written Accent Marks (Part 1)

A. El acento. Underline the stressed vowel in each of the following words.

1. doctor
2. mujer
3. mochila
4. actor
5. permiso
6. posible
7. general
8. profesores
9. universidad
10. Carmen
11. Isabel
12. biblioteca
13. usted
14. libertad
15. origen
16. animal

B. Repeticiones. Repeat the following words, imitating the speaker. The highlighted syllable receives the stress in pronunciation.

1. If a word ends in a vowel, **n,** or **s,** stress normally falls on the next-to-the-last syllable.

    sin**ce**ra   inte**re**san**te**   cua**der**nos   e**xa**men

2. If a word ends in any other consonant, stress normally falls on the last syllable.

    es**tar**   libe**ral**   profe**sor**   pa**pel**

C. Más repeticiones. Repeat the following words, imitating the speaker. The words have been divided into syllables for you. Pay close attention to which syllable receives the spoken stress.

1. Stress on the next-to-the-last syllable

    li-bro   si-lla   cla-se   me-sa   Car-men
    con-se-je-ra   li-te-ra-tu-ra   o-ri-gen   com-pu-ta-do-ra   cien-cias

2. Stress on the last syllable

    se-ñor   mu-jer   fa-vor   ac-tor   co-lor
    po-pu-lar   li-ber-tad   ge-ne-ral   sen-ti-men-tal   u-ni-ver-si-dad

D. Dictado. You will hear the following words. Each will be said twice. Listen carefully and circle the syllable that receives the spoken stress. (Check your answers in the Appendix.)

1. con-trol
2. e-le-fan-te
3. mo-nu-men-tal
4. com-pa-ñe-ra
5. bue-nos
6. us-ted

Lectura cultural: México

¿Cierto o falso? Contesta según las **Lectural culturales 1** y **2** del libro de texto.

	C	F
1. Antes de (*Before*) 1492, México no tenía (*didn't have*) ciudades grandes.	☐	☐
2. Hoy en México ya no (*no longer*) hablan idiomas (*languages*) indígenas.	☐	☐
3. Muchos turistas visitan Acapulco para ver (*to see*) a los clavadistas.	☐	☐
4. Para celebrar el Día de los Muertos, muchos mexicanos llevan comida y flores (*take food and flowers*) al cementerio.	☐	☐
5. El Chac Mool es una figura arqueológica original de los olmecas.	☐	☐
6. La cultura olmeca es la más antigua (*the oldest*) de México.	☐	☐

Paso 2 Gramática

4. Describing • Adjectives: Gender, Number, and Position

A. María Gabriela. The following sentences describe some aspects of the life of María Gabriela, a student from Argentina. In each item, scan through the adjectives to see which ones, by *form* and *meaning*, can complete the sentences. Write the appropriate ones in the space provided.

1. La ciudad de Buenos Aires es _____.
   (bonita, corta, grande, interesante, largo, pequeños)

2. Los compañeros de María Gabriela son _____.
   (amable, casado, delgados, jóvenes, simpáticos, solteras)

3. Su amiga Julia es _____.
   (delgada, gordo, importantes, nervioso, pequeña, trabajadora)

4. Sus profesoras son _____.
   (altas, impacientes, inteligentes, morena, perezosos, simpáticos)

B. Personas, objetos y lugares internacionales. Complete the following sentences with the appropriate adjective of nationality.

1. Berlín es una ciudad _____.

2. El Ferrari es un coche _____.

3. Ted Kennedy es un político _____.

4. Londres (*London*) es la capital _____.

5. Guadalajara es una ciudad _____.

6. Shakespeare y Charles Dickens son dos escritores _____.

7. París y Marsella son dos ciudades _____.

C. En busca de... (*In search of...*) Describe what you or your friends are looking for by inserting the adjectives given in parentheses *in their proper position* in these sentences. Be sure that the adjectives agree with the nouns they modify.

1. Ana busca coche. (italiano, otro) _____

2. Buscamos motocicleta. (alemán, uno) _____

3. Paco busca las novelas. (francés, otro) _____

4. Busco el drama *Romeo y Julieta*. (grande, inglés) _____

5. Jorge busca esposa. (ideal, uno) _____

D. Gramática en acción: Un poema sencillo

Paso 1. You will hear the following poem. Listen carefully and read along with the speakers, Marta and Mario.

Amigo

Fiel

Amable

Simpático

¡Lo admiro!

Amiga

Fiel

Amable

Simpática

¡La admiro!

Paso 2. Now pause and check the adjectives that can be used to describe each person without making any changes to the adjectives. (Check your answers in the Appendix.)

	FIEL	AMABLE	SIMPÁTICO	SIMPÁTICA
Marta				
Mario				

Now resume listening.

E. ¿Cómo son? Practice describing various people, using the oral and written cues. Remember to change the endings of the adjectives if necessary. (Remember to repeat the correct answer.)

MODELO: (*you see and hear*) mi profesora (*you hear*) lista →
(*you say*) Mi profesora es lista.

1. mi compañero de cuarto
2. la profesora de español
3. Bernardo
4. Amanda
5. yo (*f.*)

5. Expressing *to be* • Present Tense of *ser;* Summary of Uses (Part 2)

A. Estudiantes españoles. Muchos estudiantes en la universidad son de España. Imagina que eres uno de ellos. Jorge es de Madrid. ¿De dónde son los otros estudiantes? Usa la forma apropiada de **ser.**

Yo _____.¹
(Barcelona)

Miguel y David _____.²
(Valencia)

Tú _____.³
(Granada)

Nosotros _____.⁴
(Sevilla)

Uds. _____.⁵
(Toledo)

Vosotras _____.⁶
(Burgos)

❖**B.** **¿De dónde son estas personas?** Indicate what state or province (or country, if appropriate) the following people are from. Use the correct form of **ser.**

1. Yo _____.

2. Mi mejor (*best*) amigo/a _____.

3. Mi profesor(a) de español _____.

4. Muchos estudiantes en mi clase _____.

C. **¿De quién son estos objetos?** Ask Jorge to whom the following things belong. Then write Jorge's response.

MODELO: UD.: ¿De quién es el cuaderno?
JORGE: Es del Sr. Ortega.

Sr. Ortega

1.

la profesora

UD.: _____

JORGE: _____

2.

Cecilia

UD.: _____

JORGE: _____

3.

Sr. Alonso

UD.: _____

JORGE: _____

4.

Sres. Olivera

UD.: _____

JORGE: _____

D. Regalos. Imagine that you are giving presents to the following people. Justify each choice of presents by using one of these phrases. Add other details if you wish.

es gordo/a su televisor es viejo
desea comprar un *iPod* tienen (*they have*) cuatro niños

MODELO: diccionario bilingüe / Alberto →
El diccionario bilingüe es para Alberto. Es estudiante de lenguas.

1. programa de «Weight Watchers» / Kirstie Alley _____

_____

2. casa grande / los Sres. Walker _____

_____

3. dinero / mi hermano _____

_____

4. el televisor nuevo / mis abuelos _____

_____

E. Gramática en acción: Presentaciones (*Introductions*)

Paso 1. You will hear a brief passage about Francisco Durán and his wife, Lola Benítez. As you listen, try not to be distracted by unfamiliar vocabulary. Concentrate instead on what you *do* know and understand. You may want to take notes on the information in the passage.

_____

_____

_____

_____

Paso 2. ¿Qué recuerdas? Now pause and complete the following sentences based on the passage and your notes. ¡OJO! Use a form of the verb **ser** in the first blank of each sentence. (Check your answers in the Appendix.)

1. Marta _____ la _____ de Lola y Francisco.

2. Lola _____ _____.

3. Lola y Francisco _____ de _____.

4. Lola _____ muy _____; Francisco es _____ y moreno.

Now resume listening.

F. ¿De dónde son? Practice telling where you and your imaginary family and friends are from, using the written cues. (Remember to repeat the correct answer.)

MODELO: (*you see and hear*) mi amigo Aristides / Colombia →
(*you say*) Mi amigo Aristides es de Colombia.

1. mi amigo Lorenzo / la Argentina
2. tú / Costa Rica
3. mis abuelos / Cuba
4. mi hermano y yo / Chile

Paso 3 Gramática

6. Expressing Possession • (Unstressed) Possessive Adjectives (Part 1)

¡RECUERDA!

Uso de la preposición *de* para expresar posesión. ¿Cómo se dice en español?

    MODELO: It's Raúl's family. → Es la familia de Raúl.

1. She's Isabel's sister. _____

2. They're Mario's relatives. _____

3. They're Marta's grandparents. _____

A. **¿Cómo es tu vida** (*life*)**?** Escoge (*Choose*) la forma correcta del adjetivo posesivo, y luego (*then*) completa la oración con todos los adjetivos apropiados.

    1. Mi/Mis familia es _____.
       (grande, mediana [*average*], pequeña, pobre, rica)

    2. Nuestra/Nuestro universidad es _____.
       (grande, moderna, nueva, pequeña, vieja)

    3. Muchos de mi/mis amigos son _____.
       (casados, estudiosos, listos, perezosos, trabajadores)

    4. El coche de mi/mis padres es _____.
       (grande, nuevo, pequeño, viejo)

    5. Mi/Mis clases son _____.
       (aburridas [*boring*], grandes, interesantes, pequeñas)

    6. La madre de mi/mis mejor (*best*) amigo/a es _____.
       (alta, baja, delgada, generosa, gorda, morena, rubia, simpática)

B. **Hablando** (*Speaking*) **de la familia.** Answer affirmatively, using a possessive adjective.

    MODELO: ¿Son ellos los hijos de tu hermana? → Sí, son sus hijos.

    1. ¿Es ella la suegra de Tomás? _____

    2. ¿Es Carlos el hermano de Uds.? _____

    3. ¿Son ellos los padres de tu novia? _____

    4. ¿Son Uds. los primos de Marta? _____

    5. ¿Es Carmen la sobrina de tu mamá? _____

    6. ¿Eres el nieto / la nieta de los señores? _____

C. Gramática en acción: Invitación y posesión

Paso 1. You will hear three captions. Write the number of each caption under the correct drawing. Careful! There is an extra caption.

Paso 2. Now you will hear a series of statements. Each will be said twice. Circle **C** (**cierto**) if the statement is true or **F** (**falso**) if it is false.

1. C F 　　3. C F

2. C F 　　4. C F

a. _____ 　　　　　　b. _____

7. Expressing Actions • Present Tense of *-er* and *-ir* Verbs; Subject Pronouns (Part 2)

A. En el centro estudiantil (*student union*). Usa los verbos indicados para describir las acciones de los estudiantes.

beber Coca-Cola
comer mucho
escribir una carta
estudiar francés
leer un periódico
mirar un vídeo

1. _____

2. _____

3. _____

4. _____

5. _____

6. _____

❖**B. ¿Y tú?** Now imagine that you are at the student union. Write two more sentences telling what you and your friends usually do (or do not do) there. Remember to use the **nosotros** form.

1. _____

2. _____

C. **Gramática en acción: Un estudiante típico**

Paso 1. Dictado. You will hear the following paragraph in which Samuel introduces himself. Listen carefully and write in the missing words. (Check your answers in the Appendix before you begin **Paso 2.**)

Hola. Me llamo Samuel Flores Toledo. Soy estudiante y

_____[1] a la Universidad Nacional Autónoma

de México. _____[2] con mi familia en la

Ciudad de México. _____ café en la

mañana y _____[4] pizza y tacos con frecuencia.

_____[5] muchos libros de antropología para mi

especialización. También _____[6] muchas cartas a

mi familia. _____[7] que una educación universitaria

es muy importante. Por eso estudio y _____[8]

mucho. ¡Pero _____[9] también que es muy

importante estar con los amigos y con la familia!

Paso 2. ¿Qué recuerdas? Now pause and complete the following sentences based on the information in the passage. (Check your answers in the Appendix.)

1. Samuel _____ a la Universidad Nacional Autónoma de México.

2. Él _____ con su familia.

3. Samuel _____ café en la mañana y _____ pizza y tacos
   con frecuencia.

4. Él _____ muchos libros de antropología.

D. **Un sábado típico de la familia Robles.** Describe what happens on a typical Saturday in the Robles household, using the written and oral cues. Remember that subject pronouns are not always used in Spanish. (Remember to repeat the correct answer.)

MODELO: (*you hear*) nosotros (*you see*) estar en casa → (*you say*) Estamos en casa.

1. leer el periódico
2. escribir cartas
3. asistir a un partido (*game*) de fútbol
4. abrir una carta de mi prima
5. comer a las seis

E. **¿Quién... ?** Answer the following questions using the oral cues. Use subject pronouns only if necessary. (Remember to repeat the correct answer.)

1. ¿Quién come en la cafetería?

   MODELO: (*you hear*) Evita → (*you say*) Evita come en la cafetería.

   a. ...   b. ...   c. ...   d. ...

2. ¿Quién vive en una residencia?

   MODELO: (*you hear*) yo → (*you say*) Yo vivo en una residencia.

   a. ...   b. ...   c. ...   d. ...

Nota comunicativa: Telling How Frequently You Do Things

❖**Tú y tus amigos.** Tell about what you and your friends do or do not do. Form complete sentences by using one word or phrase from group A and one from group B. Be sure to limit yourself to writing only those things you have learned how to say in Spanish. Use the **nosotros** verb form.

      MODELO: comer → A veces comemos en la cafetería. Casi nunca comemos en casa.

   A. nunca, casi nunca, a veces, con frecuencia, todos los días

   B. aprender a, asistir, beber, deber, estudiar, leer y escribir, practicar, trabajar

   1. _____

   2. _____

   3. _____

   4. _____

   5. _____

Un poco de todo

❖**La escena** (*scene*) **universitaria.** Imagine that you have just returned home after your first few weeks at the university. Describe the people, places, and things you have seen. Form complete sentences by using one word or phrase from each of the four columns. Make five sentences with nouns from the second column and two with nouns that you supply. Watch out for agreement of adjectives! Do not use the same adjective more than once.

| mi
mis
el
la
los
las | **+** | laboratorio de lenguas
edificios
estudiantes
biblioteca
coche de mi amigo
clases
profesores
¿ ? | **+** | (no) es
(no) son | **+** | nuevo / viejo
simpático / amable / antipático
pequeño / grande / enorme
tonto / inteligente
alto / bajo
feo / bonito
joven / viejo
interesante
¿ ? |

   1. _____

   2. _____

   3. _____

   4. _____

   5. _____

   6. _____

   7. _____

¡Repasemos!

A. La familia Rivera

Paso 1. Answer these questions about the Rivera family in complete sentences. You will need to invent information about several of the characters.

Palabra útil: el ama de casa (*housewife*)

1. ¿Cuántas personas hay en la familia Rivera?

   _____

2. ¿De dónde son los padres?

   _____

3. ¿Dónde trabaja el padre ahora? ¿y la madre?

   _____

4. ¿Qué estudia el hijo mayor (*oldest*)? ¿Cuántos años tiene él? ¿Cómo es él?

   _____

   _____

5. ¿Quién es la otra señora? ¿Cuántos años tiene? ¿Cómo es?

   _____

6. ¿Cómo son el coche y la casa, y de quién(es) son?

   _____

   _____

Paso 2. Now, on a separate sheet of paper, write a descriptive paragraph about the Rivera family by combining your answers and using connecting words such as **y, pero, por eso, porque, también,** and **aunque** (*although*). Try to be as creative as possible in adding details.

B. ¿Cuál es el dibujo? You will hear a description of a drawing. Listen carefully and circle the drawing that is described. First, listen to the following new words that you will hear in the description.

el pelo	*hair*	el jardín	*garden*	prefiere	*he/she prefers*
negro	*black*	blanco	*white*		

Now pause and look at the drawings.

1.

2.

3.

C. Entrevista. You will hear a series of questions. Each will be said twice. Answer based on your experience. Pause and write the answers.

1. _____

2. _____

3. _____

4. _____

5. _____

6. _____

7. _____

❖ 🔵 **Mi diario**

Mi pariente favorito. Write a description of your favorite relative. Include the following information. Use all the adjectives you can! Refer to the vocabulary list in your textbook for additional adjectives.

- name
- relationship to you
- age (**Tiene _____ años.**)
- where he/she is from
- what he/she does for a living
- appearance
- personality

Ponte a prueba

A ver si sabes...

A. Adjectives: Gender, Number, and Position. Completa lo siguiente (*the following things*).

1. Escribe la forma correcta del adjetivo **casado**.

   a. hermana _____   **b.** primos _____

2. Escribe la forma **plural** de los adjetivos.

   a. grande _____   **b.** sentimental _____

3. Completa la tabla (*chart*) con la forma correcta de los adjetivos de nacionalidad.

FEMININE SINGULAR	*mexicana*		d		g
MASCULINE SINGULAR		a	e		h
FEMININE PLURAL		b	f	*españolas*	
MASCULINE PLURAL		c	*franceses*		i

B. Present Tense of *ser*. Match the following statements with the uses of **ser** given in the right-hand column.

1. _____ Lola es de Puerto Rico.
2. _____ La carta es para mi madre.
3. _____ Los papeles son del profesor.
4. _____ Alicia es mi prima.

   a. With **para,** to tell for whom or what something is intended.
   b. With **de,** to express possession
   c. With **de,** to express origin.
   d. To identify people and things.

C. Possessive Adjectives (Unstressed). Express the following possessive adjectives and nouns in Spanish.

1. my brother _____
2. her uncle _____
3. our grandmother _____
4. their house _____

D. Present Tense of *-er* and *-ir* Verbs. Completa la tabla con la forma correcta de los verbos.

leer

yo _____ 1
nosotros _____ 2
vosotros _____ 3

escribir

tú _____ 4
ella _____ 5
Uds. _____ 6

Prueba corta

A. La nacionalidad. Complete the following sentences with the adjective of nationality that corresponds to the country in parentheses.

MODELO: Marta es *mexicana*. (México)

1. Paolo es un estudiante _____. (Italia)
2. París es una ciudad _____. (Francia)
3. El Volkswagen es un coche _____. (Alemania)
4. Diane y Margaret son dos mujeres _____. (Inglaterra)

B. Ser. Escribe la forma apropiada del verbo **ser.**

1. La mochila no _____ nueva.

2. Yo _____ de España. ¿Tú _____ de México?

3. Burgos y Toledo _____ ciudades viejas y fascinantes.

4. El profesor y yo _____ de California.

C. Los adjetivos posesivos. Completa las oraciones con el adjetivo posesivo apropiado.

La madre de _____[1] (*my*) sobrino Mauricio se llama Cecilia. Ella es

_____[2] (*my*) cuñada. _____[3] (*My*) hermanos Enrique y Luis son

solteros. El padre de Cecilia se llama Marco; _____[4] (*her*) madre se llama Elena.

Elena y Marco son italianos, pero viven en México. Ellos piensan (*They think*) que

_____[5] (*our*) cultura es muy interesante. Todos _____[6] (*their*)

nietos son mexicanos. ¿De dónde es _____[7] (*your*) familia?

D. Los verbos. Completa las oraciones con la forma correcta del verbo apropiado de la lista.

asistir   beber   comprender   escuchar   estudiar   hablar   leer   recibir   vender

1. Nosotros no _____ mucho cuando la profesora _____

   rápidamente (*quickly*).

2. ¿(Tú) _____ música mientras (*while*) (tú) _____?

3. Mi padre nunca _____ los libros de historia.

4. ¿Siempre _____ Uds. los libros al final (*at the end*) del semestre?

5. Mi hermana siempre _____ muchos regalos y tarjetas (*cards*) el Día de

   San Valentín.

6. Yo no _____ café por la noche.

7. Nosotros _____ a esta clase todos los días (*every day*).

E. La familia de doña Isabel. You will hear a passage about doña Isabel's family. Read the passage along with the speaker and circle the numbers you hear.

¡La familia de doña Isabel es muy grande y extendida! Ella tiene **30 / 20** nietos en total, y **16 / 26** bisnietos (*great-grandchildren*). Doña Isabel tiene **89 / 99** años. Su hijo mayor, Diego, tiene **67 / 77** años. Su hija menor, Alida, tiene **64 / 54**. Doña Isabel tiene **10 / 6** hijos en total. El próximo año, todos sus hijos, nietos y bisnietos celebran los **100 / 50** años de edad de doña Isabel.

F. Cosas de todos los días. Practice talking about your imaginary family, using the written cues. When you hear the corresponding number, form sentences using the words provided in the order given, making any necessary changes or additions. (Remember to repeat the correct answer.)

MODELO: (*you see*) **1.** mi / familia / ser / muy / simpático   (*you hear*) uno →
(*you say*) Mi familia es muy simpática.

2. (nosotros) vivir / en / un / ciudad / pequeño
3. nuestro / casa / ser / bonito
4. mi / padres / siempre / leer / periódico / en / patio
5. (nosotros) siempre / comer / juntos (*together*)
6. este / noche / mi / hermanos / asistir / a / un / concierto
7. pero / yo / deber / estudiar / para / mi / clases

CAPÍTULO 3

 Paso 1 Vocabulario

De compras: La ropa

A. La ropa. Identifica la ropa que llevan estas personas. Usa el artículo indefinido.

1. a. _____

    b. _____

    c. _____

    d. _____

    e. _____

    f. _____

2. a. _____

    b. _____

    c. _____

    d. _____

    e. _____

B. De compras en México. Imagine that you are studying in Puebla, México. You ask your friend Rosa about where and how to shop. Complete her answer with the appropriate items from the list provided.

almacén	gangas	regatear
centro	mercado	tiendas
de última moda	rebajas	venden de todo
fijos		

En el _____[1] comercial de la calle Bolívar, hay un _____[2]

grande donde _____[3] Allí[a] los precios son _____[4] y muy

caros, pero la ropa es _____[5] Ahora,[b] en las _____[6]

del centro, hay muchas _____[7] O puedes ir[c] al _____.[8]

Allí los precios no son fijos y es posible _____[9] También puedes encontrar[d]

muchas _____.[10]

[a]There [b]Now [c]puedes... you can go [d]find

C. ¿Qué opinas? Completa la narración en español. Usa estas palabras: **algodón, cuero, lana, seda.**

1. La ropa interior de _____ es más fresca que (*cooler than*) la de nilón.

2. Las _____ de _____ son elegantes y bonitas.
          (*ties*)

3. Los _____ y las _____ de _____ son caros y abrigados (*warm*).
      (*sweaters*)   (*skirts*)

4. Las botas altas de _____ están de moda.

D. Identificaciones. Identify the items in the drawing after you hear the corresponding number. Begin each sentence with **Es un...**, **Es una...**, or **Son...** (Remember to repeat the correct answer.)

1. ... 2. ... 3. ... 4. ... 5. ... 6. ... 7. ... 8. ... 9. ...

¿De qué color es?

A. ¿De qué color es? Complete the sentences with the correct form of the words from the list provided. Adjectives are given in the masculine singular form. Be sure to make the adjectives agree with the nouns they are describing. Some words can be used more than once.

amarillo	azul	color café	morado	rosado
anaranjado	blanco	gris	rojo	verde

1. Las plantas son _____.

2. La bandera (*flag*) mexicana es _____, _____ y _____.
                 (*green*)   (*white*)   (*red*)

3. La bandera de los Estados Unidos es _____, _____ y

   _____.

4. La naranja (*orange*) es _____ y el limón es _____.

5. El color _____ es una combinación de blanco y negro.

6. El color _____ es una combinación de rojo y azul.

7. El color tradicional para las bebés (*baby girls*) es _____.

8. Muchos hombres hispanos llevan colores oscuros (*dark*): azul, negro y _____.

❖**B.   Mi estilo personal.** ¿Qué ropa usas en estos lugares? Menciona los colores, cuando sea (*whenever it is*) posible.

   1.   En la universidad: _____

   2.   En una cena (*dinner*) elegante: _____

   3.   En la playa (*beach*): _____

Más allá del número 100

A.   Los números. Write the following numbers in Arabic numerals.

   1.   ciento once _____

   2.   cuatrocientos setenta y seis _____

   3.   quince mil setecientos catorce _____

   4.   setecientos mil quinientos _____

   5.   mil novecientos sesenta y cinco _____

   6.   un millón trece _____

B.   ¿Cuánto cuesta? You have been asked to write six checks for ads of different sizes to be published in a Mexican newspaper. Write out in words the prices in **pesos** ($) for each ad ($2.100,00 = **dos mil cien pesos**).

   1. $28.510,00 _____

   2. $14.625,00 _____

   3. $7.354,00 _____

   4. $3.782,00 _____

   5. $1.841,00 _____

   6. $920,00 _____

C.   Dictado: El inventario del Almacén Robles. Imagine that you and a coworker are doing a partial inventory for a department store. Listen to what your coworker says, and write the numbers in numerals next to the correct items. You will hear each number twice. ¡OJO! The items are not listed in sequence. First, listen to the list of items. (Check your answers in the Appendix.)

ARTÍCULOS	NÚMERO (CANTIDAD)
pares de medias de nilón	1
camisas blancas	2
suéteres rojos	3
pares de zapatos de tenis	4
blusas azules	5
faldas negras	6

Pronunciación y ortografía • Stress and Written Accent Marks (Part 2)

A. ¿Acento escrito (*written*) o no? The following words are stressed on the underlined syllables. If a written accent is required, add it above the stressed vowel.

1. ex-<u>a</u>-men
2. lu-<u>gar</u>
3. ma-<u>tri</u>-cu-la
4. bo-<u>li</u>-gra-fo
5. <u>jo</u>-ven
6. sen-ti-men-<u>tal</u>
7. <u>Pe</u>-rez
8. e-di-<u>fi</u>-cios
9. a-le-<u>man</u>

B. Palabras divididas. The following words have been divided into syllables for you. Read them when you hear the corresponding number. (Remember to repeat the correct answer.) ¡OJO! Some of the words will be unfamiliar to you. This should not be a problem because you have pronunciation rules to guide you.

1. nor-mal
2. prác-ti-co
3. á-ni-mo
4. a-na-to-mí-a
5. cu-le-bra
6. con-ver-ti-bles
7. ter-mó-me-tro
8. co-li-brí
9. con-di-cio-nal

C. Dictado. You will hear the following words. Each will be said twice. Listen carefully and write in a written accent where required. ¡OJO! Some of the words will be unfamiliar to you. This should not be a problem because you have the rules and the speaker's pronunciation to guide you. (Check your answers in the Appendix.)

1. metrica
2. distribuidor
3. anoche
4. Rosalia
5. actitud
6. sabiduria
7. jovenes
8. magico
9. esquema

Lectura cultural: Guatemala y Honduras

Oraciones. Completa las oraciones según las **Lecturas culturales 1** y **2** del libro de texto. Usa palabras de la lista.

calendario   Copán   maya-quiché   pobre   la punta   Tegucigalpa   Tikal   volcanes

1. La capital de Honduras es _____.

2. Aunque (*Although*) la ecología de Honduras es muy rica, gran parte de la población (*population*) es _____.

3. Más del (*More than*) cuarenta por ciento de la población de Guatemala es de origen _____.

4. El _____ maya era (*was*) el más exacto de su época (*time*).

5. La ciudad más grande de la cultura maya fue (*was*) _____.

6. Algunos (*Some*) de los treinta _____ en el oeste de Guatemala son activos.

7. En las ruinas mayas de _____ hay muchos jeroglíficos y estelas.

8. La música y el baile de los garífunas se llama _____.

Paso 2 Gramática

8. Pointing Out People and Things • Demonstrative Adjectives (Part 2) and Pronouns

---

¡RECUERDA!

Formas de *este*. Escribe la forma apropiada: **este, esta, estos, estas**.

1. _____ (*This*) color está de moda este año.

2. _____ (*These*) colores son feos.

3. Me gusta _____ (*this*) camisa blanca.

4. No me gustan _____ (*these*) camisas grises.

A. ¿Este, ese o aquel? Completa las oraciones con la forma correcta de **este**, **ese** o **aquel.** Completa la última oración con su preferencia.

Necesitas comprar un coche. ¿Cuál te gusta más?

_____¹ coche es muy viejo; _____² coche es muy grande; _____³ coche

es fantástico, pero también es muy caro. Pienso comprar _____⁴ coche porque

_____.

B. ¿De quién son? You and a friend are trying to sort out to whom the following items belong. Answer your friend's questions with the appropriate demonstrative adjective. *Note:* **Aquí** (*Here*) and **allí** (*there*), like **este** and **ese** suggest closeness to, or distance from, the speaker.

> MODELO: Aquí hay unos zapatos negros. ¿Son de Pablo? → Sí, estos zapatos negros son de Pablo.
> Allí veo (*I see*) una bolsa. ¿Es de Chela? → Sí, esa bolsa es de Chela.

1. Aquí hay una chaqueta de rayas. ¿Es de Miguel? _____

2. Allí veo unos calcetines. ¿Son de Daniel? _____

3. Allí veo un impermeable. ¿Es de Margarita? _____

4. Aquí hay unos guantes (*gloves*) de cuero. ¿Son de Ceci? _____

5. Aquí hay un reloj de oro. ¿Es de Pablo? _____

6. Allí veo unos papeles. ¿Son de David? _____

C. Gramática en acción: Suéteres a buenos precios. You will hear a dialogue in which Susana goes shopping for a sweater. After listening, pause and read each statement about the dialogue. Circle **C** (**cierto**) if the statement is true or **F** (**falso**) if it is false. If the information is not contained in or cannot be inferred from the dialogue, circle **ND** (**No lo dice** [*It doesn't say*]).

1. C F ND Susana busca un suéter de rayas.

2. C F ND Los suéteres de pura lana son más caros.

3. C F ND Los suéteres de pura lana cuestan 150 quetzales.

4. C F ND Los suéteres de rayas son de acrílico y cuestan 300 quetzales.

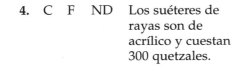

Jorge   Susana   Vendedor (*salesperson*)

Now resume listening.

D. ¿Cómo son estas cosas? Answer, using the oral cues and an appropriate form of the indicated demonstrative adjective. Remember to change the endings of the adjectives, and use **es** or **son,** as appropriate.

> MODELO: (*you see*) ese / corbatas (*you hear*) verde → (*you say*) Esas corbatas son verdes.

1. ese / botas
2. este / pantalones
3. aquel / trajes

4. aquel / faldas
5. ese / vestidos

E. Recuerdos de tu viaje a México. Your friends want to know all about your trip to Mexico. Answer their questions, using an appropriate form of the demonstrative adjective **aquel** and the oral cues.

> MODELO: (*you hear and see*) ¿Qué tal el restaurante El Charro? (*you hear*) excelente →
> (*you say*) ¡Aquel restaurante es excelente!

1. ¿Qué tal el Hotel Libertad?
2. ¿Y los dependientes del hotel?
3. ¿Qué tal la ropa del Mercado de la Merced?
4. ¿Y los parques de la capital?

9. Expressing Actions and States • *Tener, venir, preferir, querer,* and *poder;* Some Idioms with *tener*

A. Diálogo

Paso 1. Complete the following dialogue between you and a friend to make plans to go to a movie.

—¿_____[1] (*Tú:* **Querer**) ir al cine[a] esta noche?

—Hoy no _____ (*yo:* **poder**) porque _____[3] (**tener**) que estudiar

para un examen de sicología. _____[4] (**Preferir**) ir mañana.

—Bien. Entonces[b] _____[5] (*yo:* **venir**) por ti[c] mañana a las siete y media. No

_____[6] (*yo:* **querer**) llegar tarde.

[a]*ir... to go to the movies*   [b]*Then*   [c]*por... for you*

Paso 2. Now rewrite the same dialogue, replacing **yo** with the **nosotros** form and **tú** with the **Uds.** form. (Replace **por ti** with **por Uds.**)

_____

_____

_____

_____

_____

B. Conclusiones personales. Contesta con un modismo con **tener.**

1. Cuando trabajas toda la noche, ¿qué tienes en la mañana?

   _____

2. Si quieres aprender, ¿qué tienes que hacer (*do*)?

   _____

3. Si te encuentras con (*run into*) un hombre con revólver, instintivamente, ¿qué tienes?

   _____

   _____

4. Necesitas llegar a la oficina a las dos. Si son las dos menos uno, ¿qué tienes?

   _____

   _____

5. Si dices (*say*) que Buenos Aires es la capital de la Argentina, ¿qué tienes?

   _____

   _____

Buenos Aires
la Argentina

C. Luis habla con su compañero Mario. Completa el diálogo entre (*between*) Luis y Mario. *Note: / /* indica una oración nueva.

LUIS: ¿a qué hora / (tú) venir / universidad / mañana?

_____ 1

MARIO: (yo) venir / ocho y media / / ¿Por qué?

_____ 2

LUIS: ¿(yo) poder / venir / contigo? / / no / (yo) tener / coche

_____ 3

MARIO: ¡cómo no! (*of course!*) / / (yo) pasar / por ti (*for you*) / siete y media/ / ¿(tú) tener / ganas / practicar / vocabulario ahora?

_____

_____ 4

LUIS: no / / ahora / (yo) preferir / comer / algo (*something*) / / ¿(tú) querer / venir? / / (nosotros) poder / estudiar / para / examen / después (*later*)

_____

_____ 5

MARIO: bueno / idea / / (yo) creer / que / Raúl y Alicia / querer / estudiar / con nosotros

_____

_____ 6

D. Gramática en acción: Un mensaje telefónico: Dictado. You will hear the following answering machine message. It will be read twice. Listen carefully and write the missing words. (Check your answers in the Appendix.)

¡Hola, Jorge! Soy yo, Jaqui. Como tú sabes, yo siempre _____ 1 comprar la ropa en los grandes almacenes. Pero hoy no _____ 2 tiempo de ir al centro. _____ 3 comprar una camisa para Juan Miguel, para su cumpleaños mañana. Creo que _____ 4 encontrar algo en la boutique de este barrio. ¿_____ 5 ayudarme? Juanmi es muy difícil de complacer en lo que _____ 6 que ver con la moda... ¡Llámame! O mejor todavía... ¿por qué no _____ 7 a mi casa? Un millón de gracias, Jorge. Hasta pronto.

E. Es la semana de exámenes. Practice telling about what you and your friends do during exam week, using the written and oral cues. ¡OJO! Remember that subject pronouns are not always used in Spanish.

MODELO: (*you hear*) nosotros   (*you see*) tener muchos exámenes →
(*you say*) Tenemos muchos exámenes.

1. estar en la biblioteca
2. siempre venir conmigo (*with me*)
3. leer cien páginas

4. ¡ya no poder leer más!
5. querer regresar a la residencia...
6. ... pero no poder

Paso 3 Gramática

10. Expressing Destination and Future Actions •
Ir; Ir + a + Infinitive; The Contraction al

A. Una fiesta familiar. Completa las oraciones con la forma apropiada del verbo **ir**.

Muchas personas van a ir a una fiesta. Toda la familia de Ana _____.¹ Los tíos y

los abuelos de Julio _____² con los padres de Ana. Tú _____³

también, ¿verdad? Miguel y yo _____,⁴ pero yo _____⁵ a

llegar tarde.

B. El cumpleaños (*birthday*) **de Raúl.** Using **ir** + **a** + an infinitive, indicate what the following people are going to do for Raúl's birthday.

> MODELO: La fiesta es este sábado. → La fiesta va a ser este sábado.

1. Eduardo y Graciela buscan un regalo. _____

_____

2. David y yo compramos las bebidas (*drinks*). _____

_____

3. Ignacio y Pepe van con nosotros. _____

_____

4. Por eso necesitamos tu coche. _____

_____

5. Desgraciadamente (*Unfortunately*) Julio no prepara la comida. _____

_____

C. Situaciones. Imagine that a friend of yours has made the following statements. Form a response using **vamos a** + one of the phrases from the list. In each case you will be suggesting that you and your friend do something together: "Let's . . ."

mirar en el Almacén Juárez   buscar algo más barato
descansar ahora   comprar otro
estudiar esta tarde

> MODELO: Este diccionario es malo. → Vamos a comprar otro.

1. Mañana vamos a tener examen. _____

2. En esta tienda no venden buena ropa. _____

3. Los precios aquí son muy caros. _____

4. No tengo ganas de trabajar más hoy. _____

D. Gramática en acción: ¿Adónde vas? You will hear a dialogue in which Casandra asks her roommate Rosa where she is going. Then you will hear the following statements. Write the letter of the person who made each statement next to the statement.

a. Rosa   **b.** Casandra   **c.** Javier

1. _____ Voy a dar una fiesta este fin de semana.

2. _____ Voy al centro.

3. _____ Voy a comprar un vestido.

4. _____ Casandra y Rosa van a venir a mi fiesta.

E. ¿Adónde vas? You will hear a series of statements a friend might say about what you like to do or want to do. Using the words and phrases listed below, tell where you would go to do these activities. First, listen to the list.

Almacén Robles   discoteca El Ciclón   Restaurante Gallego
biblioteca   mercado   universidad

MODELO: (*you hear*) Te gusta estudiar y aprender cosas nuevas. →
(*you say*) Por eso voy a la universidad.

1. ...   **2.** ...   **3.** ...   **4.** ...   **5.** ...

F. Preguntas. You will hear a series of questions. Each will be said twice. Answer, using **ir** + **a** + infinitive and the written cues.

MODELO: (*you hear*) ¿Qué vas a comprar en la librería?   (*you see*) unos cuadernos →
(*you say*) Voy a comprar unos cuadernos.

1. tres horas
2. a casa de un amigo
3. en McDonald's
4. pantalones grises / un suéter rojo

Un poco de todo

A. De compras en San Sebastián. Complete the following paragraph with the correct form of the words in parentheses, as suggested by context. When two possibilities are given in parentheses, select the correct word.

En _____¹ (**el / la**) ciudad vasca[a] de San Sebastián, en

el norte de España, cuando la gente[b] necesita o _____²

(**querer**) ir de compras, tiene que _____³ (**ir**) a

_____⁴ (**pequeño**) tiendas que _____⁵ (**vender**)

productos _____,⁶ (**especial**) porque en San Sebastián no

permiten la construcción de _____⁷ (**grande**) almacenes.

La gente _____⁸ (**preferir**) proteger[c] a los comerciantes

vascos locales en vez de apoyar[d] a las grandes galerías _____⁹ (**español**) como El Corte

Inglés. Por eso, hay en _____¹⁰ (**este**) ciudad muchas tiendas de ropa para niños, para

mujeres y para hombres; también hay tiendas _____¹¹ (**especializado**)

como zapaterías, librerías o papelerías. Son muy _____¹² (**popular**) las tiendas que

venden artículos de piel[e] como bolsas, cinturones, gorras, guantes[f] y carteras. Claro, también

_____¹³ (**existir**) pequeñas boutiques muy _____¹⁴ (**elegante**) con productos

de moda de los más _____¹⁵ (**famoso**) nombres de la moda mundial.[g]

[a]*Basque*   [b]*people*   [c]*to protect*   [d]*en... instead of supporting*   [e]*leather*   [f]*gloves*   [g]*moda... world fashion*

B. María Montaño. Imagine that you are a new student in Dr. Prado's class. Talk about yourself and the way you feel. Complete the sentences using idioms with **tener.**

Me llamo María Montaño. _____¹ 18 años y tengo _____² de

aprender español porque quiero hablar con mis abuelos y otros parientes que viven en México.

Desgraciadamente,[a] en clase tengo _____³ de hablar. El profesor cree que debo

practicar más en el laboratorio. Él tiene _____,⁴ pero no tengo mucho tiempo

libre.[b] Trabajo muchas horas y cuando quiero estudiar, tengo mucho _____⁵

y a veces me quedo dormida.[c]

[a]*Unfortunately*   [b]*free*   [c]*me... I fall asleep*

C. **Entre amigas.** Fill in the blanks with the correct form of the infinitive or with the correct word in parentheses to complete the dialogue between Susana and Paquita.

SUSANA: Hola, Paquita. ¿Qué tal?

PAQUITA: Bien. Y tú, ¿cómo _____[1] (**estás / eres**)?

SUSANA: Muy bien. Aquí tengo algo para ti. Creo que _____[2] (**esos / estos**) textos

son _____[3] (**tu / tus**) libros de historia, ¿verdad?

PAQUITA: ¡Ay, qué bueno! Necesito _____[4] (**esos / aquellos**) libros para estudiar

para _____[5] (**nuestra / nuestro**) examen. Gracias.

SUSANA: ¿Adónde _____[6] (**ir**) ahora?

PAQUITA: Primero _____[7] (**ir**) a la biblioteca a buscar un libro y luego María y yo

_____[8] (**ir**) a estudiar. ¿Por qué no estudias con _____[9]

(**nosotros / nosotras**)?

SUSANA: Gracias por _____[10] (**tú / tu**) invitación, pero _____[11]

(**esta / este**) tarde dan[a] una película francesa y Enrique y yo _____[12]

(**querer**) ir. Tengo _____[13] (**razón / prisa**) porque él está esperándome[b]

ahora mismo.[c]

PAQUITA: Muy bien. _____[14] (**Adiós / Vamos**).

[a]*they're showing*   [b]*waiting for me*   [c]*ahora... right now*

D. **Buscando regalos para papá.** Listen to a conversation between a brother and sister, José and Ana, who are looking for gifts for their father. Do not be distracted by unfamiliar vocabulary. As you listen, circle only the items that they decide to buy. (Check your answers in the Appendix.)

¡Repasemos!

A. De compras

Paso 1. El Sr. Rivera necesita comprar dos artículos de ropa para sus vacaciones en México. Conteste las preguntas según los dibujos.

1.

2.

3.

4.

5.

6.

7.

1. ¿Qué quiere comprar el Sr. Rivera? ¿Qué tipo (*type*) de camisa busca?

   _____

2. ¿A qué hora llega a la tienda? _____

3. ¿Cómo son todas las camisas, caras o baratas? _____

   _____

4. ¿Qué camisa compra por fin (*finally*)? ¿una de veinte dólares? _____

   _____

5. Y, ¿cómo son las sandalias que venden? _____

6. ¿Adónde tiene que ir para comprar las sandalias? _____

   _____

7. ¿Regresa a casa contento o triste con sus compras? _____

   _____

Paso 2. Now, on a separate sheet of paper, convert your answers into a paragraph about Mr. Rivera's shopping trip. Use the following words to make your paragraph more coherent and connected: **pero, y, por eso, por fin, ya** (*already*).

B. Entrevista. You will hear a series of questions. Each will be said twice. Answer based on your own experience. Pause and write the answers.

1. _____

2. _____

3. _____

4. _____

5. _____

6. _____

7. _____

◆ Mi diario

Un inventario de mi ropa

Paso 1. Look in your closet and bureau drawers and take an inventory of the articles of clothing you own and the approximate number of each item. What colors are they? Now write the information in your diary.

MODELO: Tengo diez camisetas: blancas, negras, rojas y una verde.

Paso 2. Now choose three of the following situations and write a description of the clothing you typically wear in each. Include the color and fabric, if possible.

Palabras útiles

los *jean*s
la manga (*sleeve*)
de manga corta (*short-sleeved*)

de manga larga (*long-sleeved*)
los zapatos (de tenis)
los zapatos de tacón alto (*high heels*)

MODELO: Cuando estoy en la playa (*beach*), llevo...

1. en la universidad

2. en una entrevista (*job interview*)

3. en casa

4. en la playa

5. en una fiesta

6. en un *picnic* en el parque

Ponte a prueba

A ver si sabes...

A. Demonstrative Adjectives and Pronouns. Escribe el adjetivo demostrativo apropiado.

1. _____ (*this*) zapato

2. _____ (*these*) pantalones

3. _____ (*that*) bolsa

4. _____ (*those*) abrigos

5. _____ (*that, over there*) camiseta

6. _____ (*those, over there*) cinturones

B. *Tener, venir, preferir, querer,* **and** *poder;* **Some Idioms with** *tener.*

1. Completa la tabla con la forma apropiada del presente.

INFINITIVO	YO	UD.	VOSOTROS	NOSOTROS
a. poder			*podéis*	
b. querer		*quiere*		
c. venir				

2. Expresa en español los siguientes modismos con **tener.**

   a. to be afraid (of) _____

   b. to be right (wrong) _____

   c. to feel like _____

   c. to have to _____

C. *Ir; Ir + a + **Infinitive.** Rewrite the following sentences, using **ir** + **a** + *infinitive.*

1. Ellos compran ropa. _____

2. ¿No comes? _____

3. Tienen una fiesta. _____

4. Voy de compras. _____

Prueba corta

A. Los demostrativos. Rewrite the sentences, substituting the noun provided and making all the necessary changes.

   MODELO: ¿Necesitas aquel sombrero rojo?
             (corbata) → ¿Necesitas aquella corbata roja?

1. Quiero comprar esa camisa negra.

   (impermeable) _____

2. ¿Buscas estos calcetines grises?

   (traje) _____

3. Juan va a comprar esos zapatos blancos.

   (chaqueta) _____

4. Mis padres trabajan en aquel almacén nuevo.

   (tienda) _____

B. Los verbos. Completa las oraciones con la forma apropiada de uno de los verbos de la lista. (*Note:* Use each verb at least once.)

   poder   preferir   querer   tener   venir

1. Mis amigos y yo _____ a esta biblioteca todos los días para estudiar. Nuestras

   clases son difíciles y _____ que estudiar mucho.

2. —¿Qué (tú) _____ tomar, una Coca-Cola o un café?

—Yo _____ un café.

3. Si Ud. _____ prisa, debe salir (*leave*) ahora.

4. En una librería, los estudiantes _____ comprar libros, cuadernos y mochilas.

C. *Ir* + *a* + **infinitive.** Rewrite each sentence, changing the simple present tense to a construction with
ir + **a** + *infinitive*, to tell what the following people are going to do.

MODELO: Estudio mucho. → Voy a estudiar mucho.

1. Roberto lleva traje y corbata. _____

2. Busco unas chanclas baratas. _____

3. Tenemos una fiesta. _____

4. ¿Vienes a casa esta noche? _____

D. **Cosas de todos los días.** Practice talking about the price of different items of clothing, using the written
cues. When you hear the corresponding number, form sentences using the words provided in the order
given, making any necessary changes or additions. Note: **Cuesta** means *it costs*, **cuestan** means *they cost*.

MODELO: (*you see*) **1.** este / pantalones / negro / cuestan / $80   (*you hear*) uno →
(*you say*) Estos pantalones negros cuestan ochenta dólares.

2. ese / chaqueta / azul / cuesta / $127
3. aquel / botas / color café / cuestan / $215
4. este / vestido / amarillo / cuesta / $149
5. aquel / traje / gris / cuesta / $578
6. ese / ropa / cuesta / $1.069

E. **¿Qué van a llevar?** You will hear a series of situations. Tell what each person is going to wear based
on the information in each. First, listen to the possible items of clothing. ¡OJO! There is an extra item.

un abrigo de lana	un traje de baño
una camiseta de algodón	un traje y una corbata de seda
un cinturón	zapatos de tenis

MODELO: (*you hear*) Los pantalones que llevo son muy grandes. →
(*you say*) Voy a llevar un cinturón.

1. ...   **2.** ...   **3.** ...   **4.** ...   **5.** ...

F. **Apuntes** (*Notes*): **De compras con Luis.** Luis has just received a bonus from his boss. He plans to
spend all of it on clothes. Listen carefully to his narration and, as you listen, write the information
requested. Write out all numbers. First, pause and read the requested information. (Check your answers
in the Appendix.)

1. El dinero que tiene Luis: _____

2. El precio de la chaqueta: _____

3. El precio del reloj de oro (*gold*): _____

4. El material de los pantalones: _____

5. El material de las dos corbatas: _____

6. Lo que (*what*) no puede comprar: _____

7. El dinero que le queda (*remains*): _____

CAPÍTULO **4**

 Paso 1 Vocabulario

¿Qué día es hoy?

A. El horario (*schedule*) **de David.** Escribe lo que (*what*) va a hacer David esta semana.

L	M	M	J	V	S	D
banco hablar con consejero	dentista	estudiar física	laboratorio de física	examen cenar[a] con Diana	de compras concierto	playa[b]

[a]*to have dinner* [b]*beach*

MODELO: El lunes tiene que ir al banco. (El lunes va a ir al banco.)

1. El lunes también... _____

2. _____

3. _____

4. _____

5. _____

6. _____

7. _____

B. ¿Qué día es hoy? Completa las oraciones con las palabras apropiadas.

1. Hay dos días en el _____ de semana: _____ y _____.

2. _____ es el primer (*first*) día de la semana en el calendario hispánico.

3. Si hoy es martes, mañana es _____.

4. El Día de Acción de Gracias es siempre el cuarto (*fourth*) _____ de noviembre.

5. Si hoy es miércoles, _____ es viernes.

6. No puedo ir _____ sábado porque _____ sábados trabajo.

7. Tengo que estudiar mucho porque la _____ semana tengo tres exámenes.

C. **El horario** (*schedule*) **de la profesora Velásquez**

Paso 1. Dictado. Imagine that you are Professor Velásquez's secretary and that you are filling in her weekly calendar. Listen carefully as she tells you her schedule for this week, and fill in the blanks in the calendar. Some of the entries have already been made. First, pause and look at the calendar. (Check your answers in the Appendix.)

lunes	martes	miércoles	jueves	viernes
mañana 10:45 AM : Clase de conversación	mañana _____ : dentista _____ :	mañana _____ :	mañana _____ :	mañana _____ :
tarde _____ :	tarde _____ :	tarde _____ :	tarde 3:00 PM : Clase de español	tarde _____ :

Paso 2. Preguntas. Now you will hear a series of questions. Each will be said twice. Answer based on the information in **Paso 1**. Be sure to check your answers to **Paso 1** in the Appendix before beginning **Paso 2**. Follow the model.

MODELO: (*you hear*) ¿Qué días enseña la profesora una clase de conversación? →
(*you say*) El lunes y el viernes.

1. ... 2. ... 3. ... 4. ...

Los muebles, los cuartos y otras partes de la casa (Part 1)

A. **¿Qué hay en esta casa?** Identifica las siguientes partes de la casa.

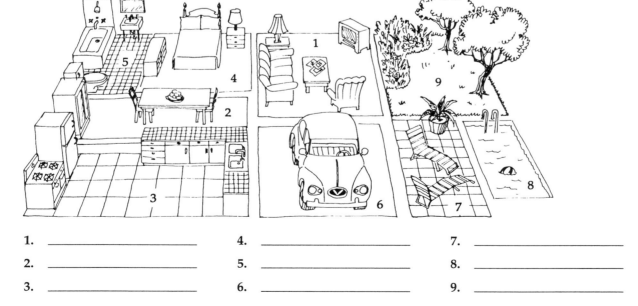

1. _____	4. _____	7. _____
2. _____	5. _____	8. _____
3. _____	6. _____	9. _____

❖**B.** **Describe tu alcoba.** Menciona los muebles que hay y el color de las paredes y de la alfombra (si la hay). Luego usa tres adjetivos para describir la alcoba en general.

_____

_____

C. **Identificación: ¿Qué hay en estos cuartos?** Identify the following items when you hear the corresponding number. Begin each sentence with **Es un...** or **Es una...** (Remember to repeat the correct answer.)

En la sala

1. ...   **2.** ...   **3.** ...   **4.** ...   **5.** ...   **6.** ...   **7.** ...

En la alcoba

8. ...   **9.** ...   **10.** ...

¿Cuándo? • Las preposiciones (Part 1)

A. **¿Antes o después?** ¿Cuándo haces estas cosas? Sigue el modelo.

> MODELO: estudiar las lecciones / tomar el examen →
> Estudio las lecciones antes de tomar el examen.

1. tener sueño / descansar _____

2. regresar a casa / asistir a clase _____

3. tener ganas de comer / estudiar _____

4. preparar la comida / ir al supermercado _____

5. lavar (*to wash*) los platos / comer _____

B. **¿Cuándo?** Tell when these people do the following things, using the oral cues. Follow the model.

> MODELO: (*you see*) Anita estudia / la clase   (*you hear*) antes de →
> (*you say*) Anita estudia antes de la clase.

1. Alicia escribe una carta / escucha la radio
2. Rosa trabaja / asistir a clases
3. Mis amigos bailan / las once de la noche
4. José lee / ir a la universidad

Pronunciación y ortografía: *b* and *v*

Spanish **b** and **v** are pronounced exactly the same way. At the beginning of a phrase, or after **m** or **n**, **b** and **v** are pronounced like the English *b*, as a stop [b]; that is, no air is allowed to escape through the lips. In all other positions, **b** and **v** are fricatives [ƀ]; that is, they are produced by allowing some air to escape through the lips. There is no equivalent for this sound in English.

A. Repeticiones. Repeat the following words and phrases, imitating the speaker. Note that the type of *b* sound you will hear is indicated at the beginning of the series.

    1. [b]   bueno viejo barato baño hombre

    2. [ƀ]   llevar libro pobre abrigo universidad

    3. [b/ƀ]   bueno / es bueno busca / Ud. busca bien / muy bien en Venezuela / de Venezuela visita / él visita

    4. [b/ƀ]   beber bebida vivir biblioteca vívido

B. Dictado. You will hear five sentences. Each will be said twice. Listen carefully and write what you hear. (Check your answers in the Appendix.)

    1. _____

    2. _____

    3. _____

    4. _____

    5. _____

Lectura cultural: El Salvador y Nicaragua

Oraciones. Completa las oraciones según las **Lecturas culturales 1** y **2** del libro de texto. Usa palabras de la lista.

activos	El Salvador	lagos	salada
cuatro	española	pelota	tiburones
cuatrocientos	indígena	pirámide	volcanes

1. El país más pequeño (*smallest*) de Centroamérica es _____.

2. Nicaragua tiene diecisiete _____ y dos _____ grandes, Nicaragua y Managua.

3. El Lago Coatepeque tiene _____ millas (*miles*) de ancho (*wide*) y _____ pies (*feet*) de hondo (*deep*).

4. En las ruinas mayas de Tazumal, en El Salvador, hay una _____ principal (*main*) y un campo (*field*) de juego de _____.

5. El volcán Masaya, cerca de (*near*) Managua, es uno de los volcanes más (*most*) _____ del mundo (*world*).

6. El Lago Nicaragua no tiene agua _____ (*salty*), pero sí tiene _____ (*sharks*).

7. La música folclórica de Nicaragua y El Salvador es una combinación de música _____ y _____.

Paso 2 Gramática

11. Expressing Actions • *Hacer, oír, poner, salir, traer,* and *ver*

A. Las actividades de Roberto. Completa las oraciones con la forma apropiada del verbo.

1. Los domingos _____ (*yo:* **ver**) mi programa favorito.

2. Ricardo y yo _____ (**salir**) con amigos los fines de semana.

3. _____ (*yo:* **Poner**) el televisor antes de ir a clases.

4. Los sábados, _____ (*yo:* **traer**) a mi perro a este parque (*park*).

5. Mis padres y yo _____ (**oír**) las noticias (*news*) de las siete.

6. Antes del examen de español, _____ (*yo:* **hacer**) los ejercicios del cuaderno.

7. _____ (*yo:* **Salir**) de la clase de matemáticas a las once de la mañana.

B. Un sábado típico. Complete the following paragraph with the correct form of **hacer, oír, poner, salir, traer,** or **ver** to tell about a typical Saturday. ¡OJO! Not all of the verbs will be used.

Por la mañana (yo) _____ [1] la radio y _____ [2] la tarea para el lunes.

Por la tarde, un amigo normalmente _____ [3] sándwiches y cerveza y comemos

juntos (*together*). Por la noche, (nosotros) _____ [4] con un grupo de amigos.

_____ [5] una película o _____ [6] a bailar.

❖**C. Preguntas personales.** Contesta con oraciones completas.

1. ¿A qué hora sales de casa los lunes para ir a la universidad?

_____

2. ¿Ves películas en casa o prefieres salir a ver películas en el cine?

_____

3. En clase, ¿haces muchas preguntas o prefieres estar callado/a (*quiet*)?

_____

4. Si quieres escuchar música, ¿qué pones, la radio o un CD? ¿Tienes una estación de radio

favorita? ¿Cuál es? _____

_____

5. ¿Qué cosas traes a clase en tu mochila? _____

6. ¿A qué hora oyes las noticias (*news*)? _____

D. Gramática en acción: Aspectos de la vida de Rigoberto. You will hear a series of statements about the following drawings. Listen carefully and write the number of each statement under the correct drawing.

a. _____   b. _____   c. _____   d. _____

E. Los jóvenes de hoy

Paso 1. Dictado. You will hear the following passage in which an adult complains about today's youth. It will be read twice. Listen carefully and fill in the missing words. (Check your answers in the Appendix.)

«¡Estos muchachos sólo quieren _____[1]! No

_____[2] sus cosas en orden en sus cuartos... Los jóvenes

de hoy día no _____[3] nada bien; no son responsables...

¡Hasta quieren _____[4] muchachas a sus cuartos!»

Paso 2. Preguntas. Now you will hear a series of questions that an adult might ask a young person. Each will be said twice. Answer based on your own experience. You will hear a possible answer. Pause and write your answers.

1. _____.

2. _____.

3. _____.

4. _____.

Now resume listening.

F. Mis compañeros y yo. Form complete sentences about yourself and others, using the oral and written cues. The last two sentences will be negative.

MODELO: (*you see*) Adela (*you hear*) hacer ejercicio →
(*you say*) Adela hace ejercicio.

1. yo   2. Tito y yo   3. tú   4. ellos   5. Marta

G. Soy buen compañero. Imagine that you want to impress your friend Sam, who is looking for a roommate. When you hear the corresponding number, form sentences that tell Sam what a good roommate you are. Make any necessary changes or additions. Repeat the correct sentence.

MODELO: (*you see and hear*) uno (*you see*) escuchar / noticias / por la mañana →
(*you say*) Escucho las noticias por la mañana.

2. no hacer / mucho / fiestas
3. siempre / hacer / cama
4. no salir / tarde / sábados

5. no poner / televisión / doce / noche
6. siempre / poner / ropa / armario

12. Expressing Actions • Present Tense of Stem-Changing Verbs (Part 2)

¡RECUERDA!					
Stem-Changing Verbs You Already Know. Complete the verb chart.					
	yo	tú	Ud., él, ella	nosotros	Uds., ellos, ellas
1. querer	_____	_____	_____	_queremos_	_____
2. preferir	_____	_prefieres_	_____	_____	_____
3. poder	_____	_____	_puede_	_____	_____

A. Preferencias. ¿Qué prefieren hacer tú y tus amigos? Completa las oraciones con la forma apropiada de los verbos entre paréntesis.

1. (**pensar**): Isabel y Fernando _____ almorzar en casa, pero Pilar y yo

   _____ salir. ¿Qué _____ hacer tú?

2. (**volver**): Nosotras _____ en tren con Sergio, pero Felipe _____

   en coche con Lola. ¿Cómo _____ Uds.?

3. (**pedir**): Por lo general Tomás _____ agua. Rita y Carmen

   _____ Coca-Cola. Pepe y yo _____ café.

B. Un día típico de Bernardo. Describe a typical schoolday for Bernardo using the words provided in the order given. Make any necessary changes, and add other words when necessary.

MODELO: comer / casa / 6:00 → Come en casa a las seis.

1. salir / casa / 7:15 _____

2. su / primera clase / empezar / ocho _____

3. si no / entender / lección, / hacer / mucho / preguntas _____

   _____

4. con frecuencia / almorzar / en / cafetería _____

5. a veces / pedir / hamburguesa / y / refresco _____

6. lunes y miércoles / jugar / tenis / con / un / amigo _____

   _____

7. su madre / servir / cena (*dinner*) / seis _____

   _____

8. hacer / la tarea / por / noche / y / dormir / siete horas _____

   _____

C. Gramática en acción: ¿Una fiesta exitosa? You will hear a series of statements about the following drawing. Circle **C** (**cierto**) if the statement is true or **F** (**falso**) if it is false. First pause and look at the drawing.

Now resume listening.

    1. C F   **2.** C F   **3.** C F   **4.** C F   **5.** C F

❖**¿Qué piensas tú?** Now pause and write the answers to the following questions.

    ¿Es una fiesta exitosa? ¿Qué piensas? ¿Por qué?

_____

_____

_____

_____

_____

D. Un sábado típico en mi casa. Tell about the activities of your fictitious family on a typical Saturday. Use the written and oral cues.

    1. yo
    2. mis padres
    3. mi hermana y yo
    4. tú

E. Entrevista con los Sres. Ruiz. Interview Mr. and Mrs. Ruiz about some of the things they like to do. Use the oral cues. You will hear an answer to each of your questions.

    MODELO: (*you hear*) jugar al tenis →
                 (*you say*) ¿Juegan al tenis? (*you hear*) No, no jugamos al tenis.

    1. ... **2.** ... **3.** ... **4.** ...

Paso 3 Gramática

13. Expressing -self/-selves • Reflexive Pronouns (Part 1)

❖**A. ¿Cierto o falso?**

		C	F
1.	Me levanto tarde los fines de semana.	☐	☐
2.	Me divierto con los amigos todas las noches.	☐	☐
3.	A veces mi padre se duerme cuando mira la televisión.	☐	☐
4.	Siempre me ducho por la noche.	☐	☐
5.	Me pongo zapatos de tenis para ir a clase.	☐	☐
6.	En la clase de español nos sentamos en un círculo.	☐	☐
7.	Me cepillo los dientes antes de vestirme.	☐	☐

B. Oraciones incompletas. Completa las oraciones con la forma apropiada del pronombre reflexivo.

1. Yo _____ llamo Juan y mi hermana _____ llama Inés.

2. Nuestros padres _____ llaman Carlos y Luisa.

3. ¿Por qué _____ pones esa blusa? Está sucia (*dirty*).

4. ¿_____ despiertan Uds. tarde los sábados?

5. Después de levantarnos, _____ bañamos y _____ vestimos.

6. ¿Dónde _____ diviertes más, en el teatro o en el cine?

C. Tú y otra persona. Cambia (*Change*) el sujeto **yo** por (*to*) **nosotros.** Haz todos los cambios necesarios.

1. Me despierto temprano. _____

2. Me visto después de ducharme. _____

3. Nunca me siento para tomar el desayuno. _____

    _____

4. En la universidad asisto a clases y me divierto. _____

    _____

5. Después de volver a casa hago la tarea. _____

    _____

6. A las doce tengo sueño, me cepillo los dientes y me acuesto. _____

    _____

7. Me duermo a las doce y media. _____

    _____

D. Gramática en acción: La rutina diaria de Andrés. You will hear a brief description of Andrés's daily routine. Then you will hear the following statements. Circle **C** (**cierto**) if the statement is true or **F** (**falso**) if it is false. If the information is not given in the description, circle **ND** (**No lo dice**).

1. C   F   ND   Andrés se levanta a las nueve de la mañana.
2. C   F   ND   Él se acuesta muy tarde.
3. C   F   ND   Se viste en el baño.
4. C   F   ND   Por lo general, Andrés tiene prisa por la mañana.

❖E. Encuesta. You will hear a series of statements about your habits. For each statement, check the appropriate response. No answers will be given. The answers you choose should be correct for you!

	SIEMPRE	CON FRECUENCIA	A VECES	¡NUNCA!
1.	☐	☐	☐	☐
2.	☐	☐	☐	☐
3.	☐	☐	☐	☐
4.	☐	☐	☐	☐
5.	☐	☐	☐	☐
6.	☐	☐	☐	☐

F. Hábitos y costumbres. Practice telling about some of the habits of the members of your fictitious family. Use the oral and written cues.

1. yo
2. mi primo y yo
3. mi hermanito
4. mis abuelos

G. ¿Qué van a hacer estas personas? When you hear the corresponding number, tell what the people in each drawing are going to do. **¡OJO!** You will be using the **ir** + **a** + infinitive construction, and you will attach the reflexive pronouns to the infinitives. First, listen to the list of verbs.

acostarse   afeitarse   ducharse   quitarse   sentarse

1.

2.

3.

4.

5.

Un poco de todo

A. El próximo sábado... Completa las oraciones con la forma correcta del verbo para describir las actividades de Juan Carlos el próximo sábado.

Los sábados _____¹ (*yo:* **levantarse**) a las nueve de la mañana, pero el sábado

de la próxima semana _____² (**tener**) que _____³ (**despertarse**)

más temprano porque _____⁴ (**querer**) ir a _____⁵ (**jugar**) al

tenis con mi amigo Daniel. Casi siempre, _____⁶ (*nosotros:* **empezar**) a las

nueve y media; si _____⁷ (*yo:* **poner**) el despertadorᵃ a las ocho y media y

_____⁸ (**salir**) de la casa a las nueve, _____⁹ (**poder**) llegar

a tiempo. Daniel y yo _____¹⁰ (**almorzar**) después de jugar al tenis. Si Daniel

_____¹¹ (**perder**) el partido,ᵇ _____¹² (*él:* **tener**) que pagar la

cuenta;ᶜ si yo _____¹³ (**perder**) el partido, yo _____¹⁴ (**tener**)

que pagar. A las dos, _____¹⁵ (*yo:* **volver**) a casa.

ᵃ*alarm clock*   ᵇ*match, game*   ᶜ*bill*

❖**B.** **Un día típico.** On a separate sheet of paper, write about your typical day this semester—what you do, and when.

Paso 1. Before you begin to write, read the verbs given and cross out those that do not apply to you. Organize the verbs you plan to use by writing **M** (**mañana**), **T** (**tarde**), **N** (**noche**) next to the appropriate infinitives. Then put each group into a logical chronological sequence.

acostarse	hacer	quitarse
afeitarse	ir	salir
almorzar	leer	sentarse a (comer)
asistir	levantarse	tomar el desayuno
bañarse/ducharse	llamar por teléfono (a)	trabajar
despertarse	mirar	vestirse
dormirse	ponerse	volver
empezar		

Paso 2. Now begin to write. Use phrases listed here, or any others, to tell *when* you do these activities and to help you organize your sentences. Connect them into three coherent paragraphs: **por la mañana, por la tarde, por la noche.**

primero, luego	siempre, todos los días	hasta	antes de
nunca	con frecuencia, a veces	durante	después de

C. **¿Cuál es su casa?** You will hear a description of Raquel and Arturo's house, read by Raquel. Listen to the description and circle the number of the drawing that matches the description.

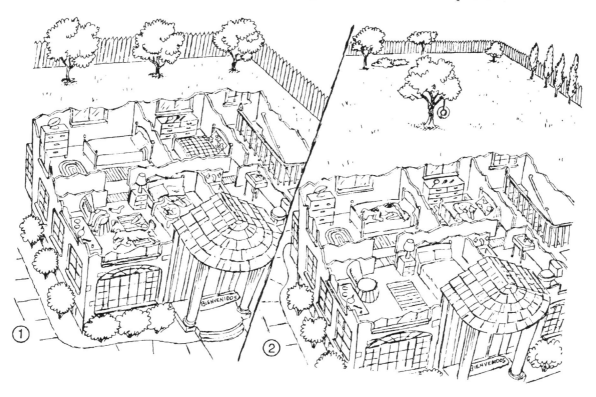

¡Repasemos!

A. Una carta. Complete this letter from Mariana to her pen pal in Bogotá, Colombia, with the correct forms of the words in parentheses. When two possibilities are given in parentheses, select the correct word.

Querida Amalia:

Me preguntas[a] cómo pasamos[b] _____[1] (**nuestro / nuestros**) fines de semana.

Pues, _____[2] (**el / los**) viernes, _____[3] (**antes de / después de**)

clases, _____[4] (*yo:* **volver**) a casa o _____[5] (**ir**) a la

_____[6] (**biblioteca / librería**) porque es un lugar tranquilo para estudiar.

Por _____[7] (**el / la**) noche, yo voy _____[8] (**a la / al**) cine

con _____[9] (**mi / mis**) amigos o _____[10] (*nosotros:* **ir**) todos

a una discoteca. Los sábados trabajo en un almacén grande. No es un trabajo difícil,[c] pero

_____[11] (**a / son**) las seis _____[12] (**de / en**) la tarde, estoy

_____[13] (**cansada / cansado**). Los domingos, _____[14] (**mi / mis**)

padres, _____[15] (**mi / mis**) hermana y yo _____[16] (**ir**)

a la iglesia, _____[17] (**leer**) el periódico y _____[18] (**mirar**) la

televisión. _____[19] (**Por / De**) la tarde, muchas veces vamos a la casa de

_____[20] (**mi / mis**) tíos. Como _____[21] (*tú:* **ver**),

_____[22] (**el / los**) fines de semana todos nosotros_____[23]

(**divertirse**).

Recuerdos cariñosos,[d] Mariana

[a]Me... *You ask me*   [b]*we spend*   [c]*difficult*   [d]Recuerdos... *Affectionate regards*

B. Entrevista. You will hear a series of questions. Each will be said twice. Answer based on your own experience. Pause and write the answers.

1. _____

2. _____

3. _____

4. _____

5. _____

6. _____

7. _____

8. _____

Mi diario

Mi casa. In your diary, write a description of your house (apartment, dorm, room, and so on). Be sure to include the following information:

- size
- name(s) and size of room(s)
- furniture in each room

- color of the walls, rug (if any), and furniture
- if there's a garage and/or yard, and what it or they are like
- your favorite place in the house (apartment, and so on) and why

Ponte a prueba

A ver si sabes...

A. *Hacer, oír, poner, salir, traer,* and *ver.* Completa la siguiente tabla.

INFINITIVO	YO	TÚ	NOSOTROS	ELLOS
1. hacer			hacemos	
2. traer				traen
3. oír		oyes		
4. poner				
5. ver				
6. salir				

B. **Present Tense of Stem-Changing Verbs**

1. What vowel changes occur in the following verb types?

    a. emp<u>e</u>zar, p<u>e</u>rder   e → _____

    b. d<u>o</u>rmir, alm<u>o</u>rzar   o → _____

    c. p<u>e</u>dir, s<u>e</u>rvir   e → _____

2. What are the two pronouns that do not show any change in the stem? _____ and _____.

3. Completa las oraciones con los siguientes verbos y preposiciones. ¡OJO! No es necesario conjugar todos los verbos.

    a. (pensar servir)   ¿Qué _____ (tú) _____?

    b. (empezar a)   Ahora (yo) _____ _____ entender.

    c. (volver a)   ¿Uds. van a _____ _____ entrar?

    d. (pedir)   Voy a _____ otra Coca-Cola.

C. Reflexive Pronouns

1. Escribe el pronombre reflexivo apropiado.

   a. yo _____ levanto   **c.** él _____ despierta   **e.** vosotros _____ acostáis

   b. tú _____ acuestas   **d.** nosotros _____ divertimos   **f.** Uds. _____ bañan

2. Cambia el plural por el singular.

   a. Nosotros nos acostamos tarde.   _____

   b. ¿Cuándo se sientan a comer?   (tú) _____

   c. Nos vestimos en cinco minutos.   _____

Prueba corta

A. Oraciones. Completa las oraciones con la forma apropiada de los verbos de la lista. (*Note:* Use each verb once.)

| divertirse | hacer | oír | salir |
| dormirse | levantarse | ponerse | sentarse |

1. Algunos (*Some*) estudiantes _____ en clase cuando están muy cansados.

2. Prefiero _____ cerca del escritorio del profesor porque no

   _____ bien.

3. Yo _____ mucho cuando salgo con mis amigos.

4. Si quieres llegar a tiempo, debes _____ temprano.

5. Para ir a un concierto al aire libre ella _____ un suéter y *jeans*.

6. (Tú) Siempre _____ muchas preguntas en clase, ¿verdad?

7. Los viernes por la noche mis amigos y yo _____ a comer y después vamos al cine.

B. Una lista. Completa la siguiente lista.

1. Escribe tres actividades que realizas (*that you do*) en la alcoba por la mañana:

   _____, _____ y _____.

2. Escribe tres actividades que realizas en el baño, después de despertarte:

   _____, _____ y _____.

3. Escribe el nombre de tres muebles de tu sala: _____,

   _____ y _____.

4. Escribe el nombre de tres cosas o muebles que piensas comprar para tu casa:

   _____, _____ y _____.

5. Escribe en qué cuartos de tu casa realizas las siguientes actividades. Usa oraciones completas.

   (**almorzar**) _____

   (**dormir**) _____

   (**estudiar**) _____

C. Asociaciones. You will hear a series of statements. Circle the location with which you associate each statement.

1. **a.** la lámpara   **b.** el comedor   **c.** la cocina
2. **a.** la sala   **b.** el baño   **c.** la alcoba
3. **a.** el sofá   **b.** el armario   **c.** el lavabo
4. **a.** la piscina   **b.** el almacén   **c.** el garaje
5. **a.** la cocina   **b.** el comedor   **c.** la sala
6. **a.** la mesita   **b.** el plato   **c.** el sillón
7. **a.** la cómoda   **b.** el estante   **c.** el jardín

D. La rutina diaria. Practice talking about your daily routine, using the written cues. When you hear the corresponding number, form sentences using the words provided in the order given, making any necessary changes or additions.

MODELO: (*you see*) **1.** (yo) despertarse y levantarse / 7:00 A.M.   (*you hear*) uno →
              (*you say*) Me despierto y me levanto a las siete de la mañana.

2. (yo) ducharse / vestirse / y/ peinarse
3. hacer / el desayuno / y / sentarse a comer
4. hacer / la cama / y / salir / de casa / 8:00
5. después de las clases / ir / al gimnasio
6. hacer ejercicio / hasta / 3:30
7. volver a casa / y / poner la televisión
8. empezar / a preparar / comida
9. por fin / acostarse / 11:00 P.M. / y / dormirse

E. Apuntes. You will hear a brief paragraph that tells about a house for sale. Listen carefully and, while listening, write in the information requested. Write all numbers as numerals. First, listen to the new vocabulary and the requested information. (Check your answers in the Appendix.)

mide	*measures*
el metro	*meter*
por	*by (as in 3 meters by 2 meters)*
el vecindario	*neighborhood*

El número de alcobas: _____ ¹

El número de baños: _____ ²

¿Cuántos metros mide la sala? _____ ³

Esta casa está cerca de _____ ⁴ y enfrente de _____. ⁵

La dirección (*address*) de la casa: _____ ⁶

CAPÍTULO **5**

Paso 1 Vocabulario

¿Qué tiempo hace hoy?

A. ¿Qué tiempo hace hoy? Describe the weather conditions in each drawing.

1. _____

2. _____

3. _____

4. _____

5. _____

6. _____

B. ¿Qué tiempo hace cuando lleva... ?

1. Marta lleva impermeable y botas. _____

2. Joselito tiene frío y lleva abrigo, dos suéteres y botas. _____

3. Carmen tiene calor y lleva traje de baño. _____

4. Samuel lleva una chaqueta de lana, pero no lleva abrigo. _____

5. Todos llevan camisetas y pantalones y están en el parque. _____

6. Nadie (*No one*) hace ejercicio hoy. _____

C. **¿Qué tiempo hace?** You will hear a series of weather conditions. Each will be said twice. Give the number of the drawing to which each corresponds, then repeat the description. First, pause and look at the drawings.

1.

2.

3.

4.

5.

6.

Los meses y las estaciones del año

A. **Meses y estaciones.** Completa las oraciones con las palabras apropiadas de esta sección.

1. El Día de los Inocentes (*April Fools' Day*) es (*date*) _____

    en los Estados Unidos.

2. Los tres meses del verano son _____, _____ y

    _____.

3. Diciembre es el primer mes del _____.

4. En la primavera hace buen tiempo, pero también _____ mucho.

5. Septiembre, octubre y noviembre son los tres meses del _____.

6. El _____ se celebra el Día de la Independencia de

    los Estados Unidos.

7. Por lo general, _____ mucho en las montañas durante el invierno.

8. Después de diciembre viene el mes de _____, y después de abril viene

    _____.

❖9. Mi cumpleaños es en (la estación de) _____.

B. **¿Cuándo es... ?** Your Peruvian friend Evangelina wants to know when certain events take place, including a birth date (**una fecha de nacimiento**), an anniversary (**un aniversario**), and a national holiday (**una fiesta nacional**). Answer, using the written cues.

MODELO: (*you hear*) ¿Cuándo es el cumpleaños de Nicolás? (*you see*) Sunday, May 4 →
(*you say*) Es el domingo, cuatro de mayo.

1. Saturday, November 22
2. Wednesday, April 14
3. February 11, 1899
4. July 4, 1776

¿Dónde está? • Las preposiciones (Part 2)

❖A. **¿Cierto o falso?** ¿Qué haces en tu clase de español?

		C	F
1.	Me siento delante del profesor.	☐	☐
2.	Prefiero sentarme detrás de un estudiante alto.	☐	☐
3.	Con frecuencia hablo con mis compañeros durante la clase.	☐	☐
4.	Siempre pongo la mochila al lado de mi silla.	☐	☐
5.	Me siento cerca de la puerta.	☐	☐
6.	Pongo los pies (*feet*) encima de la silla delante de mí.	☐	☐
7.	A veces olvido (*I forget*) libros debajo de mi silla.	☐	☐

B. **¿Dónde está España?** Mira el mapa y luego completa la descripción con la(s) palabra(s) apropiada(s). Es necesario usar algunas (*some*) palabras más de una vez (*more than once*).

al norte   al sur   al este   al oeste (*west*)   cerca   lejos (*far*)   en   entre

España y Portugal forman la Península Ibérica. Los Pirineos están _____¹ España y Francia. Francia está _____² de España y África está _____³ de España. El Mar Mediterráneo está _____⁴ de la península y el Océano Atlántico está _____.⁵

Madrid, la capital, está en el centro del país. La hermosa ciudad de Granada está _____⁶ de Madrid; Toledo está _____.⁷ La isla de Mallorca, una de las Islas Baleares, está _____⁸ el Mar Mediterráneo. Las Islas Canarias están _____⁹ de África.

❖C. ¿Quién es?

Paso 1. Draw a seating plan of the people who sit directly around you in class, and write in their names. If no one sits in one of those seats, write **nadie**.

<u>   </u>

<u>   </u>   yo   <u>   </u>

<u>   </u>

Paso 2. Ahora, en otro papel, escribe un párrafo para indicar (*indicate*) dónde se sientan tus compañeros de clase con respecto a ti. Escribe también los nombres de las personas que se sientan más lejos (*farthest*) y más cerca de la puerta.

      a mi derecha   a mi izquierda   delante de   detrás de   más lejos/cerca de

      MODELO: George se sienta delante de mí. María se sienta a mi derecha...

D. ¿Dónde está? You will hear a series of descriptions. Listen carefully and name the country, location, or item described. You will be listening for specific information about the location of the place or item. (Remember to repeat the correct answer.)

4. ...   5. ...   6. ...

1. ...   2. ...   3. ...

7. ...   8. ...   9. ...

Pronunciación y ortografía • *r* and *rr*

The letter **r** has two pronunciations in Spanish: the trilled **r** (written as **rr** between vowels or as **r** at the beginning of a word or after **l, n,** or **s**), and the flap **r,** which appears in all other positions. Because mispronunciations can alter the meaning of a word, it is important to distinguish between these two pronunciations of the Spanish **r.** For example: **coro** (*chorus*) and **corro** (*I run*).

The flap **r** is similar to the sound produced by the rapid pronunciation of *tt* and *dd* in the English words *Betty* and *ladder.*

¡RECUERDA!
The trilled **r** is spelled _____ at the beginning of a word. It is spelled _____ in the middle of a word (between vowels).

A. El sonido *rr*. Underline the examples of the trilled **rr** sound in the following words and phrases.

1. Rosa
2. caro
3. perro
4. Roberto

5. rebelde
6. un horrible error
7. una persona rara
8. Raquel es rubia.

B. Repeticiones. Listen to these word pairs. Then repeat them.

Petty / pero
sadder / Sara
motor / moro

C. Más repeticiones. Repeat the following words, phrases, and sentences, imitating the speaker.

1. arte   gracias   para   vender   triste
2. ruso   Roberto   real   reportero   rebelde   enredar   alrededor
3. burro   corral   carro   barra   corro
4. el extranjero
    el precio del cuaderno
    el nombre correcto
    Enrique, Carlos y Rosita
    las residencias
    una mujer refinada
    Puerto Rico
    El perro está en el corral.
    Soy el primo de Roberto Ramírez.
    Estos errores son raros.

D. ¿R o rr? You will hear a series of words. Each will be said twice. Circle the letter of the word you hear.

1. **a.** ahora   **b.** ahorra
2. **a.** caro   **b.** carro
3. **a.** coro   **b.** corro
4. **a.** coral   **b.** corral
5. **a.** pero   **b.** perro

Lectura cultural: Costa Rica

Oraciones. Completa las oraciones según las **Lecturas culturales 1** y **2** del libro de texto. Usa palabras de la lista.

    Arenal   ejército   Sarchí
    bañarse   neutral   veinticinco
    café   pintadas

1. Cuando hay conflictos políticos en Centroamérica, Costa Rica siempre mantiene una posición

    _____.

2. Costa Rica es un país pacífico (*peaceful*) que no tiene _____.

3. Los parques y reservas nacionales cubren (*cover*) más de _____ por ciento del

    territorio de Costa Rica.

4. Una atracción popular de Costa Rica es el Parque Nacional _____ donde los

    turistas pueden caminar (*walk*) y _____ en sus aguas termales.

5. El pueblo de _____ es famoso por su artesanía (*craftsmanship*), especialmente por

    las carretas (*carts*) _____.

6. La tierra (*earth*) volcánica de Costa Rica es ideal para cultivar (*for growing*) _____.

Paso 2 Gramática

14. ¿Qué están haciendo? • Present Progressive: *Estar + -ndo*

A. En este momento... ¿Qué están haciendo estas personas en este momento?

1. _____ Enrique Iglesias
2. _____ Antonio Banderas
3. _____ tu profesor(a)
4. _____ Jennifer López
5. _____ el presidente
6. _____ Rafael Nadal

  a. está trabajando en una película
  b. está hablando en las Naciones Unidas
  c. está cantando canciones románticas
  d. está corrigiendo (*correcting*) exámenes
  e. está jugando al tenis
  f. está haciendo un vídeo

B. La familia de Rigoberto. Describe lo que están haciendo los miembros de la familia de Rigoberto, desde su perspectiva. Usa la forma apropiada del gerundio. ¡OJO! Cuidado con los verbos que tienen un cambio en la raíz (*stem*).

1. Mi abuela está _____ (**dormir**) la siesta ahora.

2. Mi hermana María está _____ (**pedir**) $9.00 para ir al cine.

3. Mi padre está _____ (**servirse**) café.

4. Mis hermanos están _____ (**leer**) libros.

5. Mi madre está _____ (**almorzar**) con una amiga.

    Está _____ (**divertirse**).

C. Mis padres (hijos) y yo. Tus padres (hijos) siempre hacen cosas muy diferentes de las que tú haces. Cambia los infinitivos para mostrar lo que están haciendo ellos y lo que haces tú en este momento.

MODELO: leer el periódico / estudiar para un examen →
                Mis padres (hijos) están leyendo el periódico, pero yo estoy estudiando para
                un examen.

1. jugar al golf / correr en un maratón _____

_____

2. mirar la tele / aprender a esquiar _____

_____

3. leer el periódico / escuchar música _____

_____

4. acostarse / vestirme para salir _____

_____

D. Gramática en acción: ¿Qué está haciendo Elisa? Dictado. You will hear a passage that describes the activities of Elisa on her day off. Listen carefully and write the missing words. (Check your answers in the Appendix.)

Elisa es periodista. Por eso escribe mucho y habla

mucho por teléfono en su trabajo. Pero ahora no

_____¹. ¿Qué _____²?

_____³ en casa. _____⁴ música,

_____⁵ una novela y _____⁶

un café.

E. ¿Qué están haciendo? You will hear a series of sentences. Each will be said twice. Write the number of each statement next to the item that corresponds to the activity mentioned. First, listen to the list of items.

a. _____ el restaurante   d. _____ la computadora

b. _____ las bicicletas y la pelota (*ball*)   e. _____ la música

c. _____ el libro

15. ¿*Ser* o *estar*? • Summary of the Uses of *ser* and *estar*

¡RECUERDA!

¿Se usa **ser** o **estar**? Escribe el infinitivo apropiado en la columna de la izquierda. Luego completa las oraciones con la forma apropiada de **ser** o **estar** en la columna de la derecha.

1. *to talk about location of a person or thing:*

    _____

    Mis libros _____ al lado de mi silla.

2. *to talk about origin:* _____

    Mi abuela _____ de España.

3. *to express possession with* **de:**

    _____

    ¿De quién _____ este dinero?

4. *with adjectives, to express the norm or*

    inherent qualities: _____

    Los padres de Elena _____ altos.

    La nieve _____ blanca.

5. *with adjectives, to express a change from*

    the norm or to express conditions:

    _____

    Mi café _____ frío.

    Tú _____ muy guapo esta noche.

    ¿_____ Uds. ocupados?

6. *to identify people or things:*

    _____

    Nosotros _____ estudiantes.

    Miguel _____ el hijo de Julio.

7. *to express time:* _____

    _____ las dos y media.

92 *Capítulo 5*

A. Minidiálogos. Completa los diálogos con la forma apropiada de **ser** o **estar**.

1. —¿De dónde _____ tú?

   —_____ de Buenos Aires.

2. —¿De quién _____ estas cosas?

   —Creo que _____ de Ana.

3. —Estos boletos (*tickets*) _____ para Uds. Vamos a entrar ahora, ¿eh? Las puertas del

   cine ya _____ abiertas.

   —Buena idea.

4. —Pablo, ya _____ la una y media. Tenemos que _____ en el aeropuerto

   a las dos y _____ difícil encontrar (*to find*) un taxi a estas horas.

   —De acuerdo. Vamos.

5. —Juan, tu cuarto _____ muy desordenado.

   —Sí, mamá. (Yo) _____ de acuerdo, ¡pero la puerta _____ cerrada!

6. —La novia de Tito _____ cariñosa y alegre. ¿Y él?

   —Él _____ muy formal y serio.

B. Sentimientos. Complete the sentences with the forms of **estar** and the most appropriate adjectives from the following list in order to describe how you might feel in the following situations. Use each adjective only once. ¡OJO! Be careful with adjective agreement.

   aburrido/a   cansado/a   contento/a   molesto/a   nervioso/a   preocupado/a   triste

1. Cuando leo un libro que no me gusta, _____.

2. Cuando voy al cine con mis amigos, _____.

3. Antes de un examen difícil, _____.

4. Cuando mi novio/a no llama, _____.

5. Cuando mi hermano/a (compañero/a de cuarto) lleva mi chaqueta de seda favorita,

   _____.

6. Después de trabajar diez horas, _____.

7. Cuando no tengo dinero, _____.

C. Diálogo. Mari habla con Anita. Completa el diálogo con las formas apropiadas de **ser** o **estar.**

MARI: Hola, Anita. ¿Cómo _____¹?

ANITA: Todavía _____² un poco enferma de gripe.ᵃ

MARI: Ay, lo siento.ᵇ ¿Quiénes _____³ esos chicos que _____⁴ con tu hermano?

ANITA: _____⁵ nuestros primos. _____⁶ de la Argentina.

MARI: ¿Y esta guitarra? ¿De quién _____⁷?

ANITA: De mi prima Rosario. Ella _____⁸ una guitarrista fabulosa. Canta y toca comoᶜ profesional.

MARI: ¿Cuánto tiempo van a _____⁹ aquí?

ANITA: Sólo dos semanas. ¿Por qué no vienes a casa el domingo? Vamos a darᵈ una fiesta.

MARI: Encantada, gracias.

ᵃ*flu*   ᵇ*lo... I'm sorry*   ᶜ*like a*   ᵈ*give*

D. Gramática en acción: Una conversación de larga distancia. You will hear one side of a telephone conversation between a husband and his wife, who is on a business trip. Then you will hear a series of questions from the dialogue. Circle the letter of the best response to each.

1. **a.** Estoy en Nueva York.   **b.** Estoy cansada, pero estoy bien.
2. **a.** Es el Sr. Miró.   **b.** Es muy moderno.
3. **a.** Estoy trabajando.   **b.** Hace buen tiempo.
4. **a.** Hace buen tiempo.   **b.** Son las once y media.

E. ¿Qué pregunta hiciste? (*What question did you ask?*) You will hear a series of statements that contain **ser** or **estar.** Each will be said twice. Circle the letter of the question that corresponds to each.

1. **a.** ¿Cómo estás?   **b.** ¿Cómo eres?
2. **a.** ¿Cómo están?   **b.** ¿Cómo son?
3. **a.** ¿Dónde estás?   **b.** ¿De dónde eres?
4. **a.** ¿Dónde está el consejero?   **b.** ¿De dónde es el consejero?
5. **a.** ¿De quién es la blusa?   **b.** ¿De qué es la blusa?

F. ¿Quiénes son? Imagine that the people in this photograph are your relatives. Tell who they are and describe them, using the oral cues and the appropriate forms of **ser** or **estar.** All the cues are about the couple on the right. Begin your first answer with **Son...**

1. ...   2. ...   3. ...   4. ...   5. ...   6. ...

Paso 3 Gramática

16. Describing • Comparisons

❖**A.** **Opiniones.** Completa las oraciones con **más/menos... que** o **tan... como.**

1. Soy _____ alto/a _____ mi padre/madre.

2. La salud (*Health*) es _____ importante _____ el dinero.

3. Mi cuarto está _____ limpio _____ el cuarto de mi mejor amigo/a.

4. Los hermanos de Michael Jackson son _____ ricos _____ él.

5. Mi padre es _____ serio _____ mi madre.

B. **Hablando de Roberto, Ceci y Laura.** Compara las cualidades indicadas de las personas nombradas.

   MODELOS: Roberto / Ceci (delgado) → Roberto es tan delgado como Ceci.

   Roberto / Ceci (estudioso) → Roberto es más estudioso que Ceci.

1. Ceci / Laura (delgado) _____

2. Ceci / Roberto (atlético) _____

3. Roberto / Laura (introvertido) _____

4. Ceci / Laura (alto) _____

5. Roberto / Laura (estudioso) _____

6. Roberto / Ceci (moreno) _____

❖Ahora haz tres comparaciones entre tú y Roberto, Laura y/o Ceci.

7. _____

8. _____

9. _____

C. **En el centro.** Contesta según el dibujo.

1. ¿Es el cine tan alto como la tienda Casa Montaño? _____

_____

2. ¿Cuál es el edificio más pequeño de todos? _____

_____

3. ¿Cuál es el edificio más alto? _____

_____

4. ¿Es el cine tan alto como el café? _____

_____

5. ¿Es el hotel tan grande como el cine?

_____

D. **Gramática en acción: México D.F.
y Sevilla, España**

Paso 1. La comparación. Listen to a comparison
between Mexico City (**el Distrito Federal [D.F.]**)
and Sevilla.

Paso 2. ¿Qué recuerdas? Pause and complete
the following sentences based on the comparison.
(Check your answers in the Appendix.)

1. Sevilla es _____ bonita _____ la Ciudad de México.

2. Sevilla tiene _____ edificios altos _____ el D.F.

3. En el D.F. no hace _____ calor _____ en Sevilla.

4. Sevilla no tiene _____ habitantes _____ el D.F.

Now resume listening.

E. **La rutina de Alicia.** The following chart shows Alicia's routine for weekdays and weekends. You
will hear a series of statements about the chart. Each will be said twice. Circle **C** if the statement is true
or **F** if it is false, according to the chart. First pause and read the chart.

ACCIÓN	DE LUNES A VIERNES	SÁBADO Y DOMINGO
levantarse	6:30	9:30
bañarse	7:15	10:00
trabajar	8 horas	1 hora
almorzar	20 minutos	30 minutos
divertirse	1 hora	8 horas
acostarse	11:00	11:00

1. C F   **2.** C F   **3.** C F   **4.** C F   **5.** C F

F. Un desacuerdo. Imagine that you and your friend Lourdes don't agree on anything! React to her statements negatively, following the model and using the cues.

MODELO: (*you hear and see*) Los amigos son más importantes que la familia.
(*you hear*) tan → (*you say*) No, los amigos son tan importantes como la familia.

1. El invierno es más bonito que el verano.
2. Hace tanto calor en Florida como en Alaska.
3. La clase de cálculo es menos difícil que la clase de física.
4. Los niños juegan más videojuegos (*videogames*) que los adultos.

Un poco de todo

A. ¡Problemas y más problemas! Form complete sentences, using the words provided in the order given. Make any necessary changes, and add other words when necessary. Replace each ¿ ? with the appropriate form of **ser** or **estar.** Write the progressive form of the underlined verbs. Write out all numbers. Be sure that the adjectives agree with the nouns they modify. *Note:* / / indicates a new sentence.

1. Carmen / ¿ ? / ocupado / y / no / poder / ir / cine / este / noche

    _____

2. ese / camisa / ¿ ? / sucio / / (tú) deber / ponerse / otro

    _____

3. ese / tiendas / ¿ ? / cerrado / ahora / / no / (nosotros) poder / entrar

    _____

4. (nosotros) deber / llevar / el paraguas (*umbrella*) / / ¿ ? / <u>llover</u>

    _____

5. mi / primos / ¿ ? / de Lima / / Ahora / ¿ ? / (ellos) <u>visitar</u> / su / tíos / en Texas, / pero / su / madre / ¿ ? / enfermo / y / (ellos) tener / regresar / su / país / semana / viene

    _____

    _____

B. Un hermano increíble. Fill in the blanks with the correct form of the infinitive or with the correct words in parentheses to complete the narration. Write out the numbers.

Yo tengo _____¹ (**21**) años. Mi hermano Miguel tiene sólo

_____,² (**19**) pero _____³ (**ese / eso**) chico es increíble.

Estudia menos _____⁴ (**que / como**) yo, pero recibe mejores notasᵃ

_____⁵ (**de / que**) yo. También ganaᵇ más dinero _____⁶ (**de / que**)

yo, aunqueᶜ yo trabajo _____⁷ (**tanto / tan**) _____⁸ (**como / que**) él.

En realidad,ᵈ gana más _____⁹ (**de / que**) _____¹⁰ (**$200**)

a la semana, pero nunca tiene dinero _____¹¹ (**porque / por qué**) gastaᵉ todo su

dinero en ropa. ¡Le gusta _____¹² (**ser / estar**) muy de moda! Por ejemplo, cree que

necesita más _____¹³ (**de / que**) _____¹⁴ (**$150**) para

comprar zapatos de tenis. Yo creo que es una tonteríaᶠ _____¹⁵ (**paga / pagar**)

tanto por zapatos.

ᵃ*grades* ᵇ*he earns* ᶜ*although* ᵈ*En... In fact* ᵉ*he spends* ᶠ*foolish thing*

C. En la plaza Santa Ana

Paso 1. ¿Qué pasa? You will hear a series of statements about the following drawing. Each will be said twice. Circle **C** if the statement is true or **F** if it is false. First, pause and look at the drawing.

1. C F   **2.** C F   **3.** C F   **4.** C F   **5.** C F

Paso 2. Descripción. Now pause and, on a separate sheet of paper, write five sentences that describe the drawing. You can talk about the weather, what the people are doing, how they seem to be feeling, their clothing, and so on. You can also make comparisons.

¡Repasemos!

A. Composición. On a separate sheet of paper, write two short paragraphs that answer the two sets of questions below. Remember that a paragraph is not a list of numbered answers but a connected composition. Use the following connectors to make your composition more interesting and meaningful: **por eso, y, aunque** (*although*), **también, luego,** and **porque.** However, do not use **porque** to begin a sentence; use **como** (*since*). For example, the two sentences **Hace calor** and **Voy a llevar un traje de baño** can be combined in the following ways:

> Como hace calor, voy a llevar un traje de baño.
>
> Voy a llevar un traje de baño porque hace calor.

- **1.** ¿En qué mes piensas ir de vacaciones este año? ¿Qué día vas a salir?
  2. ¿Adónde vas a ir? ¿Con quién(es) vas?
  3. ¿Cuánto tiempo piensas estar allí?
  4. ¿Vas a estar en un hotel o en la casa de unos amigos?

- **1.** ¿Qué tiempo hace allí? ¿Llueve con frecuencia? ¿Nieva mucho? ¿Hay contaminación?
  2. ¿Qué ropa piensas llevar?
  3. ¿Qué cosas quieres hacer durante el día? ¿y durante la noche?
  4. ¿En qué fecha piensas volver?

B. Entrevista. You will hear a series of questions. Each will be said twice. Answer based on your own experience. Write out all numbers. Pause and write the answers.

1. _____

2. _____

3. _____

4. _____

5. _____

6. _____

Mi diario

Las estaciones. Escribe sobre tres cosas que haces, que piensas hacer o que te gusta hacer en cada estación del año.

> **Vocabulario útil:** quedarme en casa, visitar a mis abuelos (amigos), celebrar mi cumpleaños, ir a la playa, esquiar, nadar (*to swim*)

> MODELO: En la primavera me gusta ir de compras. En las vacaciones de primavera pienso visitar a mis amigos en Washington. Si todavía hay nieve, voy a esquiar (*to ski*) también. Me gusta mucho esquiar.

A. Present Progressive: *Estar + -ndo*. Completa la siguiente tabla con la forma correcta del gerundio.

VERBO	GERUNDIO	VERBO	GERUNDIO
cepillarse		hablar	*hablando*
divertirse		leer	
dormir	*durmiendo*	poner	
escribir		servir	
estudia		tener	*teniendo*

B. ¿*Ser* o *estar*? Match the statements in the left-hand column with the appropriate use of **ser** or **estar** in the right-hand column.

1. _____ Estamos muy ocupados.
2. _____ Son las nueve.
3. _____ Ella está en Costa Rica.
4. _____ El reloj es de Carlos.
5. _____ Gracias, estoy bien.
6. _____ Ella es de Costa Rica.
7. _____ Marta es alta y morena.
8. _____ Están mirando la tele.
9. _____ Es importante salir ahora.

a. to tell time
b. with **de** to express origin
c. to tell location of a person or thing
d. to form generalizations
e. with the present participle to form the progressive
f. with adjectives to express a change from the norm or to express conditions
g. with adjectives to express the norm or inherent qualities
h. to speak of one's health
i. with **de** to express possession

C. Comparisons. Subraya (*Underline*) las palabras apropiadas.

1. Paulina es (**más / tanta**) bonita (**que / como**) su hermana.
2. Tengo (**tan / tantos**) problemas (**que / como**) tú.
3. Este libro es bueno, pero el otro es (**más mejor / mejor**).
4. Tú cantas (**tan / tanto**) bien (**que / como**) Gloria.
5. Mis hermanos tienen (**tantos / menos**) clases (**que / como**) yo.

Prueba corta

A. Oraciones. Escribe oraciones con las siguientes palabras en el presente progresivo.

1. (yo) mirar / programa _____

2. Juan / leer / periódico _____

3. Marta / servir / café / ahora _____

4. niños / dormir _____

5. ¿almorzar (tú) / ahora? _____

B. ¿*Ser* o *estar*? Completa las oraciones con la forma apropiada de **ser** o **estar,** según el contexto.

1. —Buenas tardes. ¿Cómo _____ Ud., señorita?

   —_____ bien, gracias.

2. —¿De dónde _____ (tú), Pablo?

   —_____ de Bogotá, Colombia.

3. —¿En qué clase _____ Uds.?

   —_____ en la clase de Español 1.

4. —¿Qué te pasa?[a] ¿_____ enferma?

   —No, sólo _____ cansada.

5. Carlitos, debes ponerte otra camisa. Esa _____ sucia.

[a]*What's the matter with you?*

C. Arturo y Roberto. Study the following drawing. Then form complete sentences using the words provided, in the order given, to compare Arturo and Roberto.

1. Arturo / libros / Roberto _____

   _____

2. Arturo / gordo / Roberto _____

   _____

3. Roberto / alto / Arturo _____

   _____

4. Roberto / años / Arturo _____

   _____

5. Arturo / perros / Roberto _____

Arturo
22 años

Roberto
20 años

D. Comparaciones. You will hear a series of statements about the following chart. Each will be said twice. Circle **C** if the statement is true, or **F** if it is false. First, pause and read the chart.

PAÍS	POBLACIÓN (HABITANTES)	ÁREA (MILLAS CUADRADAS) (SQUARE MILES)	TEMPERATURA COSTAL / TEMPERATURA INTERIOR EN GRADOS FAHRENHEIT	NÚMERO DE USUARIOS DEL INTERNET
Costa Rica	4.133.884	19.730	90° / 63°	1.000.000
Guatemala	12.728.111	42.042	82° / 68°	756.000
Nicaragua	5.675.356	50.838	77° / 79°	140.000
México	108.700.891	756.066	120° / 61°	18.622.000

Now resume listening.

1. C   F   **2.** C   F   **3.** C   F   **4.** C   F   **5.** C   F   **6.** C   F

E. La nueva profesora costarricense. Tell about the new professor, using the written cues. When you hear the corresponding number, form sentences using the words provided in the order given, making any necessary changes or additions. You will be given a choice of verbs. Choose the correct one.

> MODELO: (*you see*) **1.** la profesora / (**ser / estar**) / Isabel Darío
> (*you hear*) uno → (*you say*) La profesora es Isabel Darío.

2. la profesora / (**ser / estar**) / de La Cruz, Costa Rica
3. La Cruz / (**ser / estar**) / lejos de la capital
4. la profesora / (**ser / estar**) / cansada por el viaje
5. ella / se (**ser / estar**) / quedando con unos amigos
6. la profesora / (**ser / estar**) / inteligente y simpática
7. los estudiantes / (**ser / estar**) / contentos con la nueva profesora

F. Hablando de viajes. Imagine that you will travel to a variety of places this year. Answer the questions you hear about each of your trips using the written cues. ¡OJO! The questions may vary slightly from those in the model. Change your answers accordingly.

> MODELO: (*you see*) 30/3 / fresco
> (*you hear*) ¿Cuándo sales para Detroit? → (*you say*) Salgo el treinta de marzo.
> (*you hear*) ¿Y qué tiempo hace allí? → (*you say*) Hace fresco.

1. 15/7 / calor
2. 1/12 / nevando
3. 10/1 / sol
4. 24/5 / viento

CAPÍTULO **6**

 **Paso 1 Vocabulario**

La comida y las comidas

A. La comida. Completa las oraciones con las palabras apropiadas de la lista a continuación.

agua	hambre	leche	sed
arroz	helado	lechuga	té
camarones	huevos	pan	tomate
carne	jugo	papas fritas	verduras
galletas	langosta	queso	zanahorias

1. Un buen desayuno típico para mucha gente (*people*) en los Estados Unidos

   es _____ de naranja, dos _____ con jamón,

   _____ tostado y café, _____ o _____.

2. Dos mariscos favoritos son los _____ y la _____.

3. Las especialidades de McDonald's son las hamburguesas y las _____.

4. El _____ mineral es una bebida favorita de la gente que (*who*) no quiere

   engordarse (*to gain weight*).

5. De (*For*) postre, ¿prefieres pastel, flan o _____ de vainilla o chocolate?

6. Un vegetariano no come _____; prefiere las _____ y las

   frutas.

7. El sándwich de jamón y _____ es popular para el almuerzo.

8. La ensalada se hace (*is made*) con _____ y _____.

9. Una combinación popular son las arvejas y las _____.

10. En la sopa de pollo hay _____ o fideos (*noodles*).

11. Cuando los niños vuelven de la escuela, tienen _____ y a veces quieren comer

    _____ con leche.

12. Cuando tengo _____, bebo agua fría.

❖**B. Preguntas personales.** Contesta estas preguntas sobre tus hábitos y preferencias con respecto a la comida.

1. ¿Dónde y a qué hora almuerzas, generalmente?

    _____

2. Cuando vuelves a casa después de tus clases o después de trabajar y tienes hambre, ¿qué te apetece (*do you feel like*) merendar? ¿frutas? ¿galletas? ¿un sándwich? ¿ ?

    Me apetece merendar _____.

3. Por lo general, ¿comes más pescado, más pollo o más carne?

    _____

C. Definiciones. You will hear a series of definitions. Each will be said twice. Circle the letter of the word defined by each.

1. **a.** la zanahoria   **b.** los huevos
2. **a.** la lechuga   **b.** la langosta
3. **a.** la leche   **b.** el vino blanco
4. **a.** un postre   **b.** un sándwich
5. **a.** el almuerzo   **b.** la cena
6. **a.** los espárragos   **b.** el agua mineral

D. Identificaciones. Identify the following foods when you hear the corresponding number. Use the definite article in your answer.

1.   2.   3.   4.

5.   6.   7.   8.

E. Categorías. You will hear a series of words. Repeat each word, telling in what category it belongs: **un tipo de carne, un marisco, una fruta, una verdura, un postre,** or **una bebida.**

MODELO: (*you hear*) el té → (*you say*) El té es una bebida.

1. ... 2. ... 3. ... 4. ... 5. ...

¿Qué sabes y a quién conoces?

❖**A.** **¿Cierto o falso?** Indica si las siguientes declaraciones son ciertas o falsas para ti.

	C	F
1. Yo sé cocinar bien.	☐	☐
2. Conozco a la familia de mi mejor amigo/a.	☐	☐
3. Mi profesor(a) sabe tocar la guitarra.	☐	☐
4. Yo también sé tocar un instrumento musical.	☐	☐
5. Conozco bien a varios estudiantes en mi clase de español.	☐	☐
6. Conozco a los dueños (*owners*) de un restaurante.	☐	☐

B. *¿Saber o conocer?* Completa las oraciones con la forma apropiada de **saber** o **conocer,** según el sentido (*meaning*).

1. Ellas no _____ a mi primo.

2. Yo no _____ a qué hora llegan del teatro.

3. ¿(*Tú*) _____ tocar el piano?

4. Necesitan _____ a qué hora vas a venir.

5. (*Nosotros*) _____ a los padres de Paquita, pero yo no _____

   al resto de su familia.

6. Queremos _____ al presidente del club.

C. **La *a* personal.** Completa las oraciones con la **a** personal, cuando sea (*whenever it is*) necesario. ¡RECUERDA! **a** + **el** = **al.**

- No veo _____[1] el dueño y no conozco _____[2] los camareros (*waiters*). Todos son nuevos.

- —¿_____[3] quién buscan Uds.?

  —Buscamos _____[4] la Srta. Estrada. Creo que no está aquí todavía.

- Mis padres conocen _____[5] este restaurante. Creen que es muy bueno.

- ¿Por qué no llamas _____[6] el camarero ahora? Quiero ver _____[7] el menú mientras

  esperamos _____[8] María Elena.

D. **¿Qué sabe y a quién conoce?**

Paso 1. Mis amigos. You will hear a brief paragraph about some of the things your friends know and whom they know. Listen and write either **sí** or **no** under the corresponding item. Two items have been done for you. (Check your answers in the Appendix before you begin **Paso 2.**)

NOMBRE	BAILAR	A JUAN	JUGAR AL TENIS	A MIS PADRES	ESTA CIUDAD
Enrique	*sí*	*no*			
Roberto					
Susana					

Paso 2. ¿Qué recuerdas? Now pause and complete the following statements with information from the completed chart. (Check your answers in the Appendix.)

1. Roberto y Susana _____ jugar al tenis.

2. Susana _____ bailar.

3. Nadie (*No one*) _____ a Juan.

4. Roberto y Enrique _____ bien la ciudad.

Now resume listening.

Pronunciación y ortografía • *d*

A. Repeticiones. Spanish **d** has two pronunciations. At the beginning of a phrase or sentence and after **n** or **l**, it is pronounced similarly to English *d* as in *dog:* [d], that is, as a stop. Listen to these words and repeat them after the speaker.

    [d]   diez   ¿dónde?   venden   condición   falda   el doctor

In all other cases, **d** is pronounced like the English sound *th* in *another* but softer: [đ], that is, as a fricative. Listen and repeat the following words.

    [đ]   adiós   seda   ciudad   usted   cuadros   la doctora

B. Entonación. Repeat the following sentences, imitating the speaker. Pay close attention to the intonation.

    ¿Dónde está el dinero?   ¿Qué estudia Ud.?

    Dos y diez son doce.   Venden de todo, ¿verdad?

C. A escoger. You will hear a series of words containing the letter **d.** Each will be said twice. Circle the letter of the **d** sound you hear.

1. a. [d]   b. [đ]   3. a. [d]   b. [đ]   5. a. [d]   b. [đ]
2. a. [d]   b. [đ]   4. a. [d]   b. [đ]

Lectura cultural: Panamá

Oraciones. Completa las oraciones según las **Lecturas culturales 1** y **2** del libro de texto. Usa palabras de la lista.

calipso	dieciséis	estadounidense	parques	San Blas
colonial	diecinueve	molas	reservas	Trinidad

1. La idea de hacer un canal en Panamá viene del siglo (*century*) _____

    y finalmente fue construido (*it was built*) en el siglo _____.

2. El Casco Antiguo es la parte _____ de la Ciudad de Panamá.

3. En Panamá hay mucha influencia _____.

4. La música más popular de Panamá es el _____ que vino (*came*) de

    _____ con los constructores (*builders*) del Canal.

5. Panamá usa el 22 por ciento de su territorio para _____ y _____.

6. Los kunas, habitantes (*inhabitants*) de las islas de _____, son famosos por la

    artesanía textil de las _____.

Paso 2 Gramática

17. Expressing *what* or *who*(*m*) • Direct Objects (Part 2): The Personal *a*; Direct Object Pronouns

A. El cumpleaños de Felipe. César Eco discusses plans for Felipe's birthday, answering everyone's questions but with a great deal of repetition. Rewrite César's answers, using direct object pronouns.

> MODELOS: —¿Quién llama a Felipe?
> —Yo llamo a Felipe. → Yo lo llamo.
>
> —¿Quién va a llevar las sillas?
> —Pepe va a llevar las sillas. (*two ways*) → Pepe va a llevarlas. (Pepe las va a llevar.)

1. —¿Quién prepara el pastel?

   —Yo preparo el pastel. _____

2. —¿Quién va a comprar los refrescos?

   —Yo voy a comprar los refrescos. (*two ways*) _____

   _____

3. —¿Quién va a hacer las galletas?

   —Dolores va a hacer las galletas. (*two ways*) _____

   _____

4. —¿Quién trae los discos?

   —Juan trae los discos. _____

5. —¿Quién invita a los primos de Felipe?

   —Yo invito a los primos de Felipe. _____

B. En casa, con la familia Buendía. Contesta las preguntas según los dibujos. Usa los pronombres del complemento directo.

1. ¿A qué hora despierta el despertador (*alarm clock*) a los padres? _____

2. ¿Quién levanta al bebé? _____

3. ¿Quién lo baña? _____

C. **Gramática en acción: De compras en el supermercado: Encuesta.** You will hear the names of various foods. Each will be said twice. Write in the blank the name of the food mentioned, then check the appropriate answer. No answers will be given. The answers you choose should be correct for you! (Check the answers for the food names in the Appendix.)

1. _____

   ☐ Siempre las como.

   ☐ Las como a veces.

   ☐ Nunca las como.

2. _____

   ☐ Siempre lo como.

   ☐ Lo como a veces.

   ☐ Nunca lo como.

3. _____

   ☐ Siempre la tomo.

   ☐ La tomo a veces.

   ☐ Nunca la tomo.

4. _____

   ☐ Siempre los como.

   ☐ Los como a veces.

   ☐ Nunca los como.

LA MODERNA MARKET
930-932 State Street • New Haven, CT • (203) 776-2333

AHORA ABIERTO EN NEW HAVEN

• TODA CLASE DE CARNES FRESCAS

• VEGETALES FRESCOS
• GROCERY

• LÍNEA COMPLETA DE PRODUCTOS MEXICANOS
La Moderna • La Morena
• La Costeña • Nestle

Solicite Nuestra Propia Longaniza y Cesina
ATENDEMOS PEDIDOS PARA NEGOCIOS

Nota comunicativa: Talking About What You Have Just Done

A. **¿Qué acaban de hacer estas personas?**

MODELO: Pete Sampras → Acaba de jugar al tenis.

1. Christina Aguilera _____

2. (en un restaurante) nosotros _____

3. (al final de la comida) el camarero _____

4. el profesor que sale de clase _____

❖5. yo, ¿ ? _____

B. **Hablando de los estudios.** You will hear a series of questions a parent or friend might ask about things you have already done. Each will be said twice. Answer, using **acabo de** and a direct object pronoun. Attach the direct object pronoun to the infinitive when you answer.

MODELO: (*you hear*) ¿Por qué no escribes la composición? → (*you say*) Acabo de escribirla.

1. ... 2. ... 3. ... 4. ...

---

18. Expressing Negation • Indefinite and Negative Words

❖**A.   Algo sobre comidas.** Indica si las siguientes declaraciones son ciertas o falsas para ti.

		C	F
1.	No quiero comer nada esta noche. No tengo hambre.	☐	☐
2.	Nadie tiene ganas de cocinar esta noche.	☐	☐
3.	No hay ninguna comida sabrosa (*tasty*) en el refrigerador.	☐	☐
4.	Y no hay nada para tomar tampoco.	☐	☐
5.	No hay ningún restaurante chino cerca de mi casa.	☐	☐
6.	Me gustan algunos platos vegetarianos.	☐	☐
7.	Ninguno de mis amigos sabe cocinar. ¡Ni yo tampoco!	☐	☐

B.   Federico, el pesimista. Tu amigo Federico es muy pesimista y siempre contesta en forma negativa. Contesta las preguntas como si fueras (*as if you were*) él. Usa la forma negativa de las palabras indicadas.

> **Palabras útiles:** contigo (*with you*)   conmigo (*with me*)

> MODELO: ¿Sirven *algo* bueno en ese restaurante? → No, no sirven nada bueno.

1.   ¿Vas a hacer *algo* interesante este fin de semana?

   No, _____.

2.   ¿*Siempre* sales con *alguien* los sábados?

   No, _____.

3.   ¿Tienes *algunos* nuevos amigos en la universidad? (¡OJO! Recuerda usar el singular.)

   No, _____.

4.   ¿*Algunas* de esas chicas son tus amigas? (¡OJO!)

   No, _____.

5.   ¿*Alguien* cena contigo *a veces*?

   No, _____.

C.   Evita, la optimista. Federico es una persona negativa pero su novia Evita es muy positiva. Escribe las reacciones positivas de Evita a los comentarios de Federico.

1.   —No quiero comer nada. La comida aquí es mala.

   —Pues, yo sí _____.

2.   —Nadie viene a atendernos (*wait on us*).

   —Pero aquí viene _____.

3.   —Nunca cenamos en un restaurante bueno.

   —Yo creo que _____.

4.   —No hay ningún plato sabroso.

   —Aquí hay _____

D. Gramática en acción: ¿Un refrigerador típico?

Paso 1. You will hear a series of questions about the following drawing. Circle the letter of the best answer to each, based on the drawing.

1. **a.** No, no hay nada. **b.** Sí, hay algo.
2. **a.** Sí, hay fruta y pan. **b.** No, no hay fruta y tampoco hay pan.
3. **a.** No, no hay ninguna manzana. **b.** Sí, hay manzanas.
4. **a.** No, nadie compra comida. **b.** Sí, alguien compra comida.

❖**Paso 2.** Now pause and write what you usually have and don't have in your refrigerator. No answers will be given.

En mi refrigerador siempre hay _____

_____

_____

Nunca hay _____

_____

_____

Now resume listening.

E. Descripción. You will hear a series of questions. Answer, according to the drawings.

MODELO: (*you hear*) ¿Hay algo en la pizarra? →
(*you say*) Sí, hay algo en la pizarra. Hay unas palabras.

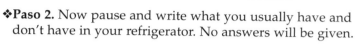

1.

2.

3.

4.

5.

F. ¡Por eso no come nadie allí! You will hear a series of questions about a very unpopular restaurant. Each will be said twice. Answer, using the double negative.

MODELO: (*you hear*) ¿Sirven algunos postres especiales? →
(*you say*) No, no sirven ningún postre especial.

1. ... 2. ... 3. ... 4. ...

Paso 3 Gramática

19. Influencing Others • Commands (Part 1): Formal Commands

A. Durante las vacaciones. The following flyer, distributed by the Spanish government, gives advice about how to prepare your house before going away on vacation. Scan it; then do the activities that follow.

Paso 1. Copy the command forms for the following infinitives from the flyer.

Título: acostumbrar _____

1. comprobar _____

2. encargar _____

3. no hacerlo _____

   dejarlas _____

4. no comentar _____

   dejar _____

5. no dejarlos _____

Paso 2. Express the basic idea of the following recommendations from the flyer by completing these sentences in English.

1. Make sure that _____

   _____.

2. Ask a neighbor to pick up

   _____.

3. Leave an extra set of keys with

   _____.

4. Don't leave notes indicating

   _____.

5. Don't leave objects of value or money

   _____.

   _____.

ACOSTUMBRE A SU CASA A QUEDARSE SOLA

DURANTE PERIODOS DE VACACIONES O AUSENCIAS PROLONGADAS

1 Compruebe que todas las posibles entradas de la casa queden perfectamente cerradas, incluyendo las ventanas que dan a patios.

2 No conviene dejar señales visibles de que su vivienda está desocupada: encargue a algún vecino la recogida de la correspondencia de su buzón.

3 Si quiere dejar un juego de llaves de reserva, no lo haga en escondites improvisados: déjelas a alguien de su confianza.

4 No comente su ausencia con personas desconocidas ni deje notas indicando cuándo piensa volver.

5 Existen diferentes entidades de crédito que durante sus vacaciones pueden hacerse cargo de sus objetos de valor: no los deje nunca en casa, ni tampoco deje dinero.

6 Conviene dejar a un vecino de confianza su dirección y teléfono de contacto mientras está usted fuera.

7 Existe la posibilidad de instalar un reloj programable que encienda y apague la luz o la radio en su vivienda, en diferentes horarios, disimulando su ausencia del domicilio.

B. Consejos. Tus amigos tienen los siguientes problemas. Dales (*Give them*) consejos apropiados con un mandato formal.

> MODELO: Estamos cansados. → Entonces, descansen.

1. Tenemos hambre. _____

2. Tenemos sed. _____

3. Mañana hay un examen. _____

4. Las ventanas están abiertas y tenemos frío. _____

5. Siempre llegamos tarde. _____

6. Somos impacientes. _____

C. ¡Qué amigos tan buenos! Your friends Emilio and Mercedes are helping you at dinner time. Answer their questions with affirmative or negative commands, as indicated. Change object nouns to pronouns.

> MODELO: ¿Lavamos (*Shall we wash*) los platos ahora? → Sí, lávenlos ahora.
> No, no los laven todavía.

1. —¿Empezamos la comida ahora? —Sí, _____.

2. —¿Servimos la cena ahora? —No, _____.

3. —¿Llamamos a tu papá ahora? —Sí, _____.

4. —¿Hacemos el café ahora? —No, _____.

5. —¿Traemos las sillas ahora? —Sí, _____.

6. —¿Ponemos la tele ahora? —No, _____.

D. Gramática en acción: Una receta para guacamole

Paso 1. You will hear the following recipe for guacamole. It contains several formal commands. Read the recipe silently, along with the speakers.

Paso 2. Now pause and write the command forms of the following infinitive verbs in the spaces. (Check your answers in the Appendix.)

1. servir: _____

2. añadir (*to add*): _____

3. mezclar (*to mix*): _____

4. cortar: _____

El guacamole

Ingredientes:
1 aguacate[a]
1 diente de ajo,[b] prensado[c]
1 tomate
jugo de un limón
sal
un poco de cilantro fresco[d]

Cómo se prepara
Corte el aguacate y el tomate en trozos[e] pequeños. Añada el jugo del limón, el ajo, el cilantro y la sal a su gusto. Mezcle bien todos los ingredientes y sírvalo con tortillas de maíz[f] fritas.

[a]*avocado* [b]*diente... clove of garlic* [c]*crushed* [d]*fresh* [e]*pieces* [f]*corn*

E. Profesora por un día... Imagine that you are the Spanish professor for the day. Practice telling your students what they should do, using the oral cues. Use **Uds.** commands.

1. ... 2. ... 3. ... 4. ... 5. ...

F. La dieta del Sr. Casiano. Mr. Casiano is on a diet and you are his doctor. He will ask you whether or not he can eat certain things. Answer his questions, using affirmative or negative commands and direct object pronouns.

> MODELO: (*you hear*) ¿Puedo comer chocolate? (*you see*) No,... →
> (*you say*) No, no lo coma.

1. No,... 2. No,... 3. No,... 4. Sí,... 5. Sí,...

Nota comunicativa: El subjuntivo

Un nuevo restaurante

Paso 1. You will hear an ad for a new restaurant that is opening soon. Listen carefully and check the appropriate boxes based on the information you hear in the ad. First, listen to the list of actions. (Check your answers in the Appendix.)

☐ hacer reservaciones   ☐ pedir una hamburguesa   ☐ pagar con tarjeta de crédito

☐ vestirse formalmente   ☐ llegar temprano   ☐ pagar al contado (*in cash*)

☐ pedir el pescado

Paso 2. Now pause and read the following recommendations. Check the recommendations that you would give a friend who wants to visit this restaurant. (Remember to check your answers to **Paso 1** in the Appendix before beginning **Paso 2.**)

1. ☐ No recomiendo que hagas reservaciones antes de ir a El Caribe.

2. ☐ Recomiendo que llegues temprano.

3. ☐ Recomiendo que vayas a El Caribe si te gusta mucho la carne.

4. ☐ Recomiendo que te vistas con ropa informal.

5. ☐ No recomiendo que lleves a toda tu familia.

6. ☐ Recomiendo que pagues con tarjeta de crédito o al contado.

Un poco de todo

A. Por teléfono. Fill in the blanks with the correct word(s) in parentheses to complete the dialogue between Ana and Pablo.

ANA: Oye, Pablo, ¿no _____[1] (**conoces / sabes**) tú _____[2]

(**a / al / el**) profesor Vargas?

PABLO: No, no _____[3] (**él / lo**) _____[4] (**sé / conozco**). ¿Por qué?

ANA: Es profesor de historia. El viernes va a dar una conferencia[a] sobre la mujer en la

Revolución mexicana. ¿No quieres ir? Yo _____[5] (**sé / conozco**) que va a

ser muy interesante.

PABLO: ¡Qué lástima![b] Casi _____[6] (**siempre / nunca**) tengo tiempo libre[c] los

viernes, pero este viernes tengo varios compromisos.[d]

ANA: Pues, yo no tengo mucho tiempo libre _____[7] (**también / tampoco**), pero

voy a asistir. _____[8] (**Al / El**) Sr. Vargas siempre usa diapositivas[e]

fascinantes y tengo ganas de verlas.

[a]dar... *give a lecture*   [b]¡Qué... *What a shame!*   [c]*free*   [d]*engagements*   [e]*slides*

B. Preparativos para una barbacoa (*barbecue*). Imagina que vives en un nuevo apartamento, donde vas a preparar una barbacoa. Contesta las siguientes preguntas sobre la barbacoa con pronombres de complemento directo.

MODELO: ¿A qué hora *me* llamas? → Te llamo a las ocho.

1. ¿Cuándo vas a preparar *la barbacoa*?

   _____

2. ¿Piensas invitar *a Juan y a su novia*?

   _____

3. ¿Puedo llamar *a dos amigas más*?

   _____

4. ¿*Te* puedo ayudar el sábado?

   _____

5. ¿Necesitas *las sillas de mi apartamento*?

   _____

C. Preparativos para la fiesta. Luisa calls to give you last-minute reminders of what to do for a party you and some friends are planning. First, write her command in the **Uds.** form. Then respond by telling her that you and José are already doing it. Use object pronouns in your response to avoid unnecessary repetition.

MODELO: limpiar la casa → LUISA: ¡Limpien la casa!

TÚ: Ya estamos limpiándola. (Ya la estamos limpiando.)

1. lavar (*to wash*) los platos   LUISA: _____

   TÚ: _____

2. hacer la ensalada   LUISA: _____

   TÚ: _____

3. preparar las verduras   LUISA: _____

   TÚ: _____

4. empezar la paella   LUISA: _____

   TÚ: _____

D. ¿Qué va a pedir Juan? Juan and his friend Marta are in a restaurant. Listen to their conversation and circle the items that Juan is going to order. In this exercise, you will practice listening for specific information. First, pause and look at the drawing.

◆ ⟩ ¡Repasemos!

A. Una cena en El Toledano. En otro papel, contesta las preguntas según los dibujos e inventa los detalles necesarios. Luego, organiza y combina tus respuestas en dos párrafos. ¡RECUERDA! Usa palabras conectivas: **por eso, Como...** (*Since . . .*), **porque, aunque** (*although*), **luego,** etcétera.

1.

2.

3.

4.

5.

6.

1. ¿Por qué llaman José y Miguel a Tomás?
2. ¿Por qué crees que deciden llevarlo a El Toledano?
3. ¿Conoce este lugar Tomás? ¿Le gusta la idea de salir con sus amigos?
4. ¿A qué hora de la noche pasan por él (*do they pick him up*)?
5. Después de llegar al restaurante, ¿en qué sitio encuentran (*do they find*) una mesa desocupada (*empty*): cerca o lejos del escenario (*stage*)?
6. ¿Por qué hay tanta gente en el restaurante?
7. ¿Qué platos pide cada joven?
8. ¿Qué escuchan durante la cena?
9. ¿Qué hacen después de comer?
10. ¿Salen del restaurante contentos y satisfechos (*satisfied*) o disgustados?

❖**B.** **Entrevista.** You will hear a series of questions. Each will be said twice. Answer based on your own experience. Use direct object pronouns in your answers, if possible. Pause and write the answers.

1. _____

2. _____

3. _____

4. _____

5. _____

6. _____

7. _____

❖ Mi diario

Algunas comidas que me gustan... ¡y otras que no! Ahora escribe en tu diario lo que te gusta mucho comer y la(s) comida(s) que no te gusta(n) nada. Si puedes, menciona los ingredientes.

> **Palabras útiles:** el cocido (*stew*), los espaguetis, las remolachas (*beets*), el rosbif (*roast beef*); caliente (*hot*), picante (*hot, spicy*); me encanta(n) (*I love*),* me gusta(n),* odiar (*to hate*); al horno (*baked, roasted*); bastante cocido (*medium*), bien cocido (*well done*), crudo (*raw*)

Ponte a prueba

A ver si sabes...

A. Direct Object Pronouns

1. Completa la tabla con la forma apropiada de los pronombres del complemento directo.

	COMPLEMENTO DIRECTO		COMPLEMENTO DIRECTO
me	*me*	us	d
you (*fam. sing.*)	a	you (*fam. pl.*)	*os*
you, him, it (*m.*)	b	you, them (*m.*)	*los*
you, her, it (*f.*)	c	you, them (*f.*)	e

---

*If something you like is a plural noun, use the plural form of **gustar** or **encantar: Me gustan las zanahorias. Me encantan las arvejas.**

2. Rewrite using a direct object pronoun for the underlined direct object noun.

   a. Yo traigo el postre. _____

   b. ¡Traiga el postre! _____

   c. ¡No traiga el postre! _____

   d. Estamos esperando al camarero. (*two ways*) _____

   _____

   e. Voy a llamar al camarero. (*two ways*) _____

   _____

B. **Negative Words.** Write the negative form of the following words or phrases.

   1. alguien _____

   2. también _____

   3. siempre _____

   4. algo _____

   5. algunos detalles (¡OJO!) _____

C. **Formal Commands.** Completa la tabla con la forma apropiada de los mandatos formales.

VERBO	MANDATO FORMAL	VERBO	MANDATO FORMAL
pensar	¹ Ud.	ser	*sea* Ud.
volver	² Ud.	buscar	⁵ Ud.
dar	³ Ud.	estar	⁶ Ud.
servir	*sirva* Ud.	saber	⁷ Ud.
ir	⁴ Ud.	decir	⁸ Ud.

Prueba corta

A. **¿Saber o conocer?** Escribe la forma apropiada de **saber** o **conocer.**

—Yo no _____¹ a la novia de Juan. ¿La _____² tú?

—No muy bien, pero (yo) _____³ que ella se llama María Elena y que

_____⁴ tocar bien la guitarra.

B. **Oraciones afirmativas.** Vuelve a escribir las oraciones en la forma afirmativa.

   1. No quiero comer nada. _____

   2. No busco a nadie. _____

   3. No hay nada para beber. _____

   4. —No conozco a ninguno de sus amigos.

      —Yo tampoco.

      _____

      _____

C. **Preguntas.** Contesta las preguntas usando pronombres de complemento directo.

1. ¿Vas a pedir la ensalada de fruta? _____

2. ¿Quieres zanahorias con la comida? _____

3. ¿Tomas café por la noche? _____

4. ¿Quién prepara la cena en tu casa? _____

D. **Mandatos formales.** Escribe la forma apropiada del mandato formal (**Uds.**) del verbo indicado.

1. _____ (*Uds.:* **Comprar**) tomates y lechuga.

2. No _____ (*Uds.:* **hacer**) ensalada hoy.

3. _____ (*Uds.:* **Traer**) dos sillas, por favor.

4. No _____ (*Uds.:* **poner**) tanto aceite en la comida.

5. Juan no está aquí todavía. _____ (*Uds.:* **Llamarlo**) ahora.

6. ¿El vino? No _____ (*Uds.:* **servirlo**) ahora.

E. **Los hispanos hablan: ¿Qué te gusta mucho comer?** In this passage, Clara tells about two dishes typical of Spain: **el cocido** and **el gazpacho.** Then you will hear a series of statements. Circle **C** if the statement is true or **F** if it is false. The following words appear in the passage.

el hueso de codillo	*leg bone (as in ham)*	el aceite de oliva	*olive oil*
la morcilla	*blood sausage*	el vinagre	*vinegar*
el pepino	*cucumber*	echarle por encima	*to sprinkle on top of it*
el pimiento	*bell pepper*	trocitos	*little bits (pieces)*
el ajo	*garlic*		

1. C   F   **2.** C   F   **3.** C   F   **4.** C   F

F. **Cosas de todos los días.** Practice talking about a new restaurant, using the written cues. When you hear the corresponding number, form sentences using the words provided in the order given, making any necessary changes or additions. When you are given a choice between verbs or words, choose the correct one.

MODELO: (*you see*) **1.** ¿(**saber / conocer**) / tú / un buen restaurante?
(*you hear*) uno → (*you say*) ¿Conoces un buen restaurante?

2. sí, / (*yo:* **saber / conocer**) / un buen restaurante
3. (**la / lo**) / acabar (ellos) de / abrir
4. (*yo:* **saber / conocer**) / al dueño (*owner*)
5. preparar (ellos) / unos camarones deliciosos
6. (**las / los**) / cocinar (ellos) / en vino blanco
7. no hay / (**algo / nada**) / malo en el menú
8. (**siempre / nunca**) / cenar (yo) allí

G. **¡Qué maleducados!** Mr. Alarcón's children have not been behaving lately, and he is constantly telling them what to do and what not to do. Play the role of Mr. Alarcón, using the oral cues.

MODELO: (*you hear*) no jugar en la sala → (*you say*) No jueguen en la sala.

1. ...   **2.** ...   **3.** ...   **4.** ...   **5.** ...

CAPÍTULO **7**

 ## Paso 1 Vocabulario
De viaje

❖**A. Tú y los viajes.** Lee las siguientes declaraciones y decide cuáles se refieren a ti.

		C	F
1.	Tengo mucho miedo de viajar en avión.	☐	☐
2.	Siempre reservo los asientos con anticipación (*in advance*).	☐	☐
3.	Cuando voy de viaje, hago las maletas a última hora (*at the last minute*).	☐	☐
4.	Siempre llevo tantas maletas que tengo que pedirle ayuda a un maletero.	☐	☐
5.	Pido un asiento en el pasillo de un avión o tren porque me gusta levantarme con frecuencia.	☐	☐
6.	Si hay una demora en la salida del avión (o del tren) no me quejo. Me siento en la sala de espera y leo un libro o voy al bar.	☐	☐

B. Viajando en avión. Completa las oraciones con la forma apropiada de las palabras de la lista. Usa cada expresión sólo una vez (*once*).

asistente	el control de	escala	salida
bajar	la seguridad	guardar	subir
boleto	demora	ida y vuelta	vuelo
cola	equipaje	pasajeros	

1. Cuando voy de viaje es más barato comprar mi _____ en el Internet.

2. Comprar un boleto de _____ es más barato que comprar dos de ida solamente (*only*).

3. Quiero _____ del avión si hace _____ en Londres (*London*).

4. Después de llegar al aeropuerto, un maletero me ayuda a facturar el _____.

5. Antes de llegar a la puerta (*gate*), hay que pasar por _____.

6. En la sala de espera hay muchos _____ que esperan su vuelo.

7. Un pasajero me _____ un asiento mientras (*while*) voy a comprar un libro.

8. Anuncian que el _____ #68 está atrasado; hay una _____ de media hora.

9. Cuando por fin anuncian la _____ de nuestro avión, los pasajeros hacemos

_____ para _____.

10. Media hora después que el avión despega (*takes off*), los _____ de vuelo sirven el

desayuno. ¡Y qué hambre tengo!

C. Escenas. Describe los dibujos con los verbos indicados. Usa el presente del progresivo cuando sea (*whenever it is*) posible.

1.

dormir, fumar, leer

2.

facturar, hacer cola, hacer una parada

3.

correr, estar atrasado, llover, subir

4.

mirar, servir algo de beber

1. _____

_____

2. _____

_____

3. _____

_____

4. _____

_____

D. Hablando de viajes... Using the oral and written cues, tell your friend Benito, who has never traveled by plane, the steps he should follow to make an airplane trip.

MODELO: (*you see*) Primero...   (*you hear*) llamar a la agencia de viajes →
(*you say*) Primero llamas a la agencia de viajes.

1. pedir...   **3.** pasar por...   **5.** Cuando anuncian la salida del vuelo, ...
2. El día del viaje,...   **4.** Después...   **6.** Por fin...

E. Identificaciones. Identify the items after you hear the corresponding number. Begin each sentence with **Es un...** , **Es una...** , or **Son...**

1. ... 2. ... 3. ... 4. ... 5. ...

De vacaciones

A. Las vacaciones

Paso 1. Identifica los objetos y lugares en el dibujo.

1. _____
2. _____
3. _____
4. _____
5. _____

Paso 2. Ahora explica qué hacen las siguientes personas.

1. El padre _____.

2. La madre _____.

3. Las hijas _____.

4. El hijo _____.

5. Toda la familia _____.

❖**B.** **Mis vacaciones.** Contesta las siguientes preguntas sobre las vacaciones que tú prefieres.

1. ¿Adónde prefieres ir de vacaciones? ¿a las montañas? ¿a la playa?

_____

2. ¿Con quién te gusta ir de vacaciones?

_____

3. ¿Cómo prefieres viajar?

_____

4. ¿Te gusta e hacer _camping_? ¿Qué se necesita para hacer _camping_?

_____

5. ¿Qué haces durante las vacaciones? ¿Te gusta sacar muchas fotos? ¿de qué? ¿Te gusta tomar el sol y nadar? ¿visitar museos o atracciones turísticas?

_____

C. **Definiciones.** You will hear a series of definitions. Each will be said twice. Circle the letter of the word that is defined by each. ¡OJO! There may be more than one answer in some cases.

1. **a.** el avión   **b.** la playa   **c.** el océano
2. **a.** el billete   **b.** la estación de trenes   **c.** el aeropuerto
3. **a.** el hotel   **b.** el restaurante   **c.** la llegada
4. **a.** el puerto   **b.** el mar   **c.** las montañas

Nota comunicativa: Other Uses of _se_ (For Recognition)

¿Cuánto sabes de estas cosas? Selecciona la respuesta más apropiada.

1. Se habla portugués en...
   a. el Paraguay.   **b.** Bolivia.   **c.** el Brasil.

2. Se factura el equipaje en...
   a. el avión.   **b.** el mostrador (_counter_).   **c.** la sala de espera.

3. Se visitan las ruinas de Machu Picchu en...
   a. Bolivia.   **b.** México.   **c.** el Perú.

4. Se ven ruinas mayas en Chichen Itzá,...
   a. Colombia.   **b.** México.   **c.** el Perú.

5. Se venden bebidas alcohólicas en...
   a. Francia.   **b.** Irán.   **c.** la Arabia Saudita.

Pronunciación y ortografía • *g*, *gu*, and *j*

A. Repeticiones. In Spanish, the letter **g** followed by **e** or **i** has the same sound as the letter **j** followed by any vowel. This sound [x] is similar to the English *h*. The pronunciation of this sound varies, depending on the region or country of origin of the speaker. Note the difference in the pronunciation of these words.

España:	Jorge	jueves	general	álgebra
el Caribe:	Jorge	jueves	general	álgebra

Repeat the following words, imitating the speaker.

1. [x] general   gigante   geranio
2. [x] jamón   Juan   pasaje

Now, say the following words when you hear the corresponding number. Repeat the correct pronunciation after the speaker.

3. gimnasio
4. giralda
5. rojo
6. jipijapa

B. El sonido [g]. When the letter **g** is followed by the vowels **a, o,** or **u** or by the combination **ue** or **ui,** its pronunciation is very similar to the letter *g* in the English word *get:* [g]. It is pronounced this way at the beginning of a word, after a pause, or after the letter **n.**

Repeat the following words, imitating the speaker.

[g] ángulo gusto gato Miguel guitarra

Now, say the following words when you hear the corresponding number. Repeat the correct pronunciation after the speaker.

1. gorila
2. grande
3. guerrilla
4. Guevara

C. El sonido [ǥ]. In all other positions, the Spanish **g** is a fricative [ǥ]. It has a softer sound produced by allowing some air to escape when it is pronounced. There is no exact equivalent for this variant in English.

Repeat the following words, imitating the speaker.

1. [ǥ] abrigo algodón el gato el gusto los gorilas
2. [g] / [ǥ] un grupo / el grupo gracias / las gracias un gato / el gato
3. [x] / [g] gigante jugos juguete

Now, read the following sentences when you hear the corresponding numbers. Repeat the correct pronunciation after the speaker.

4. ¡Qué ganga!
5. Domingo es guapo y delgado.
6. Tengo algunas amigas guatemaltecas.
7. La guitarra de Guillermo es de Gijón.

D. Dictado. You will hear four sentences. Each will be said twice. Listen carefully and write what you hear. (Check your answers in the Appendix.)

1. _____

2. _____

3. _____

4. _____

E. ¿G o j? For the following Spanish words, indicate which are pronounced as [x] (similar to English *h*) or as [g] (similar to English *g* in *gate*). Some words have both sounds.

		[x]	[g]
1.	girafa	☐	☐
2.	jugo	☐	☐
3.	geranio	☐	☐
4.	general	☐	☐
5.	guapo	☐	☐
6.	gigante	☐	☐
7.	gato	☐	☐
8.	juguete	☐	☐

Lectura cultural: La República Dominicana

¿Cierto o falso? Contesta según las **Lecturas culturales 1** y **2** del libro de texto.

		C	F
1.	La República Dominicana ocupa un tercio (*third*) de la isla La Española.	☐	☐
2.	El Teatro Nacional es un edificio colonial que data (*dates*) del siglo diecinueve.	☐	☐
3.	Anacaona, la jefa (*chief*) taína, nunca aprendió español.	☐	☐
4.	Los taínos asasinaron a (*murdered*) Anacaona.	☐	☐
5.	Se celebra el Festival Merengue en el verano.	☐	☐
6.	El lago más grande de las islas del Caribe es el Lago Enriquillo.	☐	☐

Paso 2 Gramática

20. Expressing *to who(m)* or *for who(m)* • Indirect Object Pronouns; *Dar* and *decir*

A. Formas verbales. Completa las oraciones con la forma apropiada de los verbos entre paréntesis.

(**dar**):   Hoy es el cumpleaños de Ana y todos lo celebramos con una fiesta. ¿Qué regalos le

_____[1] nosotros? Carmela le _____[2] una blusa, los padres de

Ana le _____[3] un impermeable, tú le _____[4] un suéter y yo le

_____[5] un libro.

(**decir**):   ¡No estamos de acuerdo! Yo _____[6] que quiero salir, Jorge

_____[7] que tiene que estudiar, Anita y Memo _____[8] que no

tienen suficiente dinero, y tú _____[9] que estás cansado. ¿Qué les (nosotros)

_____[10] a los otros?

B. ¿No recuerdas? Remind a friend of the things you do for him or her.

MODELO: (prestar dinero) → Te presto dinero.

1.   (comprar regalos) _____

2.   (mandar tarjetas postales) _____

3.   (invitar a almorzar) _____

4.   (explicar la tarea) _____

❖Now, on a separate sheet of paper, write three sentences to remind two other friends what you do for *them.* Use the following expressions or those above: **mandar flores, ofrecer consejos, prestar dinero.**

C. Necesito consejos. Using the cues provided, ask a friend what you should do based on the following situations.

MODELO: Mañana mi novio/a y yo vamos a un baile. (¿comprar / flores?) → ¿Le compro flores?

1.   Mi hermano necesita $25 para ir a un concierto. (¿prestar / dinero?)

_____

2.   Mi novio/a quiere saber dónde estaba (*I was*) el sábado. (¿decir / verdad [*truth*]?)

_____

3.   Esta semana es el cumpleaños de Julia y Teresa. (¿dar / fiesta?)

_____

4.   Tengo problemas en esta clase. (¿pedir ayuda / profesor?)

_____

5.   Julio y Tomás quieren otra cerveza. (¿dar / más?)

_____

D. Gramática en acción: En el aeropuerto. You will hear two brief conversations. Write the number of each next to the correct location. (Check your answers in the Appendix.)

_____ En el mostrador

_____ En el control de la seguridad

E. Las vacaciones de primavera. You will hear a brief passage about what Javier told his parents. Then you will hear a series of incomplete statements. Circle the letter of the phrase that best completes each statement.

1. **a.** nunca les pide dinero.
   b. les pide mucho dinero para sus clases.
2. **a.** pedirles dinero para este semestre.
   b. pedirles dinero para el pasaje de avión.
3. **a.** Javier les pide mucho dinero.
   b. Javier es trabajador.
4. **a.** dinero para el boleto y comida.
   b. un cheque para sus clases.

F. Descripción. When you hear the corresponding number, tell what the following people are doing, using the written cues with indirect object pronouns.

EN LA FIESTA DE ANIVERSARIO DE LOS SRES. MORENO

1. Susana: regalar
2. Miguel: mandar
3. Tito: regalar

EN CASA, DURANTE EL DESAYUNO

4. Pedro: dar
5. Marta: dar
6. Luis: servir / todos

21. Expressing Likes and Dislikes • *Gustar* (Part 2)

A. ¿Qué nos gusta de los aviones? Completa las oraciones con la forma correcta de **gustar** y la forma apropiada del complemento indirecto.

    MODELO: A mí me gusta llegar temprano al aeropuerto.

1. ¿A ti _____ sentarte en el pasillo?

2. A muchas personas no _____ hacer paradas.

3. A mí también _____ los vuelos directos.

4. A nosotros no _____ la comida que sirven en la clase turística, pero a

    Jorge _____ todo.

5. ¿Y qué línea aérea _____ a Uds.?

B. Los gustos de la familia de Ernesto. Form complete sentences to tell what type of vacation activities or places the different members of Ernesto's family like, using the words provided in the order given. Make any necessary changes, and add other words when necessary. ¡RECUERDA! Use **a** in front of the indirect object noun or pronoun.

    MODELO: su / padre / gustar / playa → A su padre le gusta la playa.

1. su / padre / gustar / vacaciones / montañas

    _____

2. su / madre / encantar / cruceros _____

3. su / hermanos / gustar / deportes acuáticos

    _____

4. nadie / gustar / viajar en autobús

    _____

5. Ernesto / gustar / sacar fotos _____

❖Now write a statement to tell what kind of vacation the different members of *your* family like. After each statement, write your reaction to their preferences using one of the following: **a mí también; pero a mí, no.**

MODELO: A mi padre le gusta la playa. A mí también. (Pero a mí, no.)

_____

_____

_____

C. Gramática en acción: Los chilenos viajeros. You will hear a series of statements about the following ad. Circle **C** if the statement is true or **F** if it is false. If the information is not contained in or cannot be inferred from the description, circle **ND** (**No lo dice**). First pause and read the ad. Do not be distracted by unfamiliar vocabulary.

Now resume listening.

1. C   F   ND
2. C   F   ND
3. C   F   ND
4. C   F   ND

D. ¡Vamos de vacaciones! Pero... ¿adónde? You and your family can't decide where to go on vacation. You will hear what each person likes. Then decide where each person would like to go, using a location from the following list. There may be more than one answer in some cases. First, listen to the list. You will hear a possible answer.

Disneylandia   las playas de México
la Florida   quedarse en casa
Nueva York   Roma

MODELO: (*you hear*) A mi padre le gusta mucho jugar al golf. →
(*you say*) Le gustaría ir a la Florida.

1. ...   2. ...   3. ...   4. ...   5. ...

E. ¿Qué te gusta? ¿Qué no te gusta? Using the written cues, tell what you like or dislike about the following situations or locations. You will hear a possible answer.

MODELO: (*you see and hear*) ¿En la universidad?   (*you see*) fiestas / exámenes →
(*you say*) Me gustan las fiestas. No me gustan los exámenes.

1. ¿En la playa?   jugar al voleibol / sol
2. ¿En un restaurante?   comida / música
3. ¿En un parque?   flores / insectos
4. ¿En la cafetería?   hablar con mis amigos / comida

⏩ Paso 3 Gramática

22. Talking About the Past (Part 1) • Preterite of Regular Verbs and of *dar*, *hacer*, *ir*, and *ser*

A. ¿Qué hicieron estas personas? Completa las oraciones con la forma apropiada de los infinitivos. ¡OJO! Recuerda los cambios ortográficos como **almorcé, empecé, hizo,** etcétera.

(yo):   Hoy _____[1] (**volver**) de la universidad a la una de la tarde.

_____[2] (**Hacerme**) un sándwich y lo _____[3] (**comer**)

sentado[a] delante del televisor. _____[4] (**Recoger**[b]) la ropa sucia

y la _____[5] (**meter**[c]) en la lavadora.[d] Antes de salir para el trabajo,

le _____[6] (**dar**) de comer[e] al perro.

(tú):   ¿Por qué no _____[1] (**asistir**) a tu clase de música esta mañana?

¿_____[2] (**Acostarte**) tarde? ¿Ya _____[3] (**empezar**) a estudiar

para el examen? ¿Adónde_____[4] (**ir**) anoche? ¿_____[5] (**Salir**)

con alguien interesante? ¿A qué hora _____[6] (**volver**) a casa?

(Eva):   El año pasado Eva _____[1] (**casarse**[f]) y _____[2] (**ir**) a vivir

a Escocia[g] con su esposo. Después de varios meses _____[3] (**matricularse**) en la

Universidad de Edimburgo y _____[4] (**empezar**) a estudiar para enfermera.[h]

Este verano _____[5] (**regresar**) para visitar a sus abuelos en Vermont por una

semana y luego _____[6] (**viajar**) a California, donde _____[7]

(**ver**) a muchos amigos y lo _____[8] (**pasar**) muy bien.[i]

(Mi amiga y yo):   El verano pasado, mi amiga Sara y yo _____[1] (**pasar**) dos meses

en Europa. _____[2] (**Vivir**) con una familia francesa en Aix-en-Provence donde

_____[3] (**asistir**) a clases en la universidad. También _____[4]

(**hacer**) viajes cortos. _____[5] (**Visitar**) la costa del sur de Francia,

_____[6] (**caminar**[j]) por las playas de Niza, _____[7] (**comer**)

muchos mariscos y _____[8] (**ver**) a muchas personas famosas allí.

(Dos científicos[k]**):**   Mi papá y otro profesor de astronomía _____[1] (**ir**) a Chile

en enero de 1986 para observar el cometa Halley. _____[2] (**Salir**) de

Los Ángeles en avión y _____[3] (**llegar**) a Santiago doce horas después.

De allí _____[4] (**viajar**) a un observatorio en los Andes donde

_____[5] (**ver**) el cometa todas las noches y _____[6] (**tomar**)

muchas fotos. La comida y el vino chilenos les _____[7] (**gustar**) mucho y

_____[8] (**volver**) de su viaje muy contentos.

[a]*seated*   [b]*To pick up*   [c]*to put*   [d]*washing machine*   [e]*le... I fed*   [f]*to get married*   [g]*Scotland*   [h]*para... to be a nurse*
[i]*lo... she had a very good time*   [j]*to walk*   [k]*scientists*

❖**B. Un viaje que hice yo**

Paso 1. Piensa en un viaje que hiciste en el pasado. Ahora subraya (*underline*) las actividades que mejor describan tus experiencias en ese viaje.

1. Viajé en... avión / barco / tren / camioneta / motocicleta / ¿ ?

2. Fui a... la playa / las montañas / hacer *camping* / otra ciudad / ¿ ?

3. Hice el viaje... con familia / con amigos / solo/a / ¿ ?

4. Fui para... visitar a amigos / ver a familia / pasar las vacaciones / ¿ ?

5. Llevé... una maleta / dos maletas / mi mochila / una tienda de campaña / ¿ ?

6. Saqué muchas fotos. / Hice vídeos. / No llevé ninguna cámara.

7. Comí... en restaurantes buenos / en casa de amigos o familia / comida rápida / ¿ ?

8. Conocí a varias personas. / No conocí a nadie. / ¿ ?

Paso 2. Ahora, en una hoja de papel aparte, combina lógicamente las oraciones que subrayaste para describir tu viaje. Usa otros detalles para hacer más interesante tu descripción.

Expresión útil: hacer reservas (*reservations*)

MODELO: El verano pasado fui a Miami con dos amigos para pasar las vacaciones, nadar y descansar.

C. Gramática en acción: Un viaje a la República Dominicana. Elisa is a reporter who recently traveled to the Dominican Republic to write an article. You will hear Elisa tell about her trip. The passage is narrated in the past.

Now pause and read the following statements. Circle **C** if the statement is true or **F** if it is false. Correct the false statements. (Check your answers in the Appendix.)

1. C   F   Elisa viajó a la República Dominicana en barco.
   _____

2. C   F   El viaje a la República Dominicana fue corto.
   _____

3. C   F   Elisa visitó muchos lugares interesantes de la isla.
   _____

4. C   F   Elisa habló con muchas personas en la República Dominicana.
   _____

5. C   F   A Elisa no le gustó su viaje.
   _____

Now resume listening.

D. ¿Qué hizo Nadia anoche? You will hear a series of statements. Each will be said twice. Write the number of each statement next to the drawing that is described by that statement. First, pause and look at the drawings. Nadia's friend is Guadalupe.

a. _____

b. _____

c. _____

d. _____

e. _____

f. _____

g. _____

h. _____

i. _____

E. ¿Qué pasó ayer? Practice telling what the following people did yesterday, using the oral and written cues. Do not say the subject pronouns in parentheses.

ANTES DE LA FIESTA

1. (yo)

2. mi compañero

3. (nosotros)

ANTES DEL EXAMEN DE QUÍMICA

4. Nati y yo

5. (tú)

6. todos

A. Cosas que pasaron el semestre pasado. Use the following expressions to tell what you did for someone else, or what someone else did for you this past semester. Use the preterite and the appropriate indirect object pronouns. Use affirmative or negative sentences, following the model.

MODELO: escribir una carta → Les escribí una carta a mis abuelos.
(No le escribí a nadie.)
(Nadie me escribió a mí.)

1. mandar tarjetas postales _____

2. regalar flores _____

3. recomendar un restaurante _____

4. ofrecer ayuda _____

5. prestar una maleta _____

6. hacer un pastel _____

B. Situaciones. Cambia los verbos al pretérito.

1. *Salgo* temprano para las clases y *me quedo* allí
toda la mañana. *Almuerzo* al mediodía[a] y a las dos *voy*
al trabajo. *Vuelvo* a casa a las ocho. *Ceno* y luego
miro una película. A las once *subo* a mi alcoba,
me quejo de la tarea, pero la *hago.* Por fin
duermo unas cinco o seis horas.

2. Luisa y Jorge *son* novios. Se *hacen* muchas
promesas[b] y él le *da* un anillo.[c] Un día
Jorge *va* a Nueva York donde *se hace*[d] actor.
Se *escriben* muchas cartas, pero nunca *vuelven*
a verse[e] más.

3. La vida simple de Simón: *Busco* trabajo el lunes,
me lo *dan* el martes, lo *pierdo* el miércoles, me
pagan el jueves, *gasto*[f] el dinero el viernes, el
sábado no *hago* nada y el domingo *descanso.*

4. *Pasamos* los días muy contentos. *Comemos* bien,
vemos a nuestros amigos y *jugamos* al tenis.

[a]*noon* [b]*promises* [c]*ring* [d]*se... he becomes* [e]*see each other* [f]*gastar = to spend*

¡Repasemos!

A. Un viaje ideal. Imagina que acabas de recibir un regalo de $5.000 de tu abuela (tía) rica. Te mandó el dinero para un viaje extraordinario. En otro papel, escríbele una carta de unas 100 palabras con la descripción de tus planes. Incluye la siguiente información.

1. ¿Adónde piensas ir y en qué mes vas a salir?

2. ¿Cómo vas a viajar?

3. ¿Qué ropa vas a llevar?

4. ¿Qué piensas hacer en ese lugar?

5. ¿Cuánto tiempo piensas estar de viaje?

6. ¿Vas a viajar solo/a o con otra persona (otras personas)?

7. ¿Dónde piensas quedarte?

MODELO:

Querida _____,

¡Mil gracias por el regalo tan fenomenal! Te escribo para darte detalles de mis planes para el viaje...

Un abrazo y muchos recuerdos cariñosos de tu (nieto/a, sobrino/a)...

B. En el periódico: Anuncios. You will hear an ad for a Mexican airline. Then you will hear a series of statements. Circle **C** if the statement is true or **F** if it is false, based on the information contained in the ad and the following chart of departures. First, listen to the following phrases you will hear in this activity.

un viaje de negocios   *a business trip*   un viaje de placer   *a trip for pleasure*

MIAMI 10 vuelos semanales

SALIDAS	LUNES	MARTES.	MIERCOLES	JUEVES	VIERNES	SABADO	DOMINGO
	11 50 Y 15 05	16 10	11 50 Y 16 10	15 15	11 50 Y 11 05	15 15	15 05

1. C F   **2.** C F   **3.** C F   **4.** C F

C. Entrevista. You will hear a series of questions. Each will be said twice. Answer based on your own experience. Pause and write the answers.

1. _____

2. _____

3. _____

4. _____

5. _____

6. _____

Mi diario

Las vacaciones. Escribe sobre unas vacaciones que tomaste *o* las de un amigo / una amiga. Incluye (*Include*) la siguiente información:

- adónde y con quién fuiste
- cuándo y cómo viajaste
- el tiempo que hizo durante las vacaciones (llovió mucho, nevó, hizo mucho calor...)
- cuánto tiempo pasaste allí
- qué cosas interesantes hiciste
- lo que te gustó más (o menos)
- si te gustaría volver a ese lugar

Expresiones útiles: esquiar
hace un año (semana, mes) = *a year (week, month) a*go
tomar el sol

Ponte a prueba

A ver si sabes...

A. Indirect Object Pronouns, *dar* and *decir*

1. Place the indirect object pronoun **le** in the correct position in the following sentences. Add accent marks as needed.

   a. Siempre _____ digo _____ la verdad a mi amiga.

   b. _____ estoy diciendo _____ la verdad a mi amiga,

   or _____ estoy diciendo _____ la verdad a mi amiga.

   c. _____ voy a decir _____ la verdad a mi amiga,

   or _____ voy a decir _____ la verdad a mi amiga.

   d. (*affirmative command, Ud.:* **decir**) ¡_____ la verdad a su amiga!

   e. (*negative command, Ud.:* **decir**) ¡_____ la verdad a su amiga!

2. Completa la siguiente tabla.

INFINITIVO	YO	TÚ	ÉL	NOSOTROS	VOSOTROS	ELLOS
a. dar		*das*				
b. decir				*decimos*		

B. Gustar. Escribe oraciones con las siguientes palabras.

1. ¿(ellos) gustar / viajar? _____

2. a mí / no / gustar / quejarse _____

3. Juan / gustar / aeropuertos _____

C. Preterite of Regular Verbs and of *dar, hacer, ir,* **and** *ser*

INFINITIVO	YO	TÚ	ÉL	NOSOTROS	VOSOTROS	ELLOS
1. dar		diste				
2. hablar			habló			
3. hacer				hicimos		
4. ir / ser					fuisteis	
5. salir						salieron

Prueba corta

A. Pronombres. Completa las oraciones con el pronombre apropiado del complemento indirecto.

1. Yo _____ compré un regalo. (a mi madre)

2. Ellos _____ escribieron una carta la semana pasada. (a nosotros)

3. Nosotros _____ compramos boletos para un concierto. (a nuestros amigos)

4. Roberto siempre _____ pide favores. (a mí)

5. ¿Qué _____ dieron tus padres para tu cumpleaños? (a ti)

B. Gustar. Usa la forma apropiada de **gustar** y el complemento indirecto.

1. A mis padres no _____ los asientos cerca de la puerta.

2. A mi mejor amigo _____ viajar solo.

3. A mí no _____ la comida que sirven en el avión.

4. A todos nosotros _____ los vuelos sin escalas.

5. Y a ti, ¿adónde _____ ir de vacaciones?

C. El pretérito. Completa las oraciones con la forma apropiada del pretérito del verbo entre paréntesis.

1. ¿A quién le _____ (*tú:* **mandar**) las flores?

2. Ayer _____ (*yo:* **empezar**) a hacer las maletas a las once.

3. Mi hermano _____ (**hacer**) un viaje al Mar Caribe.

4. ¿_____ (**Ir**) Uds. en clase turística?

5. ¿_____ (*Tú:* **Oír**) el anuncio (*announcement*) para subir al avión?

6. Ellos _____ (**volver**) de su viaje el domingo pasado.

7. Juan no me _____ (**dar**) el dinero para el boleto.

D. Cosas de todos los días: De vacaciones. Practice talking about your and your family's recent trip, using the written cues. When you hear the corresponding number, form sentences using the words provided in the order given, making any necessary changes or additions.

MODELO: (*you see*) **1.** mi familia y yo / ir de vacaciones   (*you hear*) uno →
(*you say*) Mi familia y yo fuimos de vacaciones.

2. el agente / recomendarnos / viaje a Cancún
3. (nosotros) viajar / Cancún / en avión
4. avión / no / hacer escalas
5. (nosotros) llegar / a / hotel / sin problemas
6. el recepcionista / darnos / cuarto con balcón (*balcony*)
7. mi / hermanos / nadar / la piscina (*swimming pool*)
8. (yo) tomar / el sol
9. nuestra madre / sacar / fotografías
10. nuestro padre / mandarles / tarjetas postales / a los amigos
11. gustarnos / mucho / viaje

E. Apuntes. You will hear a conversation between a tourist who is interested in traveling to Cancún and a travel agent. Listen carefully and write down the requested information. First, listen to the list of information that is being requested. (Check your answers in the Appendix.)

1. el tipo de boleto que el turista quiere: _____

2. la fecha de salida: _____

3. la fecha de regreso (*return*): _____

4. la sección y la clase en que desea a viajar: _____

5. la ciudad de la cual (*from which*) va a salir el avión: _____

6. el tipo de hotel que quiere: _____

7. el nombre del hotel en que se va a quedar: _____

CAPÍTULO **8**

Paso 1 Vocabulario
La fiesta de Javier

❖**A. Tú y las fiestas.** Indica si las siguientes declaraciones son ciertas o falsas para ti.

	C	F
1. Con frecuencia, en el Día de Acción de Gracias como demasiado y luego no me siento bien.	☐	☐
2. En la Noche Vieja bebemos, comemos, bailamos y nos divertimos mucho.	☐	☐
3. En mi universidad siempre hay una gran celebración el Cinco de Mayo.	☐	☐
4. Doy regalos el Día de los Reyes Magos.	☐	☐
5. Tengo guardadas (*I have saved*) algunas tarjetas del Día de San Valentín que me mandaron mis «viejos amores».	☐	☐
6. A veces tomo cerveza verde el Día de San Patricio.	☐	☐
7. Mi familia celebra el día de mi santo.	☐	☐
8. En la Pascua, voy a la iglesia.	☐	☐
9. Mi familia gastó mucho dinero cuando celebró la quinceañera de mi hermana (prima, sobrina).	☐	☐

B. ¿Cuánto sabes de los días festivos? Completa las oraciones con el día festivo apropiado.

el Cinco de Mayo	la Navidad	la Pascua
el Día de Año Nuevo	la Nochebuena	

1. El primero de enero es _____.

2. El 25 de diciembre los cristianos celebran _____.

3. _____ conmemora la huida (*escape*) de los judíos (*Jews*) de Egipto.

4. Muchos católicos asisten a la Misa del gallo (*midnight Mass*) durante

   _____.

5. La victoria de los mexicanos sobre los franceses en la batalla de Puebla (1862) se celebra

   _____.

C. El Día de los Inocentes. Lee la siguiente lectura sobre una fiesta popular y contesta las preguntas.

El 28 de diciembre en el mundo hispánico se celebra la fiesta tradicional que se llama el Día de los Inocentes. En esta fecha se conmemora el día en que murieron[a] muchos niños en Judea por orden de Herodes, quien esperaba hacer morir[b] al niño Jesús entre ellos.

Ese día, a la gente le gusta hacerles bromas[c] a sus amigos. Una broma común es decirle a un amigo:

—Un Sr. León te llamó hace veinte minutos[d] y quiere que lo llames porque es urgente. Aquí tienes su número de teléfono.

Todos esperan mientras el amigo inocente marca[e] el número.

—Buenos días —dice con un tono de mucha importancia—. Habla Enrique González. ¿Puedo hablar con el Sr. León, por favor? Me llamó hace unos minutos.

La joven que contesta el teléfono se ríe[f] y le dice:

—Lo siento. El Sr. León acaba de salir. ¿Quiere Ud. dejar[g] un mensaje? Yo soy su secretaria, la Srta. Elefante.

El amigo se da cuenta,[h] avergonzado,[i] de que ha llamado[j] al Jardín Zoológico[k] mientras todos le gritan[l]: —¡Por inocente, por inocente!

[a]*died* [b]*esperaba... hoped to kill* [c]*hacerles... to play tricks* [d]*hace... twenty minutes ago* [e]*dials* [f]*se... laughs* [g]*to leave* [h]*se... realizes* [i]*embarrassed* [j]*ha... he has called* [k]*Jardín... Zoo* [l]*shout*

Comprensión

1. ¿Cuál es la fecha de un día festivo en los Estados Unidos que es similar al Día de los Inocentes?

   _____

2. En el mundo hispánico, ¿qué les hace la gente a sus amigos?

   _____

3. ¿Qué significa en inglés **león**? _____

D. ¿Una fiesta familiar típica? You will hear a description of Sara's last family gathering. Then you will hear a series of statements. Circle **C** if the statement is true or **F** if it is false. If the information is not given, circle **ND** (**No lo dice**).

1. C F ND Según lo que dice Sara, las fiestas familiares normalmente son muy divertidas.

2. C F ND A la tía Eustacia le gusta discutir (*argue*) con el padre de Sara.

3. C F ND Normalmente, los primos de Sara se portan mal (*behave poorly*) en las fiestas familiares.

4. C F ND Sara no lo pasa bien nunca en las fiestas familiares.

5. C F ND Los hermanos de Sara discuten mucho con sus padres.

E. Asociaciones. With which of the following celebrations do you associate the descriptions that you hear? Each will be said twice. ¡OJO! There might be more than one possible answer in some cases.

1. a. La Navidad
   b. el Día de la Raza
   c. el cumpleaños
2. a. el Día de San Valentín
   b. la Pascua
   c. el Cuatro de Julio
3. a. el Día de los Reyes Magos
   b. el Día de Acción de Gracias
   c. el Día de los Muertos
4. a. la quinceañera
   b. el Día de los Reyes Magos
   c. el día del santo

Las emociones y los estados afectivos

A. Profesores y estudiantes. ¿Cómo reaccionan? Usa la forma apropiada de los verbos de la lista.

discutir	ponerse (avergonzado, irritado,	quejarse
enfermarse	nervioso, triste)	reírse
enojarse	portarse	

1. Cuando Julián no contesta bien en clase, se ríe porque se pone nervioso. Cuando yo no recuerdo

   la respuesta correcta, yo _____.

2. Cuando nos olvidamos de entregar (*turn in*) la tarea (*homework*) a tiempo, los profesores

   _____.

3. Cuando llega la época de los exámenes, algunos estudiantes _____

   porque no duermen lo suficiente (*enough*). Y todos _____ porque

   dicen que tienen muchísimo trabajo.

4. Generalmente, los estudiantes universitarios son responsables y _____

   bien en clase.

5. A los profesores no les gusta _____ con los estudiantes sobre las

   notas (*grades*) que les dan.

B. ¿Cómo reaccionas? Practice telling how you react to these situations, using the oral and written cues. Use the word **cuando** in each sentence.

MODELO: (*you see*) Me olvido del cumpleaños de mi madre. (*you hear*) ponerme triste →
(*you say*) Me pongo triste cuando me olvido del cumpleaños de mi madre.

1. Mis padres me quitan (*take away*) el coche.
2. Veo una película triste.
3. Saco buenas notas (*grades*).
4. Tengo que hacer cola.

Nota comunicativa. Being Emphatic

¿Qué piensas? ¡Sé enfático/a, por favor! Usa formas con **-ísimo/a.**

1. ¿Te parece larga la novela *Guerra y paz*, del autor ruso Tolstoi?

   _____

2. ¿Son ricos los Gates?

   _____

3. ¿Te sientes cansado/a después de correr diez kilómetros?

   _____

4. ¿Es cara la vida en Tokio?

   _____

5. ¿Fueron difíciles las preguntas del último examen?

   _____

Pronunciación y ortografía • c and *qu*

A. El sonido [k]. The [k] sound in Spanish can be written two ways: before the vowels **a, o,** and **u** it is written as **c;** before **i** and **e,** it is written as **qu.** The letter **k** itself appears only in words that are borrowed from other languages. Unlike the English [k] sound, the Spanish sound is not aspirated; that is, no air is allowed to escape when it is pronounced. Compare the following pairs of English words in which the first [k] sound is aspirated and the second is not.

can / scan   *cold / scold*   *kit / skit*

B. Repeticiones. Repeat the following words, imitating the speaker. Remember to pronounce the [k] sound without aspiration.

1. casa	cosa	rico	loca	roca
2. ¿quién?	Quito	aquí	¿qué?	pequeño
3. kilo	kilogramo	kerosén	kilómetro	karate

Now, when you hear the corresponding number, read the following words. Repeat the correct pronunciation after the speaker.

4. paquete	**6.** química	**8.** camarones
5. quinceañera	**7.** comida	**9.** ¿por qué?

C. Dictado. You will hear a series of words. Each will be said twice. Listen carefully and write what you hear. **¡OJO!** Some of the words may be unfamiliar to you. Concentrate on the sounds. (Check your answers in the Appendix.)

1. _____   4. _____

2. _____   5. _____

3. _____   6. _____

Lectura cultural: Cuba

Preguntas. Contesta brevemente (*briefly*) según las **Lecturas culturales 1** y **2** del libro de texto. Usa palabras y fechas de la lista.

1898	la africana	el béisbol	El Morro
1959	analfabetismo	éxodo	plantaciones de tabaco y azúcar

1. ¿En qué año subió al poder (*rose to power*) Fidel Castro? _____

2. ¿En qué año obtuvo (*obtained*) Cuba su independencia de España? _____

3. La revolución socialista en Cuba provocó un _____ de cubanos a los Estados Unidos.

4. El régimen de Castro reformó el sistema educativo, reduciendo el _____ a 5 por ciento.

5. ¿Dónde paraban (*did they used to stop*) los barcos que transportaban (*used to transport*) las riquezas (*riches*) del Nuevo Mundo? _____

6. ¿Cuál es la pasión deportiva de los cubanos? _____

7. ¿Qué se puede visitar en el Valle de Viñales? _____

8. ¿Qué influencia predomina en el «son» cubano? _____

Paso 2 Gramática
23. Talking About the Past (Part 2) • Irregular Preterites

A. ¿Cuánto sabes?

Paso 1. ¿Son ciertos o falsos los siguientes hechos históricos?

		C	F
1.	Neil Armstrong fue el primer hombre que estuvo en la luna (*moon*).	☐	☐
2.	Los Estados Unidos pusieron un satélite en el espacio antes que la Unión Soviética.	☐	☐
3.	Magallanes quiso circunnavegar el mundo, pero murió en las Filipinas a manos de los indígenas (*natives*) en 1521.	☐	☐
4.	En 1592 Cristóbal Colón pudo llegar a América.	☐	☐
5.	Hitler no quiso dominar Europa.	☐	☐
6.	Cortés no supo de la grandeza (*grandeur*) del imperio azteca hasta que (*until*) llegó a Tenochtitlán en 1519.	☐	☐
7.	Los españoles trajeron el maíz (*corn*) y el tomate a América.	☐	☐
8.	En Berlín George Bush (padre) dijo: «Yo soy un berlinés.»	☐	☐
9.	Pocos inmigrantes irlandeses vinieron a los Estados Unidos en el siglo (*century*) XIX.	☐	☐

Paso 2. Ahora tacha (*cross out*) la información incorrecta en cada respuesta falsa y corrígela (*correct it*).

B. Situaciones. Completa las oraciones con el pretérito de los verbos entre paréntesis.

Durante la Navidad: La familia Román _____[1] (**tener**) una reunión familiar muy bonita

para la Navidad. Todos sus hijos _____[2] (**estar**) presentes. _____[3]

(**Venir**) de Denver y Dallas y _____[4] (**traer**) regalos para todos. Su mamá pensaba[a]

hacer una gran cena para la Nochebuena, pero todos le _____[5] (**decir**) que no. Por la

noche todos _____[6] (**ir**) a un restaurante muy elegante donde _____[7]

(**comer**) bien, _____[8] (**poder**) escuchar música y _____[9] (**pasarlo**) bien.

Otro terremoto[b] en California: Esta mañana _____[1] (*nosotros:* **saber**) que

_____[2] (**haber**) un terremoto en California. Lo _____[3] (*yo:* **oír**)

primero en la radio y luego lo _____[4] (*yo:* **leer**) en el periódico. Algunas casas

_____[5] (**romperse**[c]), pero en general, este terremoto no _____[6]

(**hacer**) mucho daño.[d] Un experto _____[7] (**decir**): «No _____[8] (**ser**)

el primero ni va a ser el último».

[a]*was planning* [b]*earthquake* [c]*to be destroyed* [d]*damage*

C. Después del examen. Jorge y Manuel hablan en la cafetería. Completa las oraciones con la forma apropiada de los verbos entre paréntesis.

JORGE: ¿Cómo _____[1] (**estar**) el examen?

MANUEL: ¡Terrible! No _____[2] (**poder**) contestar las últimas tres preguntas porque

no _____[3] (**tener**) tiempo. ¿Por qué no _____[4] (**venir**) tú?

JORGE: _____[5] (**Querer**) venir, pero _____[6] (**estar**) enfermo todo el

día. ¿Qué preguntas _____[7] (**hacer**) el profesor?

MANUEL: Muchas, pero ahora no recuerdo ninguna. ¿_____[8] (*Tú:* **Saber**) que Claudia

_____[9] (**tener**) un accidente y tampoco _____[10] (**venir**)

al examen?

JORGE: Sí, me lo _____[11] (**decir**) María Inés esta mañana... Bueno, tengo que irme...

¡Caramba! ¿Dónde _____[12] (**poner**) mi cartera?

MANUEL: ¿No la _____[13] (**traer**) otra vez? Yo sólo _____[14] (**traer**) dos

dólares. Vamos a buscar a Ernesto. Él siempre tiene dinero.

D. Gramática en acción: La fiesta de la Noche Vieja

Paso 1. You will hear a series of statements about the following drawing. Circle **C** if the statement is true or **F** if it is false.

1. C F
2. C F
3. C F

4. C F
5. C F
6. C F

Paso 2. Now pause and circle the letter of the correct verb to indicate what each person did based on the drawing.

1. Marina _____ hablando por teléfono.
   a. pudo   b. estuvo

2. Javier y Gema le _____ un regalo a Paco.
   a. trajeron   b. quisieron

3. Sultán _____ mucho ruido.
   a. dio   b. hizo

4. Ernesto _____ su copa de champán en el televisior.
   a. puso   b. pudo

Now resume listening.

❖E. Encuesta: Hablando de lo que pasó ayer. You will hear a series of statements about what happened to you yesterday. For each statement, check the appropriate answer. No answers will be given. The answers you choose should be correct for you!

1. ☐ Sí   ☐ No   5. ☐ Sí   ☐ No

2. ☐ Sí   ☐ No   6. ☐ Sí   ☐ No

3. ☐ Sí   ☐ No   7. ☐ Sí   ☐ No

4. ☐ Sí   ☐ No   8. ☐ Sí   ☐ No

F. Una fiesta de cumpleaños. Tell what happened at the party, using the written and oral cues.

MODELO: (*you see*) estar en casa de Mario   (*you hear*) todos →
(*you say*) Todos estuvimos en casa de Mario.

1. tener que preparar la comida   3. hacer mucho ruido
2. venir con regalos   4. ¡estar estupenda!

G. Preguntas: ¿Qué pasó durante tu fiesta de cumpleaños? You will hear a series of questions. Each will be said twice. Answer, using the written cues. Use object pronouns when possible.

1. en mi casa   4. sobre una mesa
2. sí: venir todos mis tíos y primos   5. mi primo
3. a su novia

24. Talking About the Past (Part 3) • Preterite of Stem-Changing Verbs

A. Situaciones. Completa las oraciones con la forma apropiada del pretérito de uno de los verbos de la lista, según el significado de la oración.

dormirse   sentarse

1. Yo _____ delante del televisor y _____ poco después.

2. —¿A qué hora _____ Uds. a comer?

   —A las nueve y media. Y después de trabajar tanto, ¡nosotros casi _____ en la mesa!

3. Mi esposo se despertó a las dos y no _____ otra vez hasta las cinco de la mañana.

reírse   sentir (*to regret*)   **sentirse**

4. Esa película fue tan divertida que (nosotros) _____ toda la noche. Sólo Jorge

   no _____ mucho porque no la comprendió.

5. Rita y Marcial _____ mucho haber faltado (*having missed*) a tu fiesta, pero Rita

   se enfermó y _____ tan mal que se quedó en cama todo el fin de semana.

B. Gramática en acción: La quinceañera de Lupe Carrasco: Dictado. You will hear a series of sentences about the following drawing. Listen carefully and write the missing words. (Check your answers in the Appendix.)

1. Lupe _____ con un vestido blanco muy elegante.

2. Mientras cortaba el pastel de cumpleaños, Lupe _____ mucho.

3. También _____ para todas las fotos que sacaron.

4. Lupe _____ un deseo al cortar el pastel.

5. Ella _____ guardar el deseo en secreto.

6. En la fiesta _____ refrescos.

7. Todos _____ mucho en la fiesta.

8. Los invitados _____ a la una y media de la mañana.

C. La fiesta de sorpresa

Paso 1. You will hear a brief paragraph, narrated by Ernesto, about a surprise party. Listen carefully and check the appropriate actions for each person. First, pause and look at the chart. (Check your answers in the Appendix.)

PERSONA	VESTIRSE ELEGANTEMENTE	SENTIRSE MAL	DORMIR TODA LA TARDE	PREFERIR QUEDARSE EN CASA
Julia				
Verónica				
Tomás				
Ernesto (el narrador)				

Paso 2. You will hear a series of statements about the preceding paragraph. Each will be said twice. Circle **C** if the statement is true or **F** if it is false. If the information is not given, circle **ND** (**No lo dice**).

1. C   F   ND   **2.** C   F   ND   **3.** C   F   ND   **4.** C   F   ND   **5.** C   F   ND

D. ¿Qué le pasó a Antonio? Tell what happened to Antonio when you hear the corresponding number. First, listen to the beginning of the story about Antonio.

Raquel Morales invitó a Antonio a una fiesta en su casa. Antonio le dijo a Raquel que él asistiría (*would attend*), pero todo le salió mal. En primer lugar...

1. no recordar llevar refrescos
2. perder la dirección de la Srta. Morales
3. llegar muy tarde a la fiesta
4. no divertirse
5. sentirse enfermo después de la fiesta
6. acostarse muy tarde
7. dormir mal esa noche
8. despertarse a las cinco de la mañana
9. tener que ir a clases de todas formas (*anyway*)

⟩ Paso 3 Gramática

25. Expressing Direct and Indirect Objects Together • Double Object Pronouns

---

¡RECUERDA!

Direct and Indirect Object Pronouns. Cambia los complementos directos indicados o las frases indicadas (*a Ud., a nosotros, a ellos*, etcétera) a complementos pronominales. Luego identifica los pronombres (O.D. = objeto directo; O.I. = objeto indirecto).

MODELOS: No dice la verdad. (*a Uds.*) → No les dice la verdad. (O.I.)
No dice *la verdad.* → No la dice. (O.D.)

1. Yo traigo el café. (*a Ud.*) _____

2. Yo traigo *el café* ahora. _____

3. Ellos compran los boletos. (*a nosotros*) _____

4. Ellos compran *los boletos* hoy. _____

5. No hablo mucho. (*a ellas*) _____

6. No conozco bien *a tus primas.* _____

7. Queremos dar una fiesta. (*a mis padres*) _____

8. Pensamos dar *la fiesta* en casa. _____

A. ¡Promesas, promesas! (*Promises, promises!*) Estas personas prometen hacer las siguientes cosas. Vuelve a escribir lo que prometen, pero omite la repetición innecesaria del complemento directo.

MODELO: ¿Los discos? José nos trae *los discos* mañana. → ¿Los discos? José nos los trae mañana.

1. ¿El dinero? Te devuelvo (*I'll return*) *el dinero* mañana.

   _____

2. ¿Las tapas? Te traigo *las tapas* esta noche.

   _____

3. ¿La sorpresa? Nos van a revelar *la sorpresa* después.

   _____

4. ¿Los pasteles? Me prometieron *los pasteles* para esta tarde.

   _____

5. ¿Las fotos? Les mando *las fotos* a Uds. con la carta.

   _____

6. ¿La bicicleta? Le devuelvo *la bicicleta* a Pablo mañana.

   _____

7. ¿El dinero? Le doy *el dinero* a Ud. el viernes.

   _____

8. ¿Los regalos? Le muestro *los regalos* a Isabel esta noche.

   _____

¡RECUERDA!

le **les**	lo la los las	→	**se**	lo la los las	

B. La herencia (*inheritance*). Imagina que un pariente muy rico murió y les dejó (*he left*) varias cosas a ti y a diferentes personas e instituciones. ¿Qué le dejó a quién?

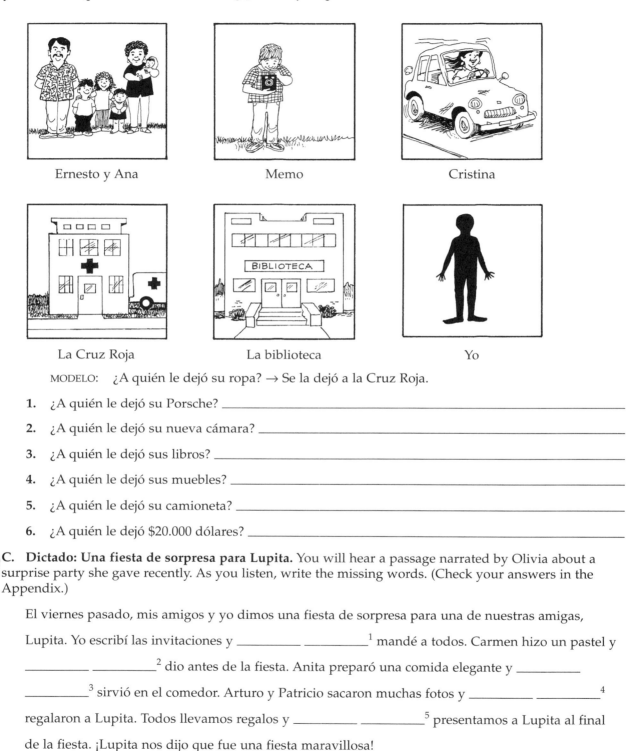

Ernesto y Ana

Memo

Cristina

La Cruz Roja

La biblioteca

Yo

MODELO: ¿A quién le dejó su ropa? → Se la dejó a la Cruz Roja.

1. ¿A quién le dejó su Porsche? _____

2. ¿A quién le dejó su nueva cámara? _____

3. ¿A quién le dejó sus libros? _____

4. ¿A quién le dejó sus muebles? _____

5. ¿A quién le dejó su camioneta? _____

6. ¿A quién le dejó $20.000 dólares? _____

C. Dictado: Una fiesta de sorpresa para Lupita. You will hear a passage narrated by Olivia about a surprise party she gave recently. As you listen, write the missing words. (Check your answers in the Appendix.)

El viernes pasado, mis amigos y yo dimos una fiesta de sorpresa para una de nuestras amigas,

Lupita. Yo escribí las invitaciones y _____ _____[1] mandé a todos. Carmen hizo un pastel y

_____ _____[2] dio antes de la fiesta. Anita preparó una comida elegante y _____

_____[3] sirvió en el comedor. Arturo y Patricio sacaron muchas fotos y _____ _____[4]

regalaron a Lupita. Todos llevamos regalos y _____ _____[5] presentamos a Lupita al final

de la fiesta. ¡Lupita nos dijo que fue una fiesta maravillosa!

D. Gramática en acción: Berta habla de la fiesta de Anita

Paso 1. You will hear a series of statements. Write the number of each statement under the corresponding drawing.

a. _____   b. _____   c. _____

Paso 2. Now pause and circle the letter of the correct object pronouns for each sentence.

1. Hice unas tapas y _____ _____ di a Anita para la fiesta.

    a. se las   **b.** me las

2. Me encantó el CD que Anita puso en la fiesta. Por eso Anita _____ _____ prestó para oírlo en casa.

    a. me lo   **b.** me la

3. Sergio sacó muchas fotos de la fiesta y _____ _____ mostró en la computadora.

    a. nos las   **b.** nos la

Now resume listening.

Paso 3. Now repeat the correct answers for **Paso 2,** imitating the speaker.

E. En casa, durante la cena. During dinner, your brother asks about the different foods that might be left. He will say each question twice. Listen carefully and circle the items to which he is referring.

> MODELO: (*you hear*) ¿Hay más?   ¿Me la pasas, por favor?
> (*you see*) la sopa   el pan   el pescado →
>
> (*you circle*) (la sopa)

1. las galletas   la fruta   el helado

2. la carne   el postre   los camarones

3. la leche   el vino   las arvejas

4. las papas fritas   la cerveza   el pastel

F. **¿Dónde está?** Carolina would like to borrow some things from you. Tell her to whom you gave each item, basing your answer on the written cues and selecting the correct pronouns. You will hear each of Carolina's questions twice.

> MODELO: (*you hear*) Oye, ¿dónde está tu diccionario?
> (*you see*) Se (**lo / la**) presté a Nicolás. Él (**lo / la**) necesita para un examen. →
> (*you say*) Se lo presté a Nicolás. Él lo necesita para un examen.

1. Se (**lo / la**) presté a Nicolás. Él (**lo / la**) necesita para un viaje.
2. Se (**los / las**) presté a Teresa. Ella (**los / las**) necesita para su fiesta.
3. Se (**la / las**) presté a Juan. Él (**la / las**) necesita para escribir un trabajo.
4. Se (**lo / la**) presté a Nina. Ella (**lo / la**) necesita para ir al parque.

Un poco de todo

A. Una carta a un amigo

Paso 1. Completa la carta que Gerardo le escribe a un amigo que vive en Acapulco. Usa el pretérito de los verbos entre paréntesis.

Querido Pepe:

La semana pasada _____[1] (*yo:* **hacer**) un corto viaje a Acapulco porque tenía[a]

una reunión con mi agente de viajes. Aunque[b] _____[2] (**estar**) ocupadísimo,

_____[3] (**querer**) visitarte, pero _____[4] (**saber**) por nuestro amigo

Luis Dávila que estabas[c] fuera[d] de la ciudad. Yo le _____[5] (**dar**) a Luis unas fotos de

la última vez que nosotros _____[6] (**estar**) juntos,[e] y le _____[7] (*yo:*

pedir) que te las diera[f] a tu vuelta[g] a Acapulco.

Espero verte durante mi próximo viaje. Recibe un abrazo[h] de tu amigo,

Gerardo

[a]*I had* [b]*Although* [c]*you were* [d]*outside, away* [e]*together* [f]*he give* [g]*a... upon your return* [h]*hug*

Paso 2. Contesta las preguntas con oraciones completas.

1. ¿Adónde hizo Gerardo un viaje? _____

2. ¿Tuvo mucho tiempo libre o estuvo ocupado? _____

3. ¿Cómo supo Gerardo que Pepe estaba fuera de Acapulco? _____

4. ¿A quién le dio las fotos? _____

B. Preguntas personales. Contesta las preguntas con oraciones completas. Usa los pronombres del complemento directo e indirecto.

> MODELO: ¿A quién le prestaste tu bicicleta? → Se la presté a mi hermano.
> (No se la presté a nadie.)

1. ¿A quién le mandaste una tarjeta de San Valentín? _____

2. ¿A quién le diste regalos de Navidad? _____

3. ¿Quién te trajo flores este año? _____

4. ¿Quién te pidió dinero este mes? _____

5. ¿Quién te hizo una fiesta para tu cumpleaños? _____

 ¡Repasemos!

A. ¡Saludos de España!

Paso 1. Lee la siguiente tarjeta postal.

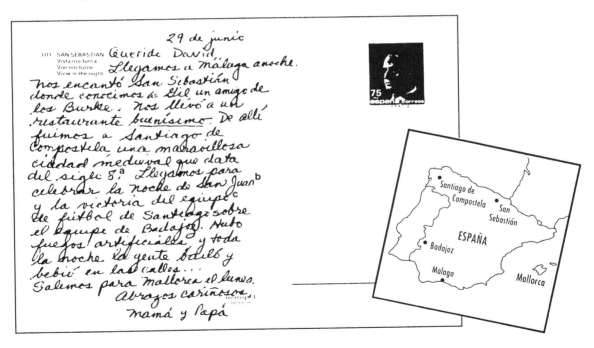

101 SAN SEBASTIAN
Vista nocturna
Vue nocturne
View in the night

> 29 de junio
> Querido David,
> Llegamos a Málaga anoche. Nos encantó San Sebastián donde conocimos a Gil, un amigo de los Burke. Nos llevó a un restaurante buenísimo. De allí fuimos a Santiago de Compostela una maravillosa ciudad medieval que data del siglo 8.ª[a] Llegamos para celebrar la noche de San Juan[b] y la victoria del equipo[c] de fútbol de Santiago sobre el equipo de Badajoz. Hubo fuegos artificiales y toda la noche la gente bailó y bebió en las calles... Salimos para Mallorca el lunes.
> Abrazos cariñosos,
> mamá y Papá

[a]data... *dates from the eighth century*   [b]Noche... fiesta tradicional que se celebra el 24 de junio   [c]*team*

Paso 2. Ahora, en otro papel, escribe una tarjeta postal a un amigo o pariente, contándole de tus vacaciones. Menciona por lo menos un lugar que visitaste y lo que viste o lo que pasó allí. Menciona también adónde piensas ir luego. Sigue el modelo de la tarjeta. Puedes inventar el viaje, si quieres.

B. Un día típico. You will hear a description of a day in Ángela's life, narrated in the past. Then you will hear a series of statements. Circle **C** if the statement is true or **F** if it is false. If the information is not given, circle **ND** (**No lo dice**).

1. C F ND   Ángela se acostó tarde ayer.

2. C F ND   Ángela se levantó a las seis y media.

3. C F ND   Ángela se puso furiosa cuando llegó a la oficina.

4. C F ND   El jefe (*boss*) le dio mucho trabajo.

5. C F ND   Los padres de Ángela viven lejos de ella.

6. C F ND   Cuando Ángela se acostó, se durmió inmediatamente.

C. Entrevista. You will hear a series of questions. Each will be said twice. Answer based on your own experience. Pause and write the answers.

1. _____
2. _____
3. _____
4. _____
5. _____
6. _____
7. _____

❖ ◗ Mi diario

Un día festivo importante. ¿Cuál es el día festivo más importante para tu familia (tus amigos)? ¿Cuándo se celebra? ¿Hay una cena especial o una fiesta? ¿Dónde es? ¿Quiénes asisten? ¿Cuáles son las costumbres (*customs*) y tradiciones más importantes para Uds.? ¿Qué comidas y bebidas se sirven? La preparación de la comida, ¿es una actividad cooperativa? ¿Lo prepara todo una sola persona?

Palabras útiles: dar las doce (*to strike 12*)

decorar el árbol (*tree*)

los fuegos artificiales (*fireworks*)

el globo (*balloon*)

normalmente (*normally*)

Ponte a prueba

A ver si sabes...

A. Irregular Preterites. Escribe las formas apropiadas de los verbos en el pretérito.

1. (estar) yo _____

2. (poder) tú _____

3. (poner) Ud. _____

4. (querer) nosotros _____

5. (saber) ellos _____

6. (tener) yo _____

7. (venir) tú _____

8. (traer) Ud. _____

9. (decir) ellos _____

10. (ir) nosotros _____

B. Preterite of Stem-Changing Verbs. Completa la siguiente tabla.

	dormir	pedir	preferir	recordar	sentirse
él/ella/Ud.					
ellos/Uds.					

C. Double Object Pronouns. Sustituye (*Substitute*) los complementos directos e (*and*) indirectos por sus respectivos pronombres.

MODELO: Alberto le sirvió *café* a *Jimena*. → Alberto _*se*_ _*lo*_ sirvió.

1. Ricardo le pidió *dinero* a *su padre*.   Ricardo _____ _____ pidió.

2. Clara le sugirió *una idea* a *Enrique*.   Clara _____ _____ sugirió.

3. Carmen les puso *los suéteres* a *sus hijos*.   Carmen _____ _____ puso.

Prueba corta

A. Oraciones. Completa las oraciones con la forma correcta del pretérito de un verbo de la lista.

conseguir   dormir   reírse
despedirse   hacer   traer
divertirse   ponerse   vestirse

1. Cuando vimos esa película cómica, todos (*nosotros*) _____ mucho.

2. Después de comer ese pescado, Marcial _____ enfermo y se acostó, pero no _____ en toda la noche.

3. Yo _____ un boleto extra para el concierto de mañana. ¿Quieres ir?

4. Marcos _____ de sus amigos y volvió a su casa.

5. Para celebrar el Año Nuevo, Mirasol _____ con ropa elegante: pantalones negros y blusa de seda. Ella _____ muchísimo bailando con sus amigos.

6. Para celebrar el Año Nuevo, nosotros _____ una fiesta y unos amigos nos _____ champán.

B. Preguntas. Contesta las preguntas con la respuesta más apropiada.

1. ¿Cuándo nos traes el café?
   a. Se lo traigo en seguida (*right away*).
   b. Te los traigo en seguida.
   c. Te lo traigo en seguida.

2. ¿Cuándo me van a lavar (*wash*) el coche?
   a. Se lo vamos a lavar esta tarde.
   b. Me lo voy a lavar esta tarde.
   c. Te lo voy a lavar esta tarde.

3. ¿Quién te sacó estas fotos?
   a. Julio me los sacó.
   b. Julio te las sacó.
   c. Julio me las sacó.

4. ¿Quién les mandó estas flores a Uds.?
   a. Ceci nos los mandó.
   b. Ceci nos las mandó.
   c. Ceci se las mandó.

5. ¿A quién le vas a regalar esa camisa?
   a. Te la voy a regalar a ti.
   b. Se lo voy a regalar a Uds.
   c. Me las vas a regalar a mí.

6. ¿A quién le sirves ese vino?
   a. Se los sirvo a Uds.
   b. Se lo sirvo a Uds.
   c. Mario nos lo sirve.

C. Preparativos para la fiesta de Gilberto. The speaker will ask you several questions about Gilberto's birthday party. You will hear each question twice. Circle the letter of the best answer for each. Pay close attention to the object nouns and pronouns you hear in the questions.

1. a. Sí, voy a mandártela.   b. Sí, voy a mandártelos.
2. a. Sí, se lo tengo que hacer.   b. Sí, te lo tengo que hacer.
3. a. Sí, nos los van a traer.   b. Sí, se los voy a traer.
4. a. No, no van a traértelas.   b. No, no van a traérmelas.
5. a. Sí, te las sirvo.   b. Sí, se los sirvo.

D. Cosas de todos los días: El cumpleaños de Gilberto. Practice talking about the surprise birthday party that you gave a friend, using the written cues. When you hear the corresponding number, form sentences using the words provided in the order given, making any necessary changes or additions.

MODELO: (*you see*) **1.** (yo) hacerle / una fiesta de sorpresa a Gilberto   (*you hear*) uno →
(*you say*) Le hice una fiesta de sorpresa a Gilberto.

2. venir / muchos de sus amigos
3. Tere / querer venir / pero / no poder
4. todos / traer / o / mandar / regalos
5. Felicia y yo / tener que preparar todo
6. Fernando y Raúl / servir los refrescos
7. Fernando / contar chistes / como siempre
8. todos / divertirse / y / reírse
9. nadie / quejarse
10. Gilberto / tener que bailar / con todas las muchachas
11. ¡(él) / ponerse / muy nervioso!

CAPÍTULO **9**

 Paso 1 Vocabulario

Los pasatiempos, diversiones y aficiones

❖**A.** **¿Qué haces?** ¿Con qué frecuencia haces estas actividades durante un fin de semana típico?

		CASI NUNCA	A VECES	CON FRECUENCIA
1.	Doy paseos (por un centro comercial, por la playa).	☐	☐	☐
2.	Hago una fiesta con algunos amigos.	☐	☐	☐
3.	Voy al cine.	☐	☐	☐
4.	Visito un museo.	☐	☐	☐
5.	Juego a las cartas.	☐	☐	☐
6.	Paseo en bicicleta.	☐	☐	☐
7.	Hago *camping* con amigos.	☐	☐	☐
8.	Entreno con un equipo deportivo (*sports*).	☐	☐	☐

❖**B.** **¿A quién le gusta... ?** ¿A cuál de tus amigos le gustan estos pasatiempos?

MODELO: (hacer *picnics*) → A Maritere le gusta hacer *picnics*.
(A ninguno de mis amigos le gusta hacer *picnics*.)

1. (montar a caballo) _____

2. (patinar) _____

3. (hacer *camping*) _____

4. (esquiar) _____

5. (nadar) _____

6. (pasear en bicicleta) _____

C. Diversiones. Completa las oraciones según los dibujos.

1.  2.  3.

1. **a.** A las personas en esta escena (*scene*) les gusta _____.

   b. Los dos hombres _____.

   c. Los tres amigos _____.

   d. La chica _____.

2. **a.** Los hombres en el parque _____.

   b. Tres personas hacen cola delante del _____ Colón.

   c. Dos personas van a visitar el _____ de Arte Moderno.

3. **Palabras útiles:** el cine   pasarlo bien

                             divertido   la película

   ELSA: Estoy cansada de estudiar. Quiero hacer algo _____.[a]

   LISA: ¿Qué te parece si vamos al _____[b] Bretón? Ponen _____[c]

               El señor de los anillos (Lord of the Rings).

   ELSA: Buena idea. Necesito salir de la casa. ¡Quiero _____[d]!

D. Gustos y preferencias. You will hear a series of descriptions of what people like to do. Each will be said twice. Listen carefully, and circle the letter of the activity or activities that are best suited to each person.

1. **a.** nadar   **b.** jugar al ajedrez   **c.** tomar el sol
2. **a.** dar fiestas   **b.** ir al teatro   **c.** ir a un bar
3. **a.** ir a un museo   **b.** hacer *camping*   **c.** hacer un *picnic*
4. **a.** pasear en bicicleta **b.** esquiar   **c.** correr
5. **a.** jugar al fútbol   **b.** ir a un museo   **c.** ir al cine

🎧 **E. Las actividades y el tiempo.** You will hear a series of descriptions of weather and activities. Write the number of the description next to the corresponding picture. ¡OJO! Listen carefully. There is an extra description.

a. _____

b. _____

c. _____

d. _____

Los quehaceres domésticos (Part 2)

A. Los aparatos domésticos. Contesta con oraciones completas.

1. ¿Para qué se usa la estufa?

_____

2. ¿En qué se prepara el café?

_____

3. ¿Qué hacemos con la lavadora y con la secadora de ropa?

_____

4. ¿Qué máquina usamos para lavar los platos?

_____

5. ¿Qué hacemos para limpiar las alfombras?

_____

6. ¿En qué tostamos el pan?

_____

7. ¿Qué aparato usamos para preparar comidas rápidamente?

_____

8. ¿Qué hace Ud. con la ropa arrugada (wrinkled)?

_____

B. Los quehaceres domésticos. Describe lo que hacen las personas en cada dibujo. Usa el presente del progresivo cuando sea (*whenever it is*) posible.

1.
2.
3.

4.
5.
6.

1. _____
2. _____
3. _____
4. _____
5. _____
6. _____

❖**¿Y tú?** Nombra tres quehaceres que prefieres *no* hacer.

_____

_____

_____

❖**C. Preguntas personales.** Haz un inventario de los aparatos eléctricos que tienes y de los que te gustaría tener en tu cocina.

Tengo _____

_____.

Me gustaría tener _____

_____.

D. Mandatos para el nuevo robot. Imagine that your family has been chosen to test a model robot in your home. Tell the robot what to do in each of the following situations, using the oral cues. ¡OJO! You will be using **Ud.** command forms.

MODELO: (*you hear*) uno   (*you see*) →
(*you say*) Lave los platos.

1.
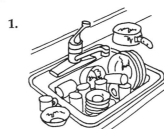

2.
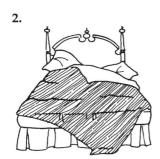

3.

4.

5.
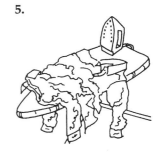

E. ¿Qué están haciendo estas personas? Tell what each person is doing. Use the present progressive in your answers. (Remember to repeat the correct answer.)

MODELO: (*you hear*) uno   (*you see*) →
(*you say*) Jorge está lavando las ventanas.

1.

2.

3.

4.

5.

A. Repeticiones. Like the [k] sound, Spanish **p** and **t** are not aspirated as they are in English. Compare the following pairs of aspirated and nonaspirated English sounds.

pin / spin   pan / span   tan / Stan   top / stop

Repeat the following words, imitating the speaker.

1.	pasar	patinar	programa	puerta	esperar
2.	tienda	todos	traje	estar	usted

Now, read the following phrases and sentences after you hear the corresponding number. Repeat the correct pronunciation after the speaker.

3. una tía trabajadora

4. unos pantalones pardos

5. Tomás, toma tu té.

6. Pablo paga el periódico.

B. Repaso: [p], [t], [k]. You will hear a series of words. Each will be said twice. Circle the letter of the word you hear.

1.	**a.**	pata	**b.**	bata		**4.**	**a.**	dos	**b.**	tos
2.	**a.**	van	**b.**	pan		**5.**	**a.**	de	**b.**	té
3.	**a.**	coma	**b.**	goma		**6.**	**a.**	callo	**b.**	gallo

C. Dictado. You will hear four sentences. Each will be said twice. Listen carefully and write what you hear. (Check your answers in the Appendix.)

1. _____

2. _____

3. _____

4. _____

Lectura cultural: Colombia

Oraciones. Completa las oraciones según las **Lecturas culturales 1** y **2** del libro de texto. Usa palabras de la lista.

altiplanos	Caribe	esculturas	oro	petróleo	platino
café	cumbia	fantásticas	Pacífico	piratas	

1. La República de Colombia tiene costas en el Mar _____ y en el Océano

_____.

2. La capital de Colombia no está en la costa. Está en los _____ del país.

3. Tres recursos (*resources*) naturales de Colombia son _____, _____

y _____, pero una de sus exportaciones principales es el _____.

4. Los españoles construyeron el Castillo en Cartagena para proteger la ciudad de los

_____.

5. En el Parque Arqueológico de San Agustín hay muchas _____ que representan

imágenes _____ y realistas.

6. Los tambores (*drums*) son instrumentos importantes en la _____ y el vallenato.

Paso 2 Gramática

26. Talking About the Past (Part 4) • Descriptions and Habitual Actions in the Past: Imperfect of Regular and Irregular Verbs

A. El cumpleaños de Clara. Lee la siguiente descripción de cómo pasaba los cumpleaños Clara López Rubio cuando era niña. Escribe las formas del imperfecto que encuentras en su descripción.

Los cumpleaños que más recuerdo son los que celebraba de pequeña. La casa siempre se llenaba de gente[a]: parientes, amiguitos míos[b] con sus padres... Mis amigos y yo debíamos hacer muchísimo ruido. Corríamos por la casa, comíamos papas fritas y luego, al final, cortábamos la torta.[c] Yo siempre era la última en recibir un pedazo[d] y eso me molestaba mucho, sobre todo[e] porque en los cumpleaños de mi amigo Pablo, él siempre era el primero porque era «el anfitrión».[f]

[a]se... *would fill up with people* [b]*of mine* [c]*pastel* [d]*piece* [e]*sobre... especialmente* [f]*host*

1. _____
2. _____
3. _____
4. _____
5. _____

6. _____
7. _____
8. _____
9. _____
10. _____

B. Recuerdos juveniles (*Youthful memories*). Completa la narración con la forma apropiada del imperfecto de los verbos entre paréntesis.

Cuando _____[1] (*yo:* **tener**) 14 años, _____[2] (*nosotros:* **vivir**)

en el campo.[a] _____[3] (*Yo:* **Ir**) al colegio[b] en una ciudad cerca de casa y a

veces _____[4] (*yo:* **volver**) tarde porque _____[5] (**preferir**)

quedarme a jugar con mis primos. Ellos a veces _____[6] (**venir**) a visitarnos,

especialmente cuando _____[7] (**ser**) el cumpleaños de mi madre. Siempre

lo _____[8] (*nosotros:* **celebrar**) con una gran fiesta y ese día mi padre

_____[9] (**hacer**) todos los preparativos y _____[10] (**cocinar**)

él mismo.[c] Nos _____[11] (**visitar**) parientes de todas partes y siempre

_____[12] (**quedarse**) algunos con nosotros por dos o tres días. Durante esos días

_____[13] (*nosotros:* **dormir**) poco porque mis primos y yo _____[14]

(**acostarse**) en la sala de recreo y allí siempre _____[15] (**haber**) gente hasta muy tarde.

Todos nosotros lo _____[16] (**pasar**) muy bien. Pero esos _____[17]

(**ser**) otros tiempos, claro.

[a]*country(side)* [b]*high school* [c]*él... himself*

C. La mujer de ayer y hoy. Compara la vida de la mujer de la década de los años 50 con la vida que lleva hoy día. Usa los infinitivos indicados. Sigue el modelo. Luego escribe dos contrastes que has observado (*you have observed*) en la vida de tu propia familia o de tus amigos.

> MODELO: tener muchos hijos / / tener familias pequeñas →
> Antes tenía muchos hijos. Ahora tiene familias pequeñas.

1. depender de su esposo / / tener más independencia económica

   _____

2. quedarse en casa / / preferir salir a trabajar

   _____

3. sólo pensar en casarse (*getting married*) / / pensar en seguir su propia carrera (*own career*)

   _____

4. su esposo sentarse a leer el periódico / / ayudarla con los quehaceres domésticos

   _____

❖5. _____

   _____

D. Gramática en acción: Los indígenas colombianos

Paso 1. Dictado. You will hear the following paragraph about the indigenous people of Colombia. Listen carefully and write the missing words. (Check your answers in the Appendix.)

Cuando los españoles llegaron al territorio que hoy es Colombia, _____[1] allí diversos pueblos indígenas que _____[2] a tres grandes familias.

LOS CHIBCHAS: _____[3] en los altiplanos y en las zonas frías de los Andes, en el interior. Su organización social _____[4] en el matriarcado.

LOS CARIBES: _____[5] la zona costera caribeña. _____[6] un pueblo guerrero y comerciante.

LOS ARAWACOS: _____[7] el interior oriental, cerca de los ríos Amazonas, Putumayo y Caquetá. _____[8] la arquitectura más avanzada de todas las tribus.

Paso 2. ¿Qué recuerdas? Now pause and complete the following sentences with words chosen from the list. There is an extra word in the list. (Check your answers in the Appendix.)

altiplanos   arquitectura   comerciante   diversos   interior

1. _____ pueblos indígenas habitaban lo que hoy es Colombia.

2. Los chibchas vivían en las zonas frías y en los _____.

3. Los caribes, un pueblo _____ y guerrero, vivían en el Caribe.

4. Los arawacos tenían la _____ más avanzada de todos los grupos indígenas.

Now resume listening.

❖**E.** **Encuesta: ¿Qué hacías y cómo eras cuando eras joven?** You will hear a series of statements about what you used to do or what you were like when you were younger. For each statement, check the appropriate answer. No answers will be given. The answers you choose should be correct for you!

1. ☐ Sí   ☐ No   4. ☐ Sí   ☐ No   6. ☐ Sí   ☐ No

2. ☐ Sí   ☐ No   5. ☐ Sí   ☐ No   7. ☐ Sí   ☐ No

3. ☐ Sí   ☐ No

F. **Describiendo el pasado: En la primaria.** Practice telling what you and others used to do in grade school, using the oral and written cues.

MODELO: (*you see*) (yo)   (*you hear*) jugar mucho → (*you say*) Jugaba mucho.

1. Rodolfo   2. (tú)   3. todos   4. (nosotros)

27. Expressing Extremes (Part 2) • Superlatives

A. **Opiniones sobre los deportes.** Expand the information in these sentences according to the model. Then give your own opinion on the line below.

MODELO: El golf es más aburrido que el fútbol. (todos) →
El golf es el deporte más aburrido de todos.
No estoy de acuerdo. El fútbol es el más aburrido.

1. El béisbol es más emocionante que el basquetbol. (todos)

     _____

     _____

2. Kobe Bryant es mejor jugador que LeBron James. (mundo)

     _____

     _____

3. El equipo de los Dallas Cowboys es peor que el de (*that of*) los 49ers. (todos)

     _____

     _____

4. El estadio (*stadium*) de Río de Janeiro, Brasil, es más grande que el de Pasadena. (mundo)

     _____

     _____

❖**B. Gramática en acción: ¡El número uno! Encuesta.** You will hear a series of statements about famous personalities. Indicate what is true, in your opinion, by checking the appropriate answers. No answers will be given. The answers you choose should be correct for you!

	ESTOY DE ACUERDO.	NO ESTOY DE ACUERDO.
1.	☐	☐
2.	☐	☐
3.	☐	☐
4.	☐	☐
5.	☐	☐
6.	☐	☐

C. Las opiniones de Margarita

Paso 1. Apuntes. You will hear a brief paragraph in which Margarita gives her opinions about a variety of topics. Listen carefully and write down her opinions. First, listen to the list of topics. (Check your answers in the Appendix.)

1. la fiesta más divertida del año: _____

2. el peor mes del año: _____

3. la mejor película del mundo: _____

4. el quehacer doméstico más aburrido: _____

❖**Paso 2.** Now pause and express your own opinions about the same topics. No answers will be given. The answers you choose should be correct for you!

En mi opinión...

1. La fiesta más divertida del año es _____

2. El peor mes del año es _____

3. La mejor película del mundo es _____

4. El quehacer doméstico más aburrido es _____

Now resume listening.

D. Sólo lo mejor... Imagine that your friend's **quinceañera** has the best of everything. Answer some questions about it, using the written cues.

MODELO: (*you see and hear*) Los vestidos son elegantes, ¿no? (*you see*) fiesta →
(*you say*) Sí, son los vestidos más elegantes de la fiesta.

1. Antonio es un chico guapo, ¿verdad? / fiesta
2. La música es buena, ¿no? / mundo
3. Y la comida, qué rica, ¿no? / mundo
4. La fiesta es divertida, ¿verdad? / año

Paso 3 Gramática

28. Getting Information (Part 2) • Summary of Interrogative Words

A. Situaciones. Imagine that you have just met Rafael Pérez, an up-and-coming baseball player. Rafael's answers are given below. Write your questions, using the appropriate interrogative from each group. Use the **Ud.** form of verbs.

¿Qué?   ¿Dónde?   ¿Adónde?   ¿De dónde?   ¿Cómo?   ¿Cuál(es)?

1. —¿_____? —Me llamo Rafael Pérez.

2. —¿_____? —(Soy) de Bayamón, Puerto Rico.

3. —¿_____? —(Vivo) En el sur de California.

4. —¿_____? —Ahora voy al estadio.

5. —¿_____? —Voy a entrenarme con el equipo.

6. —¿_____? —(Mis pasatiempos favoritos) Son jugar al tenis y nadar.

¿Cuándo?   ¿Quién(es)?   ¿Por qué?   ¿Cuánto/a?   ¿Cuántos/as?

Palabras útiles: ganar (*to earn*)   lo suficiente (*enough*)

7. —¿_____? —Empecé a jugar en 1985.

8. —¿_____? —(Mis jugadores preferidos) Son Manny Ramírez y Alex Rodríguez.

9. —¿_____? —Porque son los mejores jugadores del béisbol de todos los tiempos.

10. —¿_____? —Gano lo suficiente para vivir bien.

❖**B. Una tarjeta postal de Buenos Aires.** Here is a postcard that Sara has sent to Alfonso in the United States. Read the postcard. Then, using interrogative words, form as many questions as you can about its content to ask your classmates. You can ask questions about what it actually says as well as about what it implies.

_____

_____

_____

_____

_____

_____

Alfonso:

Hola, ¿qué tal? Hace dos días[a] que Katia y yo estamos en la Argentina. Hace mucho frío porque es agosto—en el hemisferio sur los meses de invierno son junio, julio y agosto. Los argentinos piensan que somos turistas porque llevamos camisetas y sandalias. Tienen razón... ¡y nosotras tenemos frío! ¡Qué mal escogimos[b] la ropa para este viaje! Ahora tomamos café en el hotel. Mañana pensamos comprar ropa abrigada.[c] Bueno, eso es todo por ahora.

Un abrazo[d] de
Sara

Alfonso Solís

145 Elm Street

Hudson, Ohio 44236

USA

[a]Hace... *It's been two days*   [b]¡Qué... *How badly we chose*   [c]*warm*   [d]*hug*

C. Una amiga entrometida (*nosy*). Una amiga llama a Cristina por teléfono. Completa el diálogo con las palabras interrogativas apropiadas.

AMIGA: Hola, Cristina, ¿_____[1] estás?

CRISTINA: Muy bien, gracias, ¿y tú?

AMIGA: ¡Bien, gracias! ¿_____[2] estás haciendo?

CRISTINA: Estaba estudiando con Gilberto Montero pero ya se fue.

AMIGA: ¿_____[3] es Gilberto Montero?

CRISTINA: Es un amigo de la universidad.

AMIGA: ¿Ah, sí? ¿_____[4] es?

CRISTINA: De Bogotá.

AMIGA: ¡Ah! ¡Colombiano! Y, ¿_____[5] años tiene?

CRISTINA: Veintitrés.

AMIGA: ¿_____[6] es él?

CRISTINA: Es moreno, bajo, guapo y muy simpático.

AMIGA: ¡Ajá! ¿_____[7] regresa tu amigo a su país?

CRISTINA: En julio, pero antes vamos juntos[a] a San Francisco.

AMIGA: ¡A San Francisco! ¿_____[8] van a San Francisco?

CRISTINA: Porque él quiere visitar la ciudad y yo tengo parientes allí...

AMIGA: ¿Y _____[9] van a ir? ¿En avión?

CRISTINA: No, vamos en coche.

AMIGA: ¿_____[10] coche van a usar?

CRISTINA: El coche de Gilberto. ¿Qué te parece?[b]

AMIGA: ¡Fantástico! Adiós, Cristina. Ahora tengo que llamar a Luisa.

[a]*together*   [b]¿Qué... *What do you think?*

D. Preguntas y respuestas. You will hear a series of questions. Each will be said twice. Circle the letter of the best answer to each.

1. **a.** Es de Juan.   **b.** Es negro.

2. **a.** Están en México.   **b.** Son de México.

3. **a.** Soy alto y delgado. **b.** Bien, gracias. ¿Y Ud.?

4. **a.** Mañana.   **b.** Tengo cinco.

5. **a.** Es gris.   **b.** Tengo frío.

6. **a.** Con Elvira.   **b.** Elvira va a la tienda.

7. **a.** A las nueve.   **b.** Son las nueve.

E. Gramática en acción: Un restaurante de Connecticut. You will hear a series of questions about the following ad. Circle the letter of the best response to each. First pause and read the ad.

1. **a.** El Club de Baile   **b.** El Pavo Real
2. **a.** New Haven   **b.** Garvey
3. **a.** La Orquesta Mala Fe **b.** la comida colombiana
4. **a.** el pavo   **b.** los mariscos
5. **a.** sabrosos platos   **b.** amplio y lujoso
6. **a.** Son las 11:30 de la mañana. **b.** A las 11:30 de la mañana.

F. ¿Qué dijiste? Your friend Eva has just made several statements, but you haven't understood everything she said. You will hear each statement only once. Choose either **¿Qué?** or **¿Cuál?** and form a question to elicit the information you need.

MODELO: (*you hear*) La capital del Perú es Lima.
(*you see*)   **a.** ¿qué?   **b.** ¿cuál? →
(*you say*)   **b.** ¿Cuál es la capital del Perú?

1. **a.** ¿qué?   **b.** ¿cuál?   4. **a.** ¿qué?   **b.** ¿cuál?
2. **a.** ¿qué?   **b.** ¿cuál?   5. **a.** ¿qué?   **b.** ¿cuál?
3. **a.** ¿qué?   **b.** ¿cuál?

G. Entrevista con la Srta. Moreno. Interview Ms. Moreno, an exchange student, for your campus newspaper, using the written cues. Add any necessary words. You will hear the correct question, as well as her answer. Use her name only in the first question.

MODELO: (*you hear*) uno   (*you see*)   **1.** ¿dónde? / ser →
(*you say*) Srta. Moreno, ¿de dónde es Ud.?   (*you hear*) Soy de Chile.

2. ¿dónde? / vivir   4. ¿qué? / idiomas / hablar
3. ¿dónde? / trabajar   5. ¿cuál? / ser / deporte favorito

¿Un día desastroso (*disastrous*) **o un día de suerte** (*lucky*)**?** Completa la siguiente narración haciendo estos cambios.

1. Completa la narración en el pretérito (P) o el imperfecto (I), según las indicaciones.
2. Cambia los verbos marcados con * por la forma del gerundio solamente: esquiar* → esquiando.

Hace cinco o seis semanas,[a] Fernando Sack-Soria, un joven anglohispano del sur de España,

_____[1] (**pasar:** I) unas vacaciones _____[2] (**esquiar***) en Aspen,

Colorado. Allí _____[3] (**conocer:** P) por casualidad[b] a María Soledad Villardel,

también española, pero de Barcelona. Ella _____[4] (**visitar:** I) a unos amigos que

_____ (**vivir:** I) en Aspen.

El primer encuentro[c] entre Fernando y Marisol (así llaman a María Soledad) fue casi

desastroso. Fernando _____[6] (**esquiar:** I) montaña abajo[d] a la vez[e] que

Marisol _____[7] (**estar:** I) cruzando distraída la pista de esquí.[f] Cuando Fernando

la _____[8] (**ver:** P), trató de evitar un choque.[g] _____[9] (**Doblar**[h]: P)

bruscamente[i] a la izquierda y perdió el equilibrio.[j] El joven se cayó[k] y _____[10]

(**perder:** P) uno de sus esquís. Marisol paró,[l] _____[11] (**ponerse:** P) muy avergonzada

y, casi sin pensarlo, le habló... en español.

—¡Hombre, cuánto lo siento[m]! ¡No sé dónde llevaba la cabeza[n]! ¿_____[12]

(*Tú:* **Hacerse:** P) daño[o]?

—¡No, de ninguna manera! La culpa fue mía.[p] Venía muy rápido —le dijo Fernando.

—¡Por Dios! ¡Hablas español! —contestó ella muy sorprendida.

—¡Claro! Soy español, de Jerez de la Frontera.

—Y yo, de Barcelona. ¿Qué haces por aquí?

—Ya ves, _____[13] (**esperar***) a una chica guapa con quien chocar[q] en Colorado

—dijo Fernando, _____[14] (**sacudirse***[r]) la nieve y _____[15] (**sonreír***)—.

¿Y tú?

—¿Yo? Estaba en las nubes,[s] como siempre, y casi te causé un accidente serio.

Para hacer corta la historia, desde ese día _____[16] (**hacerse**[t]: P) muy amigos y

ahora se escriben y se visitan cuando pueden.

[a]Hace... *Five or six weeks ago* [b]por... *by chance* [c]*meeting* [d]montaña... *down the mountain* [e]a... *at the same time* [f]cruzando... *crossing the ski slope absentmindedly* [g]trató... *he tried to avoid a collision* [h]*To turn* [i]*sharply* [j]*balance* [k]se... *fell down* [l]*stopped* [m]cuánto... *I'm so sorry* [n]*head* [o]Hacerse... *To hurt oneself* [p]La... *It was my fault.* [q]*to bump into* [r]*to shake off* [s]*clouds* [t]*to become*

¡Repasemos!

A. Un día típico. On a separate sheet of paper, use the following verbs or phrases in the order given to write a composition in the imperfect tense, describing a typical day when you were a high school student. Use phrases such as **casi siempre, nunca, muchas veces,** and **generalmente.**

1. despertarse
2. bañarse/ducharse
3. cepillarse los dientes
4. vestirse
5. desayunar
6. despedirse
7. ir a la escuela
8. asistir a clases
9. almorzar
10. conversar y reírse con los amigos
11. volver a casa
12. estudiar
13. sentarse a cenar a las seis
14. si no tener que estudiar
15. mirar la televisión
16. leer
17. decirle «buenas noches» a _____
18. quitarse la ropa
19. acostarse

B. ¡Nunca cambian! Mira los dibujos y describe las acciones de las personas. Usa el presente del progresivo (ahora), el pretérito (ayer) y el imperfecto (de niño/a).

Vocabulario útil

bailar
hacer ejercicio
jugar
nadar
pasear en bicicleta

Amada   Joaquín   Rosalía   Rogelio   David

1. Amada: Ahora _____

   Ayer _____

   De niña _____

2. Joaquín: Ahora _____

   Ayer _____

   De niño _____

3. Rosalía: Ahora _____

   Ayer _____

   De niña _____

4. Rogelio: Ahora _____

   Ayer _____

   De niño _____

5. David: Ahora _____

   Ayer _____

   De niño _____

C. Descripción: En casa de los Delibes. You will hear a series of statements about the following drawing. Each will be said twice. Circle **C** if the statement is true or **F** if it is false. First, pause and look at the drawing.

1. C   F
2. C   F
3. C   F
4. C   F
5. C   F
6. C   F

D. Entrevista. You will hear a series of questions. Each will be said twice. Answer based on your own experience. Pause and write the answers.

1. _____
2. _____
3. _____
4. _____
5. _____
6. _____

❖ Mi diario

Los quehaceres. ¿Qué quehaceres domésticos te tocaba hacer cuando estabas en la escuela secundaria? ¿Con qué frecuencia debías hacerlos? Escribe algo en tu diario sobre estos quehaceres.

MODELO: Yo debía hacer mi cama todos los días, ¡y lo hacía! También tenía que...

Ponte a prueba

A ver si sabes...

A. Imperfect of Regular and Irregular Verbs

    1. Completa la siguiente tabla.

	cantar	ir	leer	ser	ver
a. yo	*cantaba*				
b. nosotros					

    2. Match the following uses of the imperfect with the examples.

      a. _____ To express *time* in the past.

      b. _____ To describe a repeated or habitual action in the past.

      c. _____ To describe an action in progress.

      d. _____ To express *age* in the past.

      e. _____ To describe ongoing physical, mental, or emotional states in the past.

      f. _____ To form the past progressive.

    1. ¿Estabas estudiando?
    2. Tenía 8 años.
    3. Cenaba con mis padres cuando llamaste.
    4. Eran las doce.
    5. Siempre comíamos a las seis.
    6. No me gustaba practicar.

B. Superlatives. Completa las oraciones.

    1. (*happiest*): Soy _____ persona _____ feliz _____ mundo.

    2. (*best*): Son los _____ jugadores _____ equipo.

    3. (*worst*): Es el _____ estudiante _____ _____ clase.

C. Summary of Interrogative Words. ¿*Qué* o *cuál(es)*? Completa cada pregunta con la palabra interrogativa apropiada.

    1. ¿_____ significa (*means*) ciclismo?

    2. ¿_____ es tu teléfono?

    3. ¿_____ son tus libros?

    4. ¿_____ restaurante me recomiendas?

    5. ¿_____ es el mejor restaurante de la ciudad?

Prueba corta

A. Mafalda. Completa el párrafo con el imperfecto de los verbos entre paréntesis.

Cuando Mafalda _____ [1] (**ser**) una niña más pequeña, ella no _____ [2]
(**asistir**) a la escuela. Siempre _____ [3] (**estar**) en casa con su madre, y a veces
la _____ [4] (**ayudar**) con los quehaceres. Muchas veces, durante el día, otras
niñas que _____ [5] (**vivir**) cerca _____ [6] (**ir**) a visitarla y todas
_____ [7] (**jugar**) en el patio de su casa. Su mamá les _____ [8] (**servir**)
galletas y leche y cuando todas sus amiguitas _____ [9] (**cansarse**[a]) de jugar, ellas
_____ [10] (**volver**) a casa.

[a]*to become tired*

B. Preguntas. Completa las preguntas con la palabra o frase interrogativa apropiada.

1. ¿_____ van Uds. ahora? ¿A casa o al centro?

2. ¿_____ es la chica de pelo rubio?

3. ¿_____ se llama la profesora de francés?

4. ¿_____ están los otros estudiantes? No los veo.

5. ¿_____ es tu clase favorita este semestre? ¿Sicología o literatura?

6. ¿_____ pagaste por tu nuevo coche?

C. Recuerdos. You will hear a passage about a person's childhood memories. Then you will hear a series of questions. Circle the letter of the best answer for each.

1. **a.** Trabajaba en Panamá. **b.** Vivía en Panamá.
2. **a.** Hacía calor. **b.** No hacía calor.
3. **a.** Jugaba béisbol. **b.** Patinaba con sus amigos.
4. **a.** Iba al cine. **b.** Iba al centro.
5. **a.** Patinaba con sus padres. **b.** Patinaba con sus amigos.
6. **a.** Daba paseos en el parque. **b.** Daba paseos en el cine.
7. **a.** Su quehacer favorito era lavar los platos. **b.** No le gustaba lavar los platos.

D. Cosas de todos los días: Una niñez feliz. Practice talking about your imaginary childhood, using the written cues. When you hear the corresponding number, form sentences using the words provided in the order given, making any necessary changes or additions.

MODELO: (*you see*) **1.** (yo) / ser / niño muy feliz (*you hear*) uno →
(*you say*) Era un niño muy feliz.

2. cuando / (yo) / ser / niño, / vivir / Colombia
3. mi familia / tener / una casa / bonito / Medellín
4. mi hermana y yo / asistir / escuelas públicas
5. todos los sábados, / mi mamá / ir de compras
6. me / gustar / jugar / con mis amigos
7. los domingos / (nosotros) / reunirse / con / nuestro / abuelos

Appendix: Answers

Primera paso

Saludos y expresiones de cortesía **A.** **1.** Hola. ¿Qué tal? **2.** Buenas noches, señora Alarcón. **3.** Buenas tardes, señor Ramírez. **4.** Buenos días, señorita Cueva. **¡RECUERDA!** **1.** usted **2.** tú **3.** ¿Cómo te llamas? **4.** ¿Cómo se llama usted? **B.** **1.** ¿Qué tal? (¿Cómo estás?) **2.** ¿Y tú? **3.** hasta **4.** Hasta luego. (Hasta mañana.) **C.** **1.** Buenas **2.** está usted **3.** gracias **4.** se llama **5.** Me llamo _____. **6.** gusto **7.** Mucho gusto. (Igualmente. / Encantado/a.) **El alfabeto español** **A.** **1.** rr, ñ **2.** h **B.** **1.** ge **2.** ve (uve) **3.** equis **4.** zeta **5.** ce **6.** i **7.** Con hache **Nota comunicativa** **B. Paso 2.** **1.** C **2.** F **3.** F **4.** C **5.** C **6.** C **¿Cómo eres? (Part 1)** **H.** **1.** elegante **2.** responsable **3.** examen **4.** interesante **5.** liberal **Pronunciación y ortografía** **F.** **Paso 1.** **1.** ro*dilla* **2.** Ma*ribel* **3.** *unilateral* **4.** *salvavidas* **5.** *olvidadizo* **Paso 2.** **1.** Muñoz **2.** Robles **3.** Casimira **4.** Gamorro **Nota cultural** **A.** **1.** d **2.** a, c **3.** a, b

Segundo paso

Los números del 0 al 30; *Hay* **A.** **1.** una **2.** cuatro **3.** siete **4.** trece **5.** once **6.** un **7.** veinte **8.** veintitrés (veinte y tres) **9.** veintiséis (veinte y seis) **10.** veintiún (veinte y un) **11.** veintiuna (veinte y una) **12.** treinta **B.** **1.** 8 / ocho **2.** 11 / once **3.** 5 / cinco **4.** 6 / seis **5.** 7 / siete **6.** 22 / veintidós (veinte y dos) **7.** 30 / Treinta **Los gustos y las preferencias (Part 1)** **A.** (*Possible answers*) **1.** ¿le gusta jugar a la lotería? Sí, (No, no) me gusta. **2.** ¿le gusta la música jazz? Sí, (No, no) me gusta. **3.** ¿te gusta esquiar? Sí, (No, no) me gusta. **4.** ¿te gusta beber café? Sí, (No, no) me gusta. **¿Qué hora es?** **A.** **1.** c **2.** f **3.** d **4.** a **5.** e **6.** b **Nota comunicativa** **1.** Son las doce y veinte de la mañana. **2.** Es la una y cinco de la tarde. **3.** Son las dos en punto de la mañana. **4.** La recepción es a las siete y media de la noche. **5.** La clase es a las once menos diez de la mañana. **6.** Son las diez menos cuarto (quince) de la noche. **7.** Es la una y media de la mañana (noche). **8.** Son las ocho y cuarto (quince) de la mañana. **9.** Son las tres y veinticinco (veinte y cinco) de la tarde. **10.** Son las cuatro y diez de la mañana (noche). **¡OJO!** **a.** 4:05 P.M. **b.** 8:15 P.M. **c.** 10:50 P.M. **Lectura cultural** **1.** a **2.** c **3.** b **4.** f **5.** e **6.** d

Ponte a prueba

A ver si sabes... **A.** **1.** soy **2.** eres **3.** es **B.** **1.** Hola **2.** Buenos / Buenas / Buenas **3.** te llamas **4.** De nada / No hay de qué **C.** **1.** gusta **2.** me gusta **D.** **1.** Qué hora es **2.** Es / Son **Prueba corta** **A.** **1.** ¿Cómo se llama usted? **2.** ¿Cómo te llamas? **3.** ¿De dónde eres? **4.** Gracias. **5.** De nada. / No hay de qué. **6.** (*Possible answer*) Eres inteligente, paciente y rebelde. **7.** ¿Le gusta el jazz? **8.** ¿Te gusta el chocolate? **9.** seis / doce / quince / veintiuno / treinta **10.** las once y quince (cuarto) de la noche.

Paso 1: Vocabulario

En el salón de clase **A.** **1.** el edificio **2.** la librería **3.** la oficina **4.** la secretaria **5.** el escritorio **6.** el bolígrafo **7.** el lápiz **8.** el papel **9.** el estudiante **10.** la calculadora **11.** la ventana **12.** el cuaderno **13.** la mochila **14.** el salón de clase **15.** la silla **16.** la profesora **17.** la pizarra **18.** la puerta **19.** el libro (de texto) **20.** la biblioteca **21.** la mesa **22.** el bibliotecario **23.** el diccionario **B.** **1.** La calculadora, porque es un objeto. No es una persona. **2.** La mochila, porque es un objeto. No es un lugar. **3.** El hombre, porque es una persona. No es un objeto. **4.** El salón de clase, porque es un lugar. No es un objeto. **5.** La bibliotecaria, porque es una persona. No es un lugar. **C.** *Here is the text of Luisa's list. Check your chart against it.* A ver... para este semestre necesito algunas cosas para mis clases. Necesito cinco cuadernos, siete libros de texto, tres bolígrafos y un lápiz. También debo comprar una mochila y una calculadora. **Las materias** **A.** **1.** Gramática alemana, La novela moderna, Francés 304 **2.** Cálculo 1,

Contabilidad, Trigonometría, Computación   **3.** Antropología, Sociología urbana, Sicología del adolescente
4. Astronomía, Biología 2, Química orgánica, Física   **Nota comunicativa   A.   1.** Cuánto   **2.** A qué
hora (Cuándo)   **3.** Cómo   **4.** Cuál   **5.** Dónde   **6.** Quién   **7.** Cuándo   **8.** Qué   **B.   1.** Cómo   **2.** Quién
3. Cómo   **4.** Cuánto   **5.** Dónde   **6.** A qué hora   **7.** Qué   **Pronunciación y ortografía   A.   1.** five
2. a, e, o   **3.** i, u   **4.** strong, weak, weak   **B.   1.** es-tu-d<u>ia</u>n-te   **2.** dic-c<u>io</u>-na-r<u>io</u>   **3.** p<u>ue</u>r-ta   **4.** cua-der-no
5. bi-lin-g<u>üe</u>   **6.** gra-c<u>ia</u>s   **7.** es-cri-to-r<u>io</u>   **8.** s<u>ie</u>-te   **9.** s<u>ei</u>s   **F.   1.** *cien*ci*a*s   **2.** Patrici*o*   **3.** s*ei*s   **4.** b*ue*nos
5. *au*to   **6.** *soy*   **Lectura cultural   1.** F   **2.** F   **3.** F   **4.** C   **5.** F   **6.** C

Paso 2: Gramática

Gramática 1   A.   1. la   **2.** la   **3.** la   **4.** el   **5.** el   **6.** la   **7.** la   **8.** el   **B.   1.** un   **2.** una   **3.** un   **4.** una
5. un   **6.** una   **7.** una   **8.** un   **C.   1.** (No) Me gusta la clase de español.   **2.** (No) Me gusta la universidad.
3. (No) Me gusta la música de Bach.   **4.** (No) Me gusta el Mundo de Disney.   **5.** (No) Me gusta la
limonada.   **6.** (No) Me gusta la comida mexicana.   **7.** (No) Me gusta la física.   **8.** (No) Me gusta el
programa «American Idol».   **D.** *Español 30:* un cuaderno, un diccionario español-inglés, la novela *Don
Quijote. Cálculo 2:* un cuaderno, una calculadora, los libros de texto, la tarjeta para acceso al cuaderno
en línea   **E.   Paso 1.   1.** el   **2.** programa   **3.** el   **4.** libro   **5.** un   **6.** una   **7.** lista   **8.** novelas   **9.** el
10. problema   **11.** el   **12.** tiempo   **Gramática 2   A.   1.** las amigas   **2.** los bolígrafos   **3.** las clases
4. unos profesores   **5.** los lápices   **6.** unas extranjeras   **7.** las universidades   **8.** unos programas
B.   1. el edificio   **2.** la fiesta   **3.** una clienta   **4.** un lápiz   **5.** el papel   **6.** la condición   **7.** un problema
8. una mujer   **C.   1.** cursos   **2.** idiomas   **3.** universidades   **4.** programa residencial   **G.   1.** Hay *unos
estudiantes* en *la oficina.*   **2.** *Los diccionarios* están en *la biblioteca.*   **3.** No hay *clientes* en *la clase.*   **4.** ¿Hay
una calculadora en *la mochila?*

Paso 3: Gramática

Gramática 3   A.   1. ellas   **2.** él   **3.** yo   **4.** ellos   **5.** ellos   **6.** nosotros/as   **B.   1.** tú   **2.** vosotros / Uds.
3. Uds.   **4.** Ud.   **5.** tú / tú   **C.   1.** Él no trabaja en una oficina.   **2.** Ella no canta en japonés.   **3.** Nosotros
no tomamos cerveza en la clase.   **4.** Ella no regresa a la universidad por la noche.   **5.** Ellos no bailan
en la biblioteca.   **6.** No enseño español.   **D.   1.** hablo / canta / bailan / toman / paga / trabaja
2. escuchamos / busca / necesita   **3.** enseña / estudian / practican / regresa   **E.   1.** Él canta.   **2.** Él toca
la trompeta.   **3.** Nosotros deseamos...   **4.** Yo estudio...   **5.** Yo tomo...   **6.** Ellos toman...   **7.** Nosotros
practicamos español.   **Nota comunicativa   A.   1.** Raúl y Carmen están en el salón de clase.   **2.** Yo
estoy en la biblioteca.   **3.** Tú estás en la clase de biología.   **4.** Uds. están en el laboratorio de lenguas.
B.   1. estamos   **2.** bailan   **3.** cantan   **4.** toco   **5.** toma / escucha   **Un poco de todo   A.** (*Possible
answers*)   **1.** Sí, estudiamos español.   **2.** El Sr. (La Sra./Srta.) _____ enseña la clase.   **3.** Es de _____.
4. Hay _____ estudiantes en la clase.   **5.** Sí, (No, no) me gusta.   **6.** No, no habla inglés en la clase.
7. No, no necesitamos practicar en el laboratorio todos los días.   **8.** (La clase) Es a la (las) _____.
B.   1. (Martín) Compra libros en la librería.   **2.** Sí, hay libros en italiano.   **3.** Hay cuadernos, bolígrafos
y lápices.   **4.** Compra dos libros.   **5.** No, hablan inglés.   **6.** No, paga veintidós dólares.

Ponte a prueba

A ver si sabes...   A.   1. el / los   **2.** la / las   **3.** un / unos   **4.** una / unas   **B.   1.** busco   **2.** buscas
3. busca   **4.** buscamos   **5.** buscáis   **6.** buscan   **C.   1.** Yo no deseo tomar café.   **2.** No hablamos alemán
en la clase.   **D.   1.** nosotros estamos   **2.** estáis   **3.** están   **4.** ellos están   **Prueba corta   A.   1.** el   **2.** la
3. la   **4.** el   **5.** la   **6.** los   **7.** los   **8.** los   **B.   1.** una   **2.** unos   **3.** unos   **4.** un   **5.** una   **6.** unas   **7.** una
8. unas   **C.   1.** estudian   **2.** practico   **3.** hablamos   **4.** Toca   **5.** enseña   **6.** Necesito   **7.** regresa

CAPÍTULO 2

Paso 1: Vocabulario

La familia y los parientes   A.   1. Joaquín es el abuelo de Julián.   **2.** Julio es el primo de Julián.
3. Miguel y Mercedes son los tíos de Julián.   **4.** Estela y Julio son los primos de Julián.   **5.** Juanita es
la hermana de Julián.   **6.** Pedro y Carmen son los padres de Julián.   **7.** Chispa es el perro de Julián.
8. Tigre es el gato de Julián.   **B.   1.** sobrino   **2.** tía   **3.** abuelos   **4.** abuela   **5.** nieta   **6.** parientes

7. mascota **Nota cultural** **1.** c **2.** b **C.** Gregorio = el abuelo; Julia = la abuela; Marta = la tía; Juan = el tío; Sara = la madre; Manuel = el padre; Elena = la prima; Juanito = el primo; Manolito = el hermano **Los números del 31 al 100** **A.** **1.** cien **2.** treinta y una **3.** cincuenta y siete **4.** noventa y un **5.** setenta y seis **B.** El inventario. *45* mochilas; *99* lápices; *52* cuadernos; *74* novelas; *31* calculadoras; *100* libros de español **Los adjetivos** **B.** **1.** nuevo / pequeño **2.** grande / viejo **3.** gordo / perezoso / viejo **4.** guapo / joven / moreno **C.** **1.** No, Diana es joven y morena. **2.** No, Luis tiene 48 años. **3.** No, Carlos es soltero y delgado. **4.** No, a Luis le gusta escuchar la música clásica. **5.** No, es el siete, catorce, veintiuno, setenta y siete. **D.** **1.** bajo / feo / listo / trabajador **2.** soltero / viejo / simpático / moreno **E.** (*Possible answers*) **1.** Will Ferrell es simpático, cómico, y alto. **2.** Antonio Banderas es moreno, guapo, casado y simpático. **3.** Madonna es rica, rubia, extrovertida, independiente, rebelde y arrogante. **4.** Penélope Cruz es morena, guapa, inteligente y rica. **Pronunciación y ortografía** **A.** **1.** doctor **2.** mujer **3.** mochila **4.** actor **5.** permiso **6.** posible **7.** general **8.** profesores **9.** universidad **10.** Carmen **11.** Isabel **12.** biblioteca **13.** usted **14.** libertad **15.** origen **16.** animal **D.** **1.** con - *trol* **2.** e - le - *fan* - te **3.** mo - nu - men - *tal* **4.** com - pa - ñe - ra **5.** *bue* - nos **6.** us - *ted* **Lectura cultural** **1.** F **2.** F **3.** C **4.** C **5.** F **6.** C

Paso 2: Gramática

Gramática 4 **A.** **1.** bonita, grande, interesante **2.** delgados, jóvenes, simpáticos **3.** delgada, pequeña, trabajadora **4.** altas, impacientes, inteligentes **B.** **1.** alemana **2.** italiano **3.** estadounidense **4.** inglesa **5.** mexicana **6.** ingleses **7.** francesas **C.** **1.** Ana busca otro coche italiano. **2.** Buscamos una motocicleta alemana. **3.** Paco busca las otras novelas francesas. **4.** Busco el gran drama inglés *Romeo y Julieta.* **5.** Jorge busca una esposa ideal. **D.** *Marta:* fiel, amable, simpática; *Mario:* fiel, amable, simpático. **Gramática 5** **A.** **1.** soy de Barcelona **2.** son de Valencia **3.** eres de Granada **4.** somos de Sevilla **5.** son de Toledo **6.** sois de Burgos **C.** **1.** —¿De quién son los libros? —Son de la profesora. **2.** —¿De quién es la mochila? —Es de Cecilia. **3.** —¿De quién son los bolígrafos? —Son del Sr. Alonso. **4.** —¿De quién es la casa? —Es de los Sres. Olivera. **D.** **1.** El programa de «Weight Watchers» es para Kirstie Alley. Es gorda. **2.** La casa grande es para los Sres. Walker. Tienen cuatro niños. **3.** El dinero es para mi hermano. Desea comprar un *iPod.* **4.** El televisor nuevo es para mis abuelos. Su televisor es viejo. **E.** **1.** es / hija **2.** es / doctora **3.** son / México **4.** es / inteligente / alto

Paso 3: Gramática

Gramática 6 **¡RECUERDA!** **1.** (Ella) Es la hermana de Isabel. **2.** (Ellos) Son los parientes de Mario. **3.** (Ellos) Son los abuelos de Marta. **A.** **1.** Mi **2.** Nuestra **3.** mis **4.** mis **5.** Mis **6.** mi **B.** **1.** Sí, es su suegra. **2.** Sí, es nuestro hermano. **3.** Sí, son sus padres. **4.** Sí, somos sus primos. **5.** Sí, es su sobrina. **6.** Sí, soy su nieto. **Gramática 7** **A.** **1.** Luis come mucho. **2.** Gloria estudia francés. **3.** José y Ramón beben Coca-Cola. **4.** Inés escribe una carta. **5.** Roberto mira un vídeo. **6.** Carlos lee un periódico. **C.** **Paso 1.** **1.** asisto **2.** Vivo **3.** Bebo **4.** como **5.** Leo **6.** escribo **7.** Creo **8.** aprendo **9.** comprendo **Paso 2.** **1.** asiste **2.** vive **3.** bebe / come **4.** lee

Ponte a prueba

A ver si sabes... **A.** **1. a.** casada **b.** casados **2. a.** grandes **b.** sentimentales **3. a.** mexicano **b.** mexicanas **c.** mexicanos **d.** francesa **e.** francés **f.** francesas **g.** española **h.** español **i.** españoles **B.** **1.** c **2.** a **3.** b **4.** d **C.** **1.** mi hermano **2.** su tío **3.** nuestra abuela **4.** su casa **D.** **1.** leo **2.** leemos **3.** leéis **4.** escribes **5.** escribe **6.** escriben **Prueba corta** **A.** **1.** italiano **2.** francesa **3.** alemán **4.** inglesas **B.** **1.** es **2.** soy / eres **3.** son **4.** somos **C.** **1.** mi **2.** mi **3.** Mis **4.** su **5.** nuestra **6.** sus **7.** tu (su) **D.** **1.** comprendemos / habla **2.** Escuchas / estudias **3.** lee **4.** venden **5.** recibe **6.** bebo **7.** asistimos

CAPÍTULO 3

Paso 1: Vocabulario

De compras: La ropa **A.** **1. a.** un traje **b.** una camisa **c.** una corbata **d.** unos calcetines **e.** unos zapatos **f.** un impermeable **2. a.** un abrigo **b.** un vestido **c.** unas medias **d.** una bolsa **e.** un sombrero

B. 1. centro   2. almacén   3. venden de todo   4. fijos   5. de última moda   6. tiendas   7. rebajas   8. mercado   9. regatear   10. gangas   **C.** 1. algodón   2. corbatas / seda   3. suéteres / faldas / lana   4. cuero   **¿De qué color es?** **A.** 1. verdes   2. verde / blanca / roja   3. roja / blanca / azul   4. anaranjada / amarillo   5. gris   6. morado   7. rosado   8. color café   **Más allá del número 100** **A.** 1. 111   2. 476   3. 15.714   4. 700.500   5. 1.965   6. 1.000.013   **B.** 1. veintiocho (veinte y ocho) mil quinientos diez pesos   2. catorce mil seiscientos veinticinco (veinte y cinco) pesos   3. siete mil trescientos cincuenta y cuatro pesos   4. tres mil setecientos ochenta y dos pesos   5. mil ochocientos cuarenta y un pesos   6. novecientos veinte mil pesos   **C.** 1. 1.136   2. 567   3. 9.081   4. 3.329   5. 111   6. 843   **Pronunciación y ortografía** **A.** 3. matrícula   4. bolígrafo   7. Pérez   9. alemán   **C.** *The following words require a written accent:* 1. métrica   4. Rosalía   6. sabiduría   7. jóvenes   8. mágico   **Lectura cultural** 1. Tegucigalpa   2. pobre   3. maya-quiché   4. calendario   5. Tikal   6. volcanes   7. Copán   8. punta

Paso 2: Gramática

Gramática 8 ¡RECUERDA! 1. Este   2. Estos   3. esta   4. estas   **A.** 1. Este   2. ese   3. aquel   4. (*Possible answer*) este / es económico   **B.** 1. Sí, esta chaqueta es de Miguel.   2. Sí, esos calcetines son de Daniel.   3. Sí, ese impermeable es de Margarita.   4. Sí, estos guantes son de Ceci.   5. Sí, este reloj es de Pablo.   6. Sí, esos papeles son de David.   **Gramática 9** **A.** **Paso 1.** 1. Quieres   2. puedo   3. tengo   4. Prefiero   5. vengo   6. quiero   **Paso 2.** (*Verb forms*) Quieren / podemos / tenemos / Preferimos / venimos por Uds. / queremos   **B.** 1. Tengo sueño.   2. Tengo que estudiar mucho.   3. Tengo miedo   4. Tengo prisa.   5. Tengo razón.   **C.** 1. ¿A qué hora vienes a la universidad mañana?   2. Vengo a las ocho y media. ¿Por qué?   3. ¿Puedo venir contigo? No tengo coche.   4. ¡Cómo no! Paso por ti a las siete y media. ¿Tienes ganas de practicar el vocabulario ahora?   5. No. Ahora prefiero comer algo. ¿Quieres venir? Podemos estudiar para el examen después.   6. Buena idea. Creo que Raúl y Alicia quieren estudiar con nosotros.   **D.** 1. prefiero   2. tengo   3. Quiero   4. puedo   5. Puedes   6. tiene   7. vienes

Paso 3: Gramática

Gramática 10 **A.** 1. va   2. van   3. vas   4. vamos   5. voy   **B.** 1. Eduardo y Graciela van a buscar...   2. David y yo vamos a comprar...   3. Ignacio y Pepe van a ir...   4. Por eso vamos a necesitar...   5. Desgraciadamente Julio no va a preparar...   **C.** 1. Vamos a estudiar esta tarde.   2. Vamos a mirar en el Almacén Juárez.   3. Vamos a buscar algo más barato.   4. Vamos a descansar ahora.   **D.** 1. c   2. a   3. a   4. c   **Un poco de todo** **A.** 1. la   2. quiere   3. ir   4. pequeñas   5. venden   6. especiales   7. grandes   8. prefiere   9. españolas   10. esta   11. especializadas   12. populares   13. existen   14. elegantes   15. famosos   **B.** 1. Tengo   2. ganas   3. miedo   4. razón   5. sueño   **C.** 1. estás   2. estos   3. tus   4. esos   5. nuestro   6. vas   7. voy   8. vamos   9. nosotras   10. tu   11. esta   12. queremos   13. prisa   14. Adiós   **D.** *The following items should be circled: the plain pants, the tie, the plaid shirt, and the Stephen King novel.*

Ponte a prueba

A ver si sabes... **A.** 1. este   2. estos   3. esa   4. esos   5. aquella   6. aquellos   **B.** 1. **a.** puedo / puede / podemos   **b.** quiero / queréis / queremos   **c.** vengo / viene / venís / venimos   2. **a.** tener miedo (de)   **b.** tener razón (no tener razón)   **c.** tener ganas (de)   **d.** tener que   **C.** 1. Ellos van a comprar...   2. ¿No vas a comer?   3. Van a tener...   4. Voy a ir...   **Prueba corta** **A.** 1. Quiero comprar ese impermeable negro.   2. ¿Buscas este traje gris?   3. Juan va a comprar esa chaqueta blanca.   4. Mis padres trabajan en aquella tienda nueva.   **B.** 1. venimos / tenemos   2. prefieres (quieres) / prefiero (quiero)   3. tiene   4. pueden   **C.** 1. Roberto va a llevar traje y corbata.   2. Voy a buscar unas chanclas baratas.   3. Vamos a tener una fiesta.   4. ¿Vas a venir a casa esta noche?   **F.** 1. mil ciento veinticinco dólares   2. doscientos sesenta y cinco dólares   3. trescientos cuarenta y nueve dólares   4. lana   5. seda   6. camisa   7. dos dólares

Paso 1: Vocabulario

¿Qué día es hoy? A. (*Possible answers*) **1.** El lunes también va a (tiene que) hablar con el consejero. **2.** El martes va a (tiene que) ir al dentista. **3.** El miércoles va a (tiene que) estudiar física. **4.** El jueves va a (tiene que) ir al laboratorio de física. **5.** El viernes tiene un examen y va a cenar con Diana. **6.** El sábado va (a ir) de compras y va a ir a un concierto. **7.** El domingo va a ir a la playa. **B. 1.** fin / el sábado / el domingo **2.** El lunes **3.** miércoles **4.** jueves **5.** pasado mañana **6.** el / los **7.** próxima **C. Paso 1.** *lunes:* mañana: 10:45 A.M., clase de conversación *martes:* mañana: 8:30 A.M., dentista; 10:15 A.M., librería; tarde: 3:00 P.M., clase de español *miércoles:* mañana: 9:00 A.M., profesora Díaz; tarde: 1:00 P.M., biblioteca *jueves:* tarde: 3:00 P.M., clase de español *viernes:* mañana: 10:45 A.M., clase de conversación; tarde: 7:30 P.M., fiesta **Los muebles, los cuartos y otras partes de la casa (Part 1) A. 1.** la sala **2.** el comedor **3.** la cocina **4.** la alcoba **5.** el baño **6.** el garaje **7.** el patio **8.** la piscina **9.** el jardín **¿Cuándo? Las preposiciones (Part 1) A.** (*Possible answers*) **1.** Tengo sueño antes de descansar. **2.** Regreso a casa después de asistir a clase. **3.** Tengo ganas de comer antes de estudiar. **4.** Preparo la comida después de ir al supermercado. **5.** Lavo los platos después de comer. **Pronunciación y ortografía B. 1.** Alberto viene en veinte minutos. **2.** ¿Trabajas el viernes o el sábado? **3.** La abuela de Roberto es baja. **4.** No hay un baile el jueves, ¿verdad? **5.** ¿Vas a llevar esa corbata? **Lectura cultural 1.** El Salvador **2.** volcanes / lagos **3.** cuatro / cuatrocientos **4.** pirámide / pelota **5.** activos **6.** salada / tiburones **7.** indígena / española

Paso 2: Gramática

Gramática 11 A. 1. veo **2.** salimos **3.** Pongo **4.** traigo **5.** oímos **6.** hago **7.** Salgo **B. 1.** pongo (oigo) **2.** hago **3.** trae **4.** salimos **5.** Vemos **6.** salimos **E. Paso 1. 1.** salir **2.** ponen **3.** hacen **4.** traer **Gramática 12 ¡RECUERDA! 1.** quiero / quieres / quiere / quieren **2.** prefiero / prefiere / preferimos / prefieren **3.** puedo / puedes / podemos / pueden **A. 1.** piensan / pensamos / piensas **2.** volvemos / vuelve / vuelven **3.** pide / piden / pedimos **B. 1.** Sale de casa a las siete y cuarto (quince). **2.** Su primera clase empieza a las ocho. **3.** Si no entiende la lección, hace muchas preguntas. **4.** Con frecuencia almuerza en la cafetería. **5.** A veces pide una hamburguesa y un refresco. **6.** Los lunes y miércoles juega al tenis con un amigo. **7.** Su madre sirve la cena a las seis. **8.** Hace la tarea por la noche y duerme siete horas.

Paso 3: Gramática

Gramática 13 B. 1. me / se **2.** se **3.** te **4.** Se **5.** nos / nos **6.** te **C. 1.** Nos despertamos... **2.** Nos vestimos después de ducharnos. **3.** Nunca nos sentamos... **4.** ... asistimos... y nos divertimos. **5.** ... hacemos la tarea. **6.** ... tenemos sueño, nos cepillamos los dientes y nos acostamos. **7.** Nos dormimos... **Un poco de todo A. 1.** me levanto **2.** tengo **3.** despertarme **4.** quiero **5.** jugar **6.** empezamos **7.** pongo **8.** salgo **9.** puedo **10.** almorzamos **11.** pierde **12.** tiene **13.** pierdo **14.** tengo **15.** vuelvo

Ponte a prueba

A ver si sabes... A. 1. hago / haces / hacen **2.** traigo / traes / traemos **3.** oigo / oímos / oyen **4.** pongo / pones / ponemos / ponen **5.** veo / ves / vemos / ven **6.** salgo / sales / salimos / salen **B. 1. a.** ie **b.** ue **c.** i **2.** nosotros / vosotros **3. a.** piensas / servir **b.** empiezo a **c.** volver a **d.** pedir **C. 1. a.** me **b.** te **c.** se **d.** nos **e.** os **f.** se **2. a.** Yo me acuesto tarde. **b.** ¿Cuándo te sientas a comer? **c.** Yo me visto en cinco minutos. **Prueba corta A. 1.** se duermen **2.** sentarme / oigo **3.** me divierto **4.** levantarte **5.** se pone **6.** haces **7.** salimos **B.** (*Possible answers*) **1.** me despierto / me levanto / me visto **2.** me baño / me afeito / me cepillo los dientes **3.** el sofá, el sillón, la mesa **4.** un escritorio, una lámpara, una cama **5.** Almuerzo en la cocina. / Duermo en la alcoba. / Estudio en la sala. **E. 1.** 4 **2.** 2 **3.** 4 metros por 5 metros **4.** muchas escuelas **5.** un parque **6.** calle Miraflores, número 246

CAPÍTULO 5

Paso 1: Vocabulario

¿Qué tiempo hace hoy? A. 1. Hace (mucho) sol. **2.** Hace (mucho) calor. **3.** Hace fresco.
4. Llueve. **5.** Hace (mucho) frío. **6.** Hay mucha contaminación. **B. 1.** Llueve. **2.** Hace (mucho) frío.
3. Hace (mucho) calor. **4.** Hace fresco. **5.** Hace (muy) buen tiempo. **6.** (*Possible answer*) Hay mucha
contaminación. **Los meses y las estaciones del año A. 1.** el primero de abril **2.** junio / julio /
agosto **3.** invierno **4.** llueve **5.** otoño **6.** cuatro de julio **7.** nieva **8.** enero / mayo **¿Dónde está?**
Las preposiciones (Part 2) B. 1. entre **2.** al norte **3.** al sur **4.** al este **5.** al oeste **6.** lejos **7.** cerca
8. en **9.** al oeste (cerca) **Pronunciación y ortografía ¡RECUERDA!** r / rr **A. 1.** Rosa **3.** perro
4. Roberto **5.** rebelde **6.** un horrible error **7.** una persona rara **8.** Raquel es rubia **Lectura cultural**
A. 1. neutral **2.** ejército **3.** veinticinco **4.** Arenal / bañarse **5.** Sarchí / pintadas **6.** café

Paso 2: Gramática

Gramática 14 A. 1. c **2.** a **3.** d **4.** f **5.** b **6.** e **B. 1.** durmiendo **2.** pidiendo **3.** sirviéndose
4. leyendo **5.** almorzando / divirtiéndose **C. 1.** Mis padres (hijos) están jugando al golf, pero yo
estoy corriendo en un maratón. **2.** Mis padres (hijos) están mirando la tele, pero yo estoy aprendiendo a
esquiar. **3.** Mis padres (hijos) están leyendo el periódico, pero yo estoy escuchando música. **4.** Mis
padres (hijos) están acostándose (se están acostando), pero yo estoy vistiéndome (me estoy vistiendo)
para salir. **D. 1.** está trabajando. **2.** está haciendo **3.** Está descansando **4.** Está oyendo **5.** leyendo
6. tomando **Gramática 15 ¡RECUERDA! 1.** estar / están **2.** ser / es **3.** ser / es **4.** ser / son / es
5. estar / está / estás / Están **6.** ser / somos / es **7.** ser / Son **A. 1.** eres / Soy **2.** son / son
3. son / están **4.** es / estar / es **5.** está / Estoy / está **6.** es / es **B.** (*Possible answers*) **1.** estoy
aburrido/a **2.** estoy contento/a **3.** estoy nervioso/a **4.** estoy preocupado/a **5.** estoy molesto/a
6. estoy cansado/a **7.** estoy triste **C. 1.** estás **2.** estoy **3.** son **4.** están **5.** Son **6.** Son **7.** es
8. es **9.** estar

Paso 3: Gramática

Gramática 16 B. 1. Ceci es más delgada que Laura. **2.** Ceci es más atlética que Roberto. **3.** Roberto
es más introvertido que Laura. **4.** Ceci es tan alta como Laura. **5.** Roberto es tan estudioso como
Laura. **6.** Roberto es tan moreno como Ceci. **C. 1.** Sí, el cine es tan alto como la tienda. **2.** El café es
el (edificio) más pequeño de todos. **3.** El hotel es el más alto (de todos). **4.** No, el cine es más alto que
el café. **5.** No, el hotel es más grande que el cine. **D. Paso 2. 1.** tan / como **2.** menos / que
3. tanto / como **4.** tantos / como **Un poco de todo A. 1.** Carmen está ocupada y no puede ir al
cine esta noche. **2.** Esa camisa está sucia. Debes ponerte otra. **3.** Esas tiendas están cerradas ahora.
No podemos entrar. **4.** Debemos llevar el paraguas. Está lloviendo. **5.** Mis primos son de Lima; ahora
están visitando a sus tíos en Texas, pero su madre está enferma y tienen que regresar a su país la semana
que viene. **B. 1.** veintiún **2.** diecinueve **3.** ese **4.** que **5.** que **6.** que **7.** tanto **8.** como **9.** de
10. doscientos dólares **11.** porque **12.** estar **13.** de **14.** ciento cincuenta dólares **15.** pagar

Ponte a prueba

A ver si sabes... A. cepillándose / divirtiéndose / escribiendo / estudiando / leyendo / poniendo /
sirviendo **B. 1.** f **2.** a **3.** c **4.** i **5.** h **6.** b **7.** g **8.** e **9.** d **C. 1.** más / que **2.** tantos / como
3. mejor **4.** tan / como **5.** menos / que **Prueba corta A. 1.** Estoy mirando un programa. **2.** Juan
está leyendo el periódico. **3.** Marta está sirviendo el café ahora. **4.** Los niños están durmiendo.
5. ¿Estás almorzando ahora? **B. 1.** está / Estoy **2.** eres / Soy **3.** están / Estamos **4.** Estás / estoy
5. está **C. 1.** Arturo tiene tantos libros como Roberto. **2.** Arturo es más gordo que Roberto. **3.** Roberto
es más alto que Arturo. **4.** Roberto es menor (tiene dos años menos) que Arturo. **5.** Arturo tiene menos
perros que Roberto.

CAPÍTULO 6

Paso 1: Vocabulario

La comida y las comidas **A.** **1.** jugo / huevos / pan / té / leche **2.** camarones / langosta **3.** papas fritas **4.** agua **5.** helado **6.** carne / verduras **7.** queso **8.** lechuga / tomate **9.** zanahorias **10.** arroz **11.** hambre / galletas **12.** sed **¿Qué sabes y a quién conoces?** **B.** **1.** conocen **2.** sé **3.** Sabes **4.** saber **5.** Conocemos / conozco **6.** conocer **C.** **1.** al **2.** a **3.** A **4.** a **5.** Ø **6.** al **7.** Ø **8.** a **D.** **Paso 1.** ENRIQUE: *Sí:* bailar, a mis padres; *No:* a Juan, jugar al tenis, esta ciudad. ROBERTO: *Sí:* bailar, jugar al tenis, a mis padres; *No:* a Juan, esta ciudad. SUSANA: *Sí:* jugar al tenis, a mis padres, esta ciudad; *No:* bailar, a Juan. **Paso 2.** **1.** saben **2.** no sabe **3.** conoce **4.** no conocen **Lectura cultural** **1.** dieciséis / diecinueve **2.** colonial **3.** estadounidense **4.** calipso / Trinidad **5.** parques / reservas **6.** San Blas / las molas

Paso 2: Gramática

Gramática 17 **A.** **1.** Yo lo preparo. **2.** Yo voy a comprarlos. / Yo los voy a comprar. **3.** Dolores va a hacerlas. / Dolores las va a hacer. **4.** Juan los trae. **5.** Yo los invito. **B.** **1.** Los despierta a las seis y media. **2.** El padre lo levanta. **3.** La madre lo baña. **C.** *Here are the foods that were mentioned:* **1.** las galletas **2.** el atún **3.** el agua mineral **4.** los frijoles **Nota comunicativa** (*Possible answers*) **1.** Acaba de cantar y bailar. **2.** Acabamos de comer. **3.** Acaba de traer la cuenta. **4.** Acaba de enseñar. **Gramática 18** **B.** **1.** No, no voy a hacer nada interesante. **2.** No, nunca (jamás) salgo con nadie los sábados. **3.** No, no tengo ninguno (ningún nuevo amigo). **4.** No, ninguna (de esas chicas) es mi amiga. **5.** No, nadie cena conmigo nunca (jamás). **C.** **1.** ... quiero (comer) algo. La comida aquí es buena. **2.** ... alguien. **3.** ... siempre cenamos en un restaurante bueno. **4.** ... algunos platos sabrosos.

Paso 3: Gramática

Gramática 19 **A.** **Paso 1.** *Título:* acostumbre **1.** compruebe **2.** encargue **3.** no lo haga / déjelas **4.** no comente / deje **5.** no los deje **Paso 2.** **1.** your house is well locked **2.** your mail **3.** someone you know **4.** when you will return **5.** in your house **B.** (*Possible answers*) **1.** Entonces, coman algo. **2.** Entonces, beban (tomen) algo. **3.** Entonces, estudien. **4.** Entonces, ciérrenlas. **5.** Entonces, lleguen (salgan) (más) temprano. **6.** Entonces, no sean impacientes. **C.** **1.** empiécenla ahora **2.** no la sirvan todavía **3.** llámenlo ahora **4.** no lo hagan todavía **5.** tráiganlas ahora **6.** no la pongan todavía **D.** **Paso 2.** **1.** sirva **2.** añada **3.** mezcle **4.** corte **Nota comunicativa** **Paso 1.** **1.** *You should have checked:* hacer reservaciones, pedir el pescado, llegar temprano, pagar con tarjeta de crédito, pagar al contado **Un poco de todo** **A.** **1.** conoces **2.** al **3.** lo **4.** conozco **5.** sé **6.** siempre **7.** tampoco **8.** El **B.** (*Possible answers*) **1.** Voy a prepararla (La voy a preparar) este sábado. **2.** Sí, pienso invitarlos (los pienso invitar). **3.** Sí, puedes llamarlas (las puedes llamar) si quieres. **4.** Sí, me puedes ayudar (puedes ayudarme). **5.** Sí, las necesito. **C.** **1.** ¡Laven los platos! / Ya los estamos lavando. (Ya estamos lavándolos.) **2.** ¡Hagan la ensalada! / Ya la estamos haciendo. (Ya estamos haciéndola.) **3.** ¡Preparen las verduras! / Ya las estamos preparando. (Ya estamos preparándolas.) **4.** ¡Empiecen la paella! / Ya la estamos empezando. (Ya estamos empezándola.)

Ponte a prueba

A ver si sabes... **A.** **1. a.** te **b.** lo **c.** la **d.** nos **e.** las **2. a.** Yo lo traigo. **b.** ¡Tráigalo! **c.** ¡No lo traiga! **d.** Estamos esperándolo. / Lo estamos esperando. **e.** Voy a llamarlo. / Lo voy a llamar. **B.** **1.** nadie **2.** tampoco **3.** nunca / jamás **4.** nada **5.** ningún detalle **C.** **1.** piense **2.** vuelva **3.** dé **4.** vaya **5.** busque **6.** esté **7.** sepa **8.** diga **Prueba corta** **A.** **1.** conozco **2.** conoces **3.** sé **4.** sabe **B.** **1.** Quiero comer algo. **2.** Busco a alguien. **3.** Hay algo para beber. **4.** —Yo conozco a algunos de sus amigos. —Yo también. **C.** (*Possible answers*) **1.** No, no voy a pedirla. (No, no la voy a pedir.) Sí, las quiero. **3.** No, no lo tomo por la noche. **4.** Yo la preparo. **D.** **1.** Compren **2.** hagan **3.** Traigan **4.** pongan **5.** Llámenlo **6.** lo sirvan

Paso 1: Vocabulario

De viaje **B.** **1.** boleto **2.** ida y vuelta **3.** bajar / escala **4.** equipaje **5.** el control de la seguridad **6.** pasajeros **7.** guarda **8.** vuelo / demora **9.** salida / cola / subir **10.** asistentes **C.** (*Possible answers*) **1.** En la sala de espera (En la sección de no fumar) un hombre está durmiendo; en la sección de fumar dos pasajeros están fumando y una mujer está leyendo el periódico. **2.** Los pasajeros están haciendo cola para facturar su equipaje. El vuelo 68 a Madrid hace una parada en Chicago. **3.** Está lloviendo. Un hombre está corriendo porque está atrasado. Los otros pasajeros están subiendo al avión. **4.** Los asistentes de vuelo están sirviendo algo de beber. Los pasajeros están mirando una película. **De vacaciones** **A.** **Paso 1.** **1.** las montañas **2.** la tienda de campaña **3.** la playa **4.** la camioneta **5.** el mar / el océano **Paso 2.** (*Possible answers*) **1.** El padre saca fotos (de la madre). **2.** La madre toma el sol en la playa. **3.** Las hijas juegan en la playa. **4.** El hijo nada en el mar/océano. **5.** Toda la familia hace *camping*. **Nota comunicativa** **1.** c **2.** b **3.** c **4.** b **5.** a **Pronunciación y ortografía** **D.** **1.** Don Guillermo es viejo y generoso. **2.** Por lo general, los jóvenes son inteligentes. **3.** Juan estudia geografía y geología. **4.** A mi amiga Gloria le gustan los gatos. **E.** **1.** [x] **2.** [x], [g] **3.** [x] **4.** [x] **5.** [g] **6.** [x], [g] **7.** [g] **8.** [x], [g] **Lectura cultural** **1.** F **2.** F **3.** F **4.** F **5.** C **6.** C

Paso 2: Gramática

Gramática 20 **A.** **1.** damos **2.** da **3.** dan **4.** das **5.** doy **6.** digo **7.** dice **8.** dicen **9.** dices **10.** decimos **B.** **1.** Te compro regalos. **2.** Te mando tarjetas postales. **3.** Te invito a almorzar. **4.** Te explico la tarea. **C.** **1.** ¿Le presto el dinero? **2.** ¿Le digo la verdad? **3.** ¿Les doy una fiesta? **4.** ¿Le pido ayuda al profesor? **5.** ¿Les doy más? **D.** En el mostrador: 2; En el control de seguridad: 1 **Gramática 21** **A.** **1.** te gusta **2.** les gusta **3.** me gustan **4.** nos gusta / le gusta **5.** les gusta **B.** **1.** A su padre le gustan las vacaciones en las montañas. **2.** A su madre le encantan los cruceros. **3.** A sus hermanos les gustan los deportes acuáticos. **4.** A nadie le gusta viajar en autobús. **5.** A Ernesto le gusta sacar fotos.

Paso 3: Gramática

Gramática 22 **A.** *yo:* **1.** volví **2.** Me hice **3.** comí **4.** Recogí **5.** metí **6.** di *tú:* **1.** asististe **2.** Te acostaste **3.** empezaste **4.** fuiste **5.** Saliste **6.** volviste *Eva:* **1.** se casó **2.** fue **3.** se matriculó **4.** empezó **5.** regresó **6.** viajó **7.** vio **8.** pasó *Mi amiga y yo:* **1.** pasamos **2.** Vivimos **3.** asistimos **4.** hicimos **5.** Visitamos **6.** caminamos **7.** comimos **8.** vimos *Dos científicos:* **1.** fueron **2.** Salieron **3.** llegaron **4.** viajaron **5.** vieron **6.** tomaron **7.** gustaron **8.** volvieron **C.** **1.** F: Viajó en avión. **2.** Falso: Fue largo. **3.** C **4.** C **5.** F: A Elisa le gustó mucho el viaje. **Un poco de todo** **A.** (*Possible answers*) **1.** Les mandé tarjetas postales a mis abuelos. (No le mandé tarjetas postales a nadie. / Nadie me mandó tarjetas postales a mí.) **2.** Le regalé flores a mi madre. (No le regalé flores a nadie. / Nadie me regaló flores a mí.) **3.** Les recomendé un restaurante a mis amigos. (No le recomendé un restaurante a nadie. / Nadie me recomendó un restaurante a mí.) **4.** Le ofrecí ayuda a una amiga. (No le ofrecí ayuda a nadie. / Nadie me ofreció ayuda a mí.) **5.** Le presté una maleta a mi hermano. (No le presté una maleta a nadie. / Nadie me prestó una maleta a mí.) **6.** Le hice un pastel a un amigo. (No le hice un pastel a nadie. / Nadie me hizo un pastel a mí.) **B.** **1.** Salí / me quedé / Almorcé / fui / Volví / Cené / miré / subí / me quejé / hice / dormí **2.** fueron / hicieron / dio / fue / se hizo / escribieron / volvieron **3.** Busqué / dieron / perdí / pagaron / gasté / hice / descansé **4.** Pasamos / Comimos / vimos / jugamos

Ponte a prueba

A ver si sabes... **A.** **1. a.** Siempre le digo... **b.** Le estoy diciendo... / Estoy diciéndole... **c.** Le voy a decir... / Voy a decirle... **d.** Dígale... **e.** No le diga... **2. a.** doy / da / damos / dais / dan **b.** digo / dices / dice / decís / dicen **B.** **1.** ¿Les gusta viajar? **2.** A mí no me gusta quejarme. **3.** A Juan le gustan los aeropuertos. **C.** **1.** di / dio / dimos / disteis / / dieron **2.** hablé / hablaste / hablamos / hablasteis / hablaron **3.** hice / hiciste / hizo / hicisteis / hicieron **4.** fui / fuiste / fue / fuimos /

fueron   **5.** salí / saliste / salió / salimos / salisteis   **Prueba corta   A.   1.** le   **2.** nos   **3.** les   **4.** me
5. te   **B.   1.** les gustan   **2.** le gusta   **3.** me gusta   **4.** nos gustan   **5.** te gusta   **C.   1.** mandaste
2. empecé   **3.** hizo   **4.** Fueron   **5.** Oíste   **6.** volvieron   **7.** dio   **E.   1.** un boleto de ida y vuelta
2. el doce de noviembre   **3.** el veintisiete de noviembre   **4.** la sección de no fumar, clase turística
5. Chicago   **6.** uno que esté cerca de la playa y que tenga aire acondicionado   **7.** Hotel Presidente

CAPÍTULO 8

Paso 1: Vocabulario

La fiesta de Javier   B.   1. el Día de Año Nuevo   **2.** la Navidad   **3.** La Pascua   **4.** la Nochebuena   **5.** el
Cinco de Mayo   **C.   1.** Es el primero de abril.   **2.** Les hace bromas.   **3.** Significa *lion*.   **Las emociones
y los estados afectivos.   A.** (*Possible answers*)   **1.** me pongo avergonzado/a   **2.** se enojan (se ponen
irritados)   **3.** se enferman / se quejan   **4.** se portan   **5.** discutir   **Nota comunicativa.   1.** Sí, me parece
larguísima.   **2.** Sí, son riquísimos.   **3.** Sí, me siento cansadísimo/a.   **4.** Sí, es carísima.   **5.** Sí, fueron
dificilísimas.   **Pronunciación y ortografía   C.   1.** quemar   **2.** quince   **3.** campaña   **4.** compras
5. coqueta   **6.** comedor   **Lectura cultural   1.** 1959   **2.** 1898   **3.** éxodo   **4.** analfabetismo   **5.** El Morro
6. el béisbol   **7.** plantaciones de tabaco y azúcar   **8.** la africana

Paso 2: Gramática

Gramática 23   A.   Paso 1.   1. C   **2.** F   **3.** C   **4.** F   **5.** F   **6.** C   **7.** F   **8.** F   **9.** F   **Paso 2.   2.** La
Unión Soviética puso un satélite en el espacio antes que los Estados Unidos.   **4.** En 1492...   **5.** Hitler
sí quiso dominar Europa.   **7.** Los españoles llevaron el maíz y el tomate a Europa.   **8.** John Kennedy
dijo: «Yo soy un berlinés».   **9.** Muchos inmigrantes irlandeses vinieron a los Estados Unidos en el siglo
XIX.   **B.** *Durante la Navidad:*   **1.** tuvo   **2.** estuvieron   **3.** Vinieron   **4.** trajeron   **5.** dijeron   **6.** fueron
7. comieron   **8.** pudieron   **9.** lo pasaron   *Otro terremoto...*   **1.** supimos   **2.** hubo   **3.** oí   **4.** leí   **5.** se
rompieron   **6.** hizo   **7.** dijo   **8.** fue   **C.   1.** estuvo   **2.** pude   **3.** tuve   **4.** viniste   **5.** Quise   **6.** estuve
7. hizo   **8.** Supiste   **9.** tuvo   **10.** vino   **11.** dijo   **12.** puse   **13.** trajiste   **14.** traje   **Gramática 24   A.   1.** me
senté / me dormí   **2.** se sentaron / nos dormimos   **3.** se durmió   **4.** nos reímos / se rio   **5.** sintieron /
se sintió   **B.   1.** se vistió   **2.** se rio   **3.** se sonrió   **4.** pidió   **5.** prefirió   **6.** sirvieron   **7.** se divirtieron
8. se despidieron   **C.   Paso 1.**   *You should have checked the following actions for each person: Julia:* vestirse
elegantemente; *Verónica:* vestirse elegantemente; *Tomás:* sentirse mal, dormir toda la tarde, preferir
quedarse en casa; *Ernesto (el narrador):* vestirse elegantemente

Paso 3: Gramática

Gramática 25   ¡RECUERDA!   1. Yo le traigo el café. (O.I.)   **2.** Yo lo traigo ahora. (O.D.)   **3.** Ellos nos
compran los boletos. (O.I.)   **4.** Ellos los compran hoy. (O.D.)   **5.** No les hablo mucho. (O.I.)   **6.** No las
conozco bien. (O.D.)   **7.** Queremos darles una fiesta. (O.I.)   **8.** Pensamos darla en casa. (O.D.)   **A.   1.** ¿El
dinero? Te lo devuelvo mañana.   **2.** ¿Las tapas? Te las traigo el jueves.   **3.** ¿La sorpresa? Nos la van a
revelar después.   **4.** ¿Los pasteles? Me los prometieron para esta tarde.   **5.** ¿Las fotos? Se las mando a
Uds. con la carta.   **6.** ¿La bicicleta? Se la devuelvo a Pablo mañana.   **7.** ¿El dinero? Se lo doy a Ud. el
viernes.   **8.** ¿Los regalos? Se los muestro a Isabel esta noche.   **B.** (*Possible answers*)   **1.** Se lo dejó a
Cristina.   **2.** Se la dejó a Memo.   **3.** Se los dejó a la biblioteca.   **4.** Se los dejó a la Cruz Roja.   **5.** Se la
dejó a Ernesto y Ana.   **6.** ¡Me los dejó a mí!   **C.   1.** se las   **2.** me lo   **3.** nos la   **4.** se las   **5.** se los
Un poco de todo   A.   Paso 1.   1. hice   **2.** estuve   **3.** quise   **4.** supe   **5.** di   **6.** estuvimos   **7.** pedí
Paso 2.   1. Hizo un viaje a Acapulco.   **2.** Estuvo ocupado.   **3.** Su amigo Luis Dávila se lo dijo.   **4.** Se las
dio a Luis.   **B.** (*Possible answers*)   **1.** Se la mandé a mi novio/a.   **2.** Se los di a mi familia y a mis amigos.
3. Nadie me las trajo.   **4.** Mi hermano me lo pidió.   **5.** Mis amigos me la hicieron.

Ponte a prueba

A ver si sabes...   A.   1. estuve   **2.** pudiste   **3.** puso   **4.** quisimos   **5.** supieron   **6.** tuve   **7.** viniste
8. trajo   **9.** dijeron   **10.** fuimos   **B.**   *él/ella/Ud.:* durmió / pidió / prefirió / recordó / se sintió

ellos/Uds.: durmieron / pidieron / prefirieron / recordaron / se sintieron   **C.**   **1.** se lo   **2.** se la **3.** se los   **Prueba corta**   **A.**   **1.** nos reímos   **2.** se puso / durmió   **3.** conseguí   **4.** se despidió   **5.** se vistió / se divirtió   **6.** hicimos / trajeron   **B.**   **1.** a   **2.** a   **3.** c   **4.** b   **5.** a   **6.** b

CAPÍTULO 9

Paso 1: Vocabulario

Los pasatiempos, diversiones y aficiones   **C.**   **1. a.** hacer *camping*   **b.** juegan a las cartas   **c.** dan un paseo   **d.** toma el sol   **2. a.** juegan al ajedrez   **b.** Teatro   **c.** Museo   **3. a.** divertido   **b.** cine   **c.** la película **d.** pasarlo bien   **Los quehaceres domésticos**   **A.**   **1.** Se usa la estufa para cocinar.   **2.** Se prepara el café en la cafetera.   **3.** Lavamos y secamos la ropa.   **4.** Usamos el lavaplatos.   **5.** Pasamos la aspiradora. **6.** Tostamos el pan en la tostadora.   **7.** Usamos el microondas.   **8.** La plancho.   **B.**   **1.** La mujer está sacudiendo los muebles.   **2.** El chico está sacando la basura.   **3.** El hombre está lavando (limpiando) la ventana.   **4.** El hombre está barriendo el suelo.   **5.** El niño está haciendo la cama.   **6.** La mujer está poniendo la mesa.   **Pronunciación y ortografía**   **C.**   **1.** Paco toca el piano para sus parientes.   **2.** Los tíos de Tito son de Puerto Rico.   **3.** ¿Por qué pagas tanto por la ropa?   **4.** Tito trabaja para el padre de Pepe. **Lectura cultural**   **1.** Caribe / Pacífico   **2.** altiplanos   **3.** (*Possible answers*) petróleo / oro / platino / café **4.** piratas   **5.** esculturas / fantásticas   **6.** cumbia

Paso 2: Gramática

Gramática 26   **A.**   **1.** celebraba   **2.** se llenaba   **3.** debíamos   **4.** Corríamos   **5.** comíamos **6.** cortábamos   **7.** era   **8.** me molestaba   **9.** era   **10.** era   **B.**   **1.** tenía   **2.** vivíamos   **3.** Iba   **4.** volvía **5.** prefería   **6.** venían   **7.** era   **8.** celebrábamos   **9.** hacía   **10.** cocinaba   **11.** visitaban   **12.** se quedaban **13.** dormíamos   **14.** nos acostábamos   **15.** había   **16.** pasábamos   **17.** eran   **C.**   **1.** Antes dependía de su esposo. Ahora tiene más independencia económica.   **2.** Antes se quedaba en casa. Ahora prefiere salir a trabajar.   **3.** Antes sólo pensaba en casarse. Ahora piensa en seguir su propia carrera.   **5.** Antes su esposo se sentaba a leer el periódico. Ahora (su esposo) la ayuda con los quehaceres domésticos.   **D.**   **Paso 1.** **1.** había   **2.** pertenecían   **3.** Vivían   **4.** se basaba   **5.** Habitaban   **6.** Era   **7.** Ocupaban   **8.** Tenían **Paso 2.**   **1.** Diversos   **2.** altiplanos   **3.** comerciante   **4.** arquitectura   **Gramática 27**   **A.**   **1.** (*Possible answers*) El béisbol es el deporte más emocionante de todos.   **2.** Kobe Bryant es el mejor jugador del mundo.   **3.** El equipo de los Dallas Cowboys es el peor equipo de todos.   **4.** El estadio de Río de Janeiro, Brasil, es el estadio más grande del mundo.   **C.**   **Paso 1.**   **1.** el carnaval   **2.** mayo   **3.** *Como agua para chocolate*   **4.** pasar la aspiradora

Paso 3: Gramática

Gramática 28   **A.**   **1.** ¿Cómo se llama (Ud.)?   **2.** ¿De dónde es (Ud.)?   **3.** ¿Dónde vive (Ud.)? **4.** ¿Adónde va (Ud.) ahora?   **5.** ¿Qué va a hacer (Ud.)?   **6.** ¿Cuáles son sus pasatiempos favoritos? **7.** ¿Cuándo empezó (Ud.) a jugar?   **8.** ¿Quiénes son sus jugadores preferidos?   **9.** ¿Por qué (son sus preferidos)?   **10.** ¿Cuánto gana (Ud.) al año?   **C.**   **1.** cómo   **2.** Qué   **3.** Quién   **4.** De dónde   **5.** cuántos **6.** Cómo   **7.** Cuándo   **8.** Por qué   **9.** cómo   **10.** Qué   **Un poco de todo**   **A.**   **1.** pasaba   **2.** esquiando **3.** conoció   **4.** visitaba   **5.** vivían   **6.** esquiaba   **7.** estaba   **8.** vio   **9.** Dobló   **10.** perdió   **11.** se puso **12.** Te hiciste   **13.** esperando   **14.** sacudiéndose   **15.** sonriendo   **16.** se hicieron

Ponte a prueba

A ver si sabes...   **A.**   **1. a.** iba / leía / era / veía   **b.** cantábamos / íbamos / leíamos / éramos / veíamos   **2. a.** 4   **b.** 5   **c.** 3   **d.** 2   **e.** 6   **f.** 1   **B.**   **1.** Soy *la* persona *más* feliz *del* mundo.   **2.** Son los *mejores* jugadores *del* equipo.   **3.** Es el *peor* estudiante *de la* clase.   **C.**   **1.** Qué   **2.** Cuál   **3.** Cuáles **4.** Qué   **5.** Cuál   **Prueba corta**   **A.**   **1.** era   **2.** asistía   **3.** estaba   **4.** ayudaba   **5.** vivían   **6.** iban **7.** jugaban   **8.** servía   **9.** se cansaban   **10.** volvían   **B.**   **1.** Adónde   **2.** Quién   **3.** Cómo   **4.** Dónde **5.** Cuál   **6.** Cuánto